T0355491

The Bible Told Them So

The Bible Told Them So

*How Southern Evangelicals Fought to
Preserve White Supremacy*

J. RUSSELL HAWKINS

OXFORD
UNIVERSITY PRESS

Oxford University Press is a department of the University of Oxford. It furthers
the University's objective of excellence in research, scholarship, and education
by publishing worldwide. Oxford is a registered trade mark of Oxford University
Press in the UK and certain other countries.

Published in the United States of America by Oxford University Press
198 Madison Avenue, New York, NY 10016, United States of America.

© Oxford University Press 2021

Library of Congress Cataloging-in-Publication Data
Names: Hawkins, J. Russell, author.
Title: The Bible told them so : how Southern Evangelicals fought to
preserve white supremacy / by J. Russell Hawkins.
Description: New York, NY : Oxford University Press, [2021] |
Includes bibliographical references and index.
Identifiers: LCCN 2020058623 (print) | LCCN 2020058624 (ebook) |
ISBN 9780197571064 (hardback) | ISBN 9780197571071 (epub)
Subjects: LCSH: South Carolina—Church history—20th century. |
Segregation—Religious aspects—Christianity. | Segregation—
South Carolina—History—20th century. | Christians, White—
South Carolina—History. | White supremacy movements—Religious aspects—Christianity. |
Baptists—South Carolina. | Methodists—South Carolina. |
Racism—Religious aspects—Christianity. | South Carolina—Race relations.
Classification: LCC BR555.S6 H39 2021 (print) |
LCC BR555.S6 (ebook) | DDC 261.709757/09045—dc23
LC record available at https://lccn.loc.gov/2020058623
LC ebook record available at https://lccn.loc.gov/2020058624

DOI: 10.1093/oso/9780197571064.001.0001

5 7 9 8 6

Printed by Sheridan Books, Inc., United States of America

for Kristi, my love

Contents

Acknowledgments

I made my first trip to South Carolina to conduct the research that would eventually become this book in 2006. One of the difficulties with a project that spans fourteen years is the accumulation of debts so numerous that they are impossible to fully remember, let alone repay. What follows is a meager attempt to, at a minimum, acknowledge some of those debts. I hope that the people named below recognize their influence on this project far exceeds the brief mention I am able to give them.

Financial support for researching this book came in part from the Southern Baptist Historical Library and Archives, Baylor University's Institute for Oral History, the University of South Carolina's Institute for Southern Studies, Rice University's Dean Currie Fund, and Indiana Wesleyan University's Lilly Scholarship Fund and Sabbatical Grant Award. The generosity of these various entities allowed me to pursue research in nineteen different archives in half a dozen states. While a cursory glance through the notes will reveal that some of those archival visits were more fruitful than others, the archivists at each and every stop were unfailingly helpful and went out of their way to provide me with the materials I knew I needed and point me to more that *they* knew I needed. Among this group of archivists, Bill Sumners, Graham Duncan, Kate Moore, Herb Hartsook, and Phillip Stone deserve special recognition for sharing their insights, expertise, and camaraderie during my visits to their respective collections.

John B. Boles oversaw this project in its early stages as a graduate dissertation at Rice University and pushed me to extend my arguments and analysis as it evolved into a monograph. Along the way, John has been an unwavering source of encouragement and kindness. Those of us who have been students of Dr. Boles know how fortunate we are to have been recipients of his brilliance and generosity. Michael Emerson's scholarship on race and evangelical Christianity also played a significant role in shaping the ideas found in these pages during their nascent stage at Rice and in their final form in this book. Michael's professional and personal advice and guidance over the years have been indispensable to me. Early in my career I was fortunate to participate in a three week interdisciplinary seminar that Michael convened at Calvin

University in 2010 on the topic of race in American religion. A decade later, many of the relationships forged during that seminar continue to endure and the arguments in this book have been strengthened by the historians, theologians, and sociologists Michael gathered together that summer: Ed Blum, Tanya Brice, Ryon Cobb, Korie Edwards, Paul Gordiejew, Luke Harlow, Kimberly Hill, Karen Joy Johnson, Rebecca Kim, Mark Mulder, Jerry Park, Julie Park, Regina Shands Stoltzfus, and Erica Wong. Another member of our group, theologian Bruce Fields, passed away before this book's publication, but his influence helped shaped not only this book but my own life as well.

It has been a pleasure working with Oxford University Press again, and I am especially grateful for Cynthia Read and Brent Matheny who shepherded this project along. In addition to designing the incredible cover, Oxford also lined up stellar anonymous readers whose helpful suggestions and trenchant critiques made for a much better final product.

As helpful as the anonymous readers were, so too have been the innumerable colleagues and peers who have provided invaluable feedback at different points in the writing of this book. Three deserve special mention. Carolyn Dupont has been generous with her analysis of my work in its various stages and the insights drawn from her research of Mississippi evangelicals helped sharpen my own conclusions. In addition to commenting on chapter drafts, Wes Phelps has served as my roommate at many academic conferences over the years where he has endured a decade's worth of discussions about this book and its arguments. Finally, Luke Harlow has read drafts of seemingly everything I have written going back to our earliest days together as new graduate students at Rice and has never failed to provide suggestions that improve my analysis and arguments at every turn. Carolyn, Wes, and Luke have all made this a significantly better book.

My academic home the past twelve years has been in the John Wesley Honors College at Indiana Wesleyan University. My honors college colleagues have been the best I could have wanted and I have lost track of the number of drafts I have asked them to read or conversations about race and evangelicalism I have subjected them to. These fine individuals include Annastasia Bonczyk, Brian Clark, Lena Crouso, Lanta Davis, Lexi Eikelboom, Kirsten Guidero, Amy Peeler, Lance Peeler, Todd Ream, Jason Runyan, Jeff Tabone, Sara Scheuneman, Anneke Stasson, Julia VanderMolen, Lisa Toland Williams, and Sameer Yadav. It has been a gift to be part of this interdisciplinary community where my own research has been pushed and deepened by the insights and scholarship of these incredible peers. Two additional honors college colleagues warrant further recognition. David Riggs has been my dean since the day I arrived at Indiana Wesleyan and has been nothing but supportive of my research and teaching from the start. I am thankful for both his professional leadership and personal friendship. I had the good fortune of having an office across the hall from Charles Bressler for my first seven years at Indiana Wesleyan and learned how to teach and interact with students and colleagues by following his example. Charles read every single word of this book in its manuscript form. And after I incorporated his feedback, he read every word again. With his keen editorial eye, Charles improved this book immensely. Thank you, kind sir!

Many students over the years have enrolled in my honors seminars on religion and the civil rights movement and have helped sift through the archival material that is the basis of so much of this book. Two students in particular served as research assistants at key points in the book's production and deserve their own mention. Early on, Stephen German accompanied me on a week-long research trip to South Carolina and went through countless boxes and folders to amass a significant amount of the evidence presented in the book. Allison Tinch, meanwhile, provided invaluable support in the final stages, hunting down sources, double checking endnotes, and providing helpful feedback on final drafts. A hearty thanks to Steve and Tinch for their contributions to this project.

I have been fortunate to be part of two intentionally multiracial churches in Texas and Indiana during the duration of writing this book. City of Refuge Church in Houston was my church home when this project began and REAL Community Covenant Church in Marion is where my family and I attend at its publication. My church families in both these congregations have been a source of support and inspiration to me over the years and give me hope that the history found in this book may yet be redeemed.

My biological family has likewise been a source of indispensable encouragement in the course of bringing this book into being. My father and mother, James and Carolyn Hawkins, nurtured my love of history at a young age with every quarter deposited at my "president's stand." Along with my sisters, Emily Dennis and Kathryn Lalli, my parents have been consistent supporters—and served as my imagined readers—throughout the writing of this book.

My sons, Caleb and Micah, have listened to (and occasionally even requested) countless lectures on American history during family hikes and bike rides over the years. In addition to pushing me to make my stories interesting and relevant, they have been a source of incalculable pride and joy and have helped me maintain much needed balance and perspective about the important things in life.

Finally, this book would never have been finished without the encouragement and support of my wife, Kristi. She more than anyone else in my life has lived with this book for the past fourteen years. Kristi has sacrificed countless evenings and weekends to ensure that I finish this project and never stopped believing I could even when I gave her every reason to do so. She is my biggest supporter, proudest promoter, and best friend. This book is dedicated to her, along with the promise that the next one won't take so long.

Introduction

"As Old as the Scriptures ... "

On a June afternoon in 1963, nearly 250 religious leaders gathered in the East Room of the White House. Hailing from all corners of the country and representing different faiths and multiple Christian denominations, the clerics assembled that late-spring Monday at the invitation of President John F. Kennedy to discuss how American pastors, priests, and rabbis could rally support for Kennedy's recent call for sweeping civil rights legislation. Less than a week before this meeting with the clergy, Kennedy couched black equality in explicitly moral terms during a televised address to the nation that Martin Luther King Jr. later called "one of the most eloquent, profound, and unequivocal pleas for justice and the freedom of all men ever made by any President." With his bold speech, Kennedy positioned his administration on the side of the black demonstrators organizing and marching in the streets of southern cities that year. But the President understood that persuading Congress to pass a bill elevating black Americans from second-class citizen status required more than well-crafted speeches. For this reason, Kennedy followed his televised address with a campaign to sell his proposal to groups whose power and influence in American society would benefit the civil rights crusade. Governors, labor leaders, educators, lawyers, hotel and theater owners—all were summoned to the White House to hear the president discuss the need for new civil rights legislation. Kennedy's staff reserved June 17 for the nation's religious leaders to receive the presidential pitch, and as Kennedy prepared for his meeting with the clerics, his aides reminded the president to tailor his remarks to this particular group by emphasizing "the moral position of the churches on the question of racial equality."[1] The president indicated he understood.

The assembled clergymen respectfully rose from their gilded chairs as Kennedy strode into the East Room for their meeting, his characteristic charm on full display. Smiling, the president welcomed the group to "this old house," invited them to have a seat, and expressed his hope that the media's

The Bible Told Them So. J. Russell Hawkins, Oxford University Press. © Oxford University Press 2021.
DOI: 10.1093/oso/9780197571064.003.0001

absence from the gathering would allow Kennedy and his guests to have a candid conversation regarding the need for a civil rights law. Kennedy told the men that while his main objective that day was to hear their thoughts, the president nonetheless felt obliged to offer a few introductory remarks: "I would hope each religious group would—and again I don't think we can say this too often—underscore the moral position of racial equality," the president said. "There is bound to be resentments against Washington. There is bound to be resentment against outsiders. The more we can make this . . . a community action, with moral overtones and not merely a political effort, the better off we will be." Recalling his staff's instructions, Kennedy reiterated his charge that civil rights was a moral issue before opening the floor to suggestions that his administration could heed to maximize support from people of faith for his proposed legislation.[2]

Around the room hands went up, and the president signaled to individuals eager to express their views. "I am very happy this meeting was held because the holding of this meeting is a recognition of the fact by the entire country that this is a moral problem, essentially," said a local minister from Washington, DC. "It may have economic, legal and social overtones," he continued, "but we as religious men must consider it solely the essential thing that it is, a moral problem." Similar comments continued in the East Room as northern clergymen of liberal theological persuasions suggested means for communicating the righteousness of civil rights to their parishioners.[3]

But when Kennedy called on the raised hand of Albert Garner, a Baptist minister from Florida, the meeting took an unexpected turn. Rising to address Kennedy, Garner informed the president and his fellow clergy that he and other white people of the "Southland" were certainly in agreement that civil rights was a moral issue, but not in the same way the others in the room viewed it. Instead, Garner noted that many southern white Christians like himself actually held a "strong moral conviction" that "racial integration . . . is against the will of their Creator." After all, Garner reasoned, "segregation is a principle of the Old Testament and . . . prior to this century neither Christianity nor any denomination of it ever accepted the integration philosophy." Since Kennedy and his fellow clergy in the East Room were intent on casting civil rights in a moral light, Garner wondered if the president had "any remedy by which we can change these [southern white Christians'] moral convictions and religious convictions of people in the Bible and do you feel that these convictions are absolutely wrong?"[4]

If Kennedy was startled by Garner's question, his surprise did not show. Instead, the president brushed aside Garner's query—one account claimed Kennedy easily dismissed "this familiar bugaboo"—responding that perceived biblical injunctions against interracial mixing remained matters of personal religious convictions, not public policy. His administration's concern, Kennedy informed Garner, was not to force the social intermingling of the races. Rather, the White House sought only the "equality of jobs and a chance to get an education, so you can get a job, and a chance to move freely through this country and stop at places where others stop."[5]

Before Garner yielded the floor, he fired a second question to Kennedy. Could the president suggest ways to calm southern white fears "on the moral issue of this mixing from [the] high school level down?"[6] Once again, Kennedy parried Garner's question, this time dispatching the minister's concern by declaring that school desegregation fell under the purview of the nation's courts. But Kennedy ended his exchange with Garner on a conciliatory note: "I realize how difficult it is," the Catholic president told the Baptist preacher, "but we are asking your people to do what only seems fair and not cut across their religious convictions."[7]

Just two days after Kennedy's meeting with the religious leaders, the president submitted a civil rights bill to Congress that started the legislation on its long and difficult journey to eventual passage. In the intervening months, white Christians in the South proved that Albert Garner had not misrepresented them during his White House visit. On a Wednesday evening in August 1963, five hundred miles south of Washington, DC, members of a Southern Baptist church in Hanahan, South Carolina, called a special meeting after their midweek Bible study to discuss Kennedy's proposed law. Although the president had hoped congregations like Hanahan Baptist would help make straight the path for civil rights in the 1960s, the faithful Baptists gathered that summer evening in this small community outside of Charleston voted to "take a firm stand against the present civil rights legislation." Describing themselves as "Christ centered" and "Bible believing," these Hanahan Baptists saw no contradiction between their Christian faith and their opposition to a law they perceived as forcing them to accept black Americans as their equal.[8] The Hanahan Baptists were not alone. Across the South, white Christians thought the president was flaunting Christian orthodoxy in pursuing his civil rights agenda. "Where does Mr. Kennedy get his views and rules?" queried one white southerner for many during the national debate over civil rights. "Certainly not from the Holy Bible of God and Jesus Christ."[9]

Although Kennedy would not live to see the realization of his desired law, a little more than a year after he proposed his hallmark bill, the 1964 Civil Rights Act became law. This watershed legislation was followed the next year by the 1965 Voting Rights Act, an equally if not more important law in the quest for black equality. Taken together, these two acts fundamentally altered the American South more quickly than the region's residents could have ever foreseen. The passage of such revolutionary legislation immediately aided the black southerners' defeat of Jim Crow so much so that Kennedy's in-house historian, Arthur Schlesinger Jr., predicted that twenty-first-century historians would struggle to explain why liberal achievements like the Civil Rights Act and Voting Rights Act took so long to be enacted. Schlesinger wondered how was it that for more than a century after the end of slavery, white Americans countenanced the "systematic dehumanization" of their fellow black citizens.[10]

Standing before Kennedy in the East Room of the White House in June 1963, Albert Garner had provided an answer to Schlesinger's rhetorical question for those who were able to hear. The president of the United States, however, did not have such ears. Kennedy simply could not comprehend the truth Garner was communicating: based on their religious beliefs, southern white Christians thought integration was evil. When Kennedy told Garner he wanted southern white Christians to do only what was fair and not violate their religious beliefs, the president was inventing a dichotomy between their Christian faith and racial attitudes that few white southerners would recognize or even accept. As demonstrated by the Hanahan Baptists, religious convictions forged by reading and interpreting scripture and following inherited traditions formed many white Christians' sense of fairness regarding black equality. Asking white southerners to ignore their religious beliefs in pursuit of racial equality was seemingly asking the impossible. These white southerners did not undertake their resistance to black equality *in spite* of their religious convictions, but their faith *drove* their support of Jim Crow segregation. Central to the drama for racial justice that unfolded during America's civil rights years lay an indisputable religious conflict between black Christian activists and their white Christian antagonists, both of whom confidently, proudly, and often joyously claimed God's favor for their political stance.

An intramural Christian dispute over God's position on civil rights is perhaps difficult to imagine in the twenty-first century. Devout Christians who read their Bibles, prayed to Jesus, and sincerely believed God desired segregation—people like Albert Garner and the Hanahan Baptists—are most often left out of public remembrances and popular culture portrayals of the civil rights movement. These segregationist Christians' absence in popular civil rights accounts makes it difficult to grasp the religious dimensions of resistance to the black freedom struggle, inadvertently lending credence that black protestors alone were motivated by their faith. Hollywood films and best-selling novels set in the civil rights years, for instance, almost invariably include scenes of activists packed in the pews of black churches with freedom songs ringing out and powerful sermons soaring from pulpits to recruit and fortify foot soldiers in the march to black equality. And these depictions are not wrong. Historians such as David L. Chappell and Lewis V. Baldwin have accurately shown that a deep and abiding Christian faith forged in and through experiences of oppression energized many black civil rights activists and helped sustain them throughout their freedom struggle.[11] As Chappell underscores, black Christianity rooted in the prophetic tradition made the civil rights movement *move*.[12]

But another version of Christianity is seldom portrayed in the well-known renditions of the civil rights movement that many Americans celebrate: the Christianity characterized and articulated by Albert Garner standing in the East Room of the White House, insisting that white southerners' biblical defense of segregation was hermeneutically correct. This version of Christianity allowed Hanahan Baptists to move seamlessly from studying their Bibles to denouncing civil rights legislation on the same Wednesday evening. It is the version of Christianity practiced by a large percentage of southern white evangelicals, justifying their resistance to racial equality during the civil rights years. In the previous century, a significant number of white southerners found in their holy scripture coupled with church traditions a blueprint for racial segregation, not a call to universal brotherhood. The present book tells their story, offering an account of white Christians like Garner and the Hanahan Baptists, who sincerely believed racial integration violated God's will. The pages that follow explain how southern white Christians reached such theological conclusions and illustrate how this version of Christianity adapted to defend segregation's righteousness even after the gains of the civil rights movement.

The Bible Told Them So takes as its vantage point an underexplored corner of Dixie in the study of white resistance to civil rights: South Carolina. Although South Carolina has a similar history as other southern states in the civil rights era—peaceful protestors facing down violent defenders of Jim Crow, Citizens' Councils using economic intimidation to thwart black gains, reactionary politicians vowing never to integrate—the state's massive resistance story occupies far less space in Americans' collective memory than its Deep South neighbors. By examining white evangelicals' fight to thwart civil rights gains in the Palmetto State, this book breaks new ground in our understanding of religious massive resistance in South Carolina while providing a fuller understanding of segregationist Christianity's purchase in the South.

In the same way that *The Bible Told Them So* derives its arguments primarily from South Carolina, its study of white evangelical Christians is limited chiefly to the state's Southern Baptists and Methodists.[13] In the context of midcentury South Carolina evangelicalism, however, examining "only" Baptists and Methodists is hardly a limit at all. In the mid-twentieth century, the percentage of southerners who identified as Protestant Christian was extraordinarily high; nine of ten southerners identified as such in 1954. The percentages also had significant persistence. By 1966, the percentage of Protestant southerners had slipped only three points to 87 percent.[14] While no specific data exists concerning the percentage of South Carolinians identifying as Protestant during the years covered in this book (1955–1970), it is reasonable to believe the state reflected the same percentages as the region to which it belonged, at or near 90 percent. South Carolina is no exception to the Baptist and Methodist numerical dominance that scholars have shown existed throughout the South in the second half of the twentieth century. Indeed, among Protestant Christians in South Carolina in the mid-1960s, over 80 percent identified as a Baptist or a Methodist.[15] South Carolina's white Southern Baptists and Methodists thus provide a numerically significant sample for a study of white evangelicals' racial perspectives and feelings.

In addition to their sheer volume, Southern Baptists and Methodists provide useful groups to study because their unique forms of church governance enabled the two groups to respond differently to racial issues. Congregational and autonomous in their polity, each Southern Baptist church governs itself independently of a church hierarchy or denominational oversight. Consequently, when sending representatives to state and national meetings of Southern Baptists, individual churches pointedly send "messengers," not "delegates." *Delegates* have power to act on behalf of a church, whereas

Baptist *messengers* are allowed only to communicate the desire of their congregation and then report back to their churches news and statements from the Baptist convention. As church representatives, messengers can vote to accept or reject reports and proposals at the convention meetings, but none of these reports or proposals is binding upon the churches within the denomination.[16] Methodists, on the other hand, have an episcopal and bureaucratic church polity in which congregations submit to the authority of bishops and to other denominational structures of power. Unlike Southern Baptist churches, individual Methodist churches cede authority to members of the laity and clergy who serve as "delegates" to denominational meetings and conduct binding business on behalf of the represented churches and conferences at such gatherings.

Taken as a whole, white Southern Baptists and Methodists in South Carolina were remarkably similar in their belief in and support of segregationist Christianity. Yet the significant difference between Southern Baptist and Methodist church governance caused the two groups to pursue different strategies to maintain and protect segregation in their churches, schools, and denominations. As will be seen in the chapters ahead, the particulars of church polity required Southern Baptists and Methodists to navigate issues of race in different ways at various times during the civil rights period. Accounting for these differences provides a fuller understanding of segregationist Christianity's influence during and after the civil rights period.

The Bible Told Them So makes two central and interconnected arguments. First, the book argues that many white South Carolinians who resisted the civil rights movement were animated by a Christian faith influenced by biblical exegesis that deemed racial segregation as divinely ordered. A complete understanding of southern white resistance to civil rights requires wrestling with this unique hermeneutic. Prior to a recent historiographical turn, southern evangelicalism's role in fueling white animus toward the black freedom struggle was understudied or even downplayed within civil rights scholarship.[17] Recently, however, a growing number of scholars have demonstrated the power that religious belief held for white evangelical resistance to the civil rights movement.[18] *The Bible Told Them So* contributes to this important crop of scholarship by offering a fulsome explication of the biblical interpretations white evangelicals used to construct their segregationist theology. At the same time, the book demonstrates how such theology fueled southern white Christians' defense of Jim Crow segregation in their society and churches. Drawn from a particular biblical reading, segregationist theology became the lifeblood of a segregationist Christianity around which many white southerners ordered their lives in the 1950s. The first two chapters of this book document this story. In so doing, *The Bible Told Them So* demonstrates that the efforts of white Christians in South Carolina to block the racial gains of their black neighbors harmonized with similar efforts that historians such as Carolyn DuPont, Ansley Quiros, and Stephen Haynes have documented in other southern locales. This book's first argument, then, extends the current historiography, further revealing the ubiquity of white evangelical resistance to black equality throughout the South while deepening our understanding of Christianity's centrality to southern white resistance to civil rights.

The book's last three chapters contain its second central argument and represent a departure from rather than extension of the current scholarship of religious massive resistance. Tracing the continuation of segregationist Christianity after the significant gains of the civil rights movement in the mid-1960s, I argue that segregationist theology did not cease with the political achievements of the civil rights movement. Historically speaking, Albert Garner's appeal in the White House to a biblically inspired justification for segregation occurred during the twilight of legal segregation. As noted previously, not thirteen months after Garner stood in front of President Kennedy, Jim Crow had crumbled under the weight of a powerful civil rights act, and the following year black southerners had successfully secured voting rights. It is tempting to interpret the religious objections Garner raised in 1963 to integration as the last gasp of a belief system soon to be relegated to history's dustbin. As I show in the pages ahead, however, the biblically inspired segregationist Christianity Garner represented did not die. Indeed, in the years after 1965, segregationist Christianity evolved and persisted in new forms that would become mainstays of southern white evangelicalism by the 1970s: colorblind individualism and a heightened focus on the family.

Segregationist Christianity's capacity to evolve beyond a biblical literalism defending Jim Crow in the 1950s and take on the form of colorblind familial protection by the 1970s was a product of white evangelicalism's insulated subculture. While the 1964 Civil Rights Act and 1965 Voting Rights Act forced a fundamental transformation of the broader southern society, southern white evangelicals' claim to religious liberty in their private schools, church buildings, and denominations provided safe harbor for continued segregation, denying the black freedom struggle power to change white evangelicalism. As southern society acquiesced to the changes wrought by the civil rights movement in the late 1960s, however, white evangelicals felt pressure to justify their support of segregation in new terms. A new "colorblind" form of segregationist Christianity allowed southern evangelicals to maintain social standing by eschewing appeals to the overt segregationist theology they had made freely a decade hence. But, as this book argues, the linkages between the explicitly theological Christian segregation in the 1950s and its more subtle version in the 1970s must not be overlooked. Caught in the tension between their sincere beliefs that God desired segregation and their reticence to publicly vocalize such ideas for fear of seeming bigoted or intolerant, southern white evangelicals eventually arrived at a strategy that embraced both colorblindness and protection of the family as measures to maintain both segregation and respectable social standing. Such a strategy, I argue, took root, blossomed, and spread widely throughout the evangelical subculture in the early 1970s, setting white evangelicals on a detrimental path for race relations in the decades ahead.

Understanding the argument presented in the following pages requires a clarification for the way the word "theology" is used in this book.[19] To claim that white Christians who used religious justifications to defend segregation in the South were employing a "theology" is not to claim that these individuals were drawing upon a codified or systematic argumentation of racial separation. Although I attempt in Chapter 2 to provide the contours of such a systematized segregationist theology, few rank-and-file Christians thought in these terms. Even fewer of these individuals making religious arguments against integration would have considered such acts as "doing theology" or conceived of themselves as theologians. Assigning the term "theology" is therefore attributing a level of category sophistication to white religious conservatives that likely only a handful would have assumed for themselves. Segregationist theology, then, must be properly understood as the myriad arguments white southerners made against integration using either the Bible or the broader natural world.

Such a definition is not intended to imply that segregationist theology lacked sophistication of thought or sincerity of belief by those who employed it. Nor should segregationist theology be understood solely as an endeavor of the Christian laity. To the contrary, southern ministers were instrumental in both teaching and spreading segregationist theology throughout the region. While some of these clergy published their formulations of segregationist theologies in pamphlets, books, and sermons, most toiled away in the obscurity of the ubiquitous small churches that dotted the southern landscape, content to make their views on segregation known only to their congregations in their weekly sermons.

Although ministerial participation in defending racial segregation should not be discounted, the importance of the laity for segregationist theology's ultimate purchase cannot be overemphasized. As historians have noted, because the democratic strain of evangelicalism in the American context usually means "it is the *people* who are custodians of orthodoxy," it mattered little that segregationist theology did not pass muster with the seminary-trained theologians of the day who made up a small minority of southern white churchgoers.[20] As long as the majority of white southern Christians—in either actual numbers or mere perception—believed that the Bible they read and the natural world they observed endorsed the separation of the races, they continued to work against attempts at racial integration. And, as will become clear in the chapters ahead, white southerners in the twentieth century had little difficulty seeing segregation written in either the book of nature or the Good Book itself.

Following this introduction, Chapter 1 begins the story of segregationist Christianity with an exploration of the tensions that arose in southern evangelicalism between local church congregations and state- and national-level bodies in the wake of the 1954 *Brown* decision. Such tensions reveal how Southern Baptists and Methodists negotiated the heightened antagonism that emerged between denominational leaders and the people in the pews over civil rights issues in the mid-1950s. The chapter opens with South Carolina Southern Baptist churches rejecting broader Southern Baptist Convention efforts to advocate for civil rights in religious language and concludes with lay South Carolina Methodists defending the White Citizens' Councils against criticism from a small number of Methodist clergy. Both these studies reveal the effective authority of local congregations in directing southern white churches' responses to matters of race in the civil rights years. This chapter highlights that the congregational-level perspective gives the best vantage point for understanding white evangelicalism's response to the civil rights movement, regardless of church polity.

Chapter 2 explicates the theology behind the resistive response of southern evangelicals described in the previous chapter. This chapter explains *why* conservative white Christians opposed civil rights reforms by arguing that a significant percentage of these Christians constructed a theology from both the natural world and biblical texts in which God was viewed as the author of segregation, one who desired that racial separatism be maintained.

Referencing letters, sermons, pamphlets, and books, this chapter documents how segregationist theology was crafted, defended, and deployed throughout the 1950s and 1960s in the South. It also demonstrates how such a theology birthed a segregationist Christianity that became common in southern white churches, proving influential in shaping the social and political responses white southerners had to the civil rights movement. Segregationist theology enjoyed enough adherents among church laity and clergy to prevent southern white evangelical churches from participating in the cause to extend equal treatment to African Americans and often served as the basis for active resistance to that cause.

Of course, despite the desires of segregationist Christians, change did come to the South by the mid-1960s. The book's last three chapters detail how segregationist theology lived on and evolved in the face of the broader legal and social gains black Americans achieved after 1964. While the world changed around them, white Baptists and Methodists fought to maintain white supremacy in arenas where they retained power: their church colleges, denominational structures, and households. Chapter 3 highlights the continued influence of segregationist theology in evangelical circles even as segregationist ideas began losing purchase outside that sphere in the mid-1960s. The centerpieces of this chapter are parallel narratives detailing the desegregation of Wofford College and Furman University, the respective flagship institutions of the Methodist and Baptist denominations in South Carolina. In describing the battles between school administrators who sought to desegregate their institutions and the laity of the state's two largest evangelical denominations who resisted such measures, this chapter emphasizes white evangelicals' continued opposition to black civil rights even as the broader southern culture was forced by the federal government to acquiesce on integration in institutions of higher education. Segregationist theology remained influential for a majority of white Baptists and Methodists who voted against desegregating the church schools in the mid-1960s and who withdrew their support when the colleges integrated against these Christians' desires.

Chapter 4 traces the transformation of segregationist theology into ideas of colorblind individualism in the early 1970s. This chapter narrates the integration of the United Methodist denomination to demonstrate how white evangelicals adopted a language of colorblindness in an attempt to subvert racial integration. The story of South Carolina's Methodists illuminates ways that religious ideas can adapt to the imperatives of the culture in which they reside. Accordingly, this chapter demonstrates that while evangelicals were still influenced by traditional notions of segregationist theology, the growing acceptance of racial equality in American society dictated the need for a new rhetoric to keep segregationist Christianity in line with cultural benchmarks of acceptability. Colorblind individualism proved to be such rhetoric.

Finally, Chapter 5 examines how by the early 1970s white evangelicals utilized the emerging rhetoric of colorblindness in service to the defense of their households. When the Supreme Court forced South Carolina to enact substantive desegregation of the state's public schools in the closing years of the 1960s, white Christian parents interpreted the move as a threat to their children's well-being. In response, these parents helped create private religious schools that functioned as havens, they believed, for keeping their children safe. White Christian parents rarely discussed race, maintaining instead that they were merely following God's mandate to shepherd their children by creating schools with stricter behavioral standards and higher educational expectations than the integrated public schools. But this chapter documents how these private schools, in actuality, represented another bastion of religiously motivated resistance to racial equality and how they helped extend the legacy of segregationist Christianity into the twenty-first century.

Although *The Bible Told Them So* is a study of the twentieth century, the book's five chapters open with a short vignette from the nineteenth century corresponding to the history examined in each respective chapter. The inclusion of these brief prologues at the start of each chapter affirms James Baldwin's powerfully articulated truth that "the great force of history comes from the fact that we carry it within us, are unconsciously controlled by it in many ways, and history is literally *present* in all that we do. It could scarcely be otherwise, since it is to history that we owe our frames of reference, our identities, and our aspirations."[21] The twentieth-century Christians whose stories appear in the pages ahead were deeply influenced by the history they inherited from the century before. Indeed, the segregationist Christianity explored in this book in many respects is merely a continuation and persistence of the white supremacy that has existed across time in the South under many different guises. Recognizing such continuity and persistence is crucial for understanding the present. Segregationist Christianity's ability to evolve and persist means the history described in this book has ramifications for American evangelicalism today, a truth I demonstrate in the book's epilogue.

When John Kennedy appeared on television screens across the country to announce his civil rights bill the week before his showdown with Albert Garner in the East Room, the president declared from the Oval Office that the racial crisis facing the nation was "as old as the Scriptures." Kennedy was right to invoke scripture in his articulation of the racial problem, but not as a marker of time. Instead, as the president learned in his exchange with Albert Garner the following week, scripture was a significant *source* of the problem Kennedy sought to solve. The pages ahead explain why.

1

Not in Our Church

Congregational Backlash to *Brown v. Board of Education*

*William Tecumseh Sherman and his soldiers entered Orangeburg, South
Carolina, in February 1865, only weeks before the horrific war they were
fighting marked its fourth year. The Union general had recently completed
his destructive march across Georgia. Having reached the Atlantic coast, he
turned his army north, determined to bring the full force of military might
against South Carolina, the seedbed of the Confederacy. Sherman had
initiated "total war" during his campaign—destroying anything of military
value as a way to break southern morale—and arriving in Orangeburg,
his federal troops were keen on introducing the town to Sherman's style of
warfare. The county courthouse, depot, and "a good deal of cotton" were
all set aflame, sacrifices to Sherman's war strategy.[1] Although not burned,
Orangeburg's First Baptist Church also played a part in Sherman's foray
through the city. Situated directly across the street from the courthouse, the
church grounds proved convenient for Sherman's men to stable horses and
stockpile supplies while torching the rebels' governmental seat. From the
front steps of the church, Union soldiers watched as flames devoured the
Orangeburg County courthouse on the opposite side of Russell Street. After
two days, Sherman's army departed the church grounds, leaving behind the
smoldering ruins of the courthouse across the street.[2]*

*Three decades after Sherman's uninvited stopover in their community,
white women of Orangeburg set out to redeem the desecration the general's
visit had wrought. They planned to erect a monument honoring those who
had donned Confederate gray during the war and the cause for which they
fought. By 1893, the women's preparation and fundraising efforts were completed. On an autumn day that year, Orangeburg citizens gathered for a
dedication ceremony at the site of the former courthouse. Eager to see the
fruit of the women's efforts, the crowd eventually grew so large that it spilled
across Russell Street onto the First Baptist grounds, providing celebrants the
same vantage point that federal troops had enjoyed decades earlier while*

The Bible Told Them So. J. Russell Hawkins, Oxford University Press. © Oxford University Press 2021.
DOI: 10.1093/oso/9780197571064.003.0002

the courthouse burned. After a prayer by Reverend S. P. H. Elwell and the reading of a letter sent for the occasion by former governor and Confederate general Wade Hampton, the monument was unveiled: a thirty-three-foot stone pedestal capped with a statue of a Confederate soldier, a tribute to those who died defending "our rights, our honor, and our homes."³

But the ceremony was not purely celebratory. It was also a time for somber reflection on the meaning of the Confederacy and the reason for the veterans' sacrifice. For this purpose, the Orangeburg women invited Colonel James Armstrong to address the crowd. In his oratory, the former Confederate officer moved the crowd, vividly recounting the "grand memories and glorious recollections which beautify and ennoble and immortalize the cause" for which the men of Orangeburg and all of South Carolina had given their lives a generation before. Thanking the "noble women" who brought the monument into being, Armstrong reminded his listeners of the importance of such memorials. The statue of the Confederate soldier, forever in uniform with his rifle at his side, would remind all who looked up to his perch "to guard the memories of our fallen comrades, ever to have faith in the righteousness of our cause . . . that cause which the broken shield of the Confederacy resting above the pulseless breast of our President Davis, is as stainless as a star."⁴ The Confederacy had been defeated, but as Armstrong made clear, its purpose remained holy and just.

Armstrong received a "thunderous hurrah" from the crowd—including four hundred former Confederate veterans whose presence lent the ceremony additional honor and solemnity—until a band struck up a rendition of "Dixie" to close the ceremony.⁵ As the crowd dispersed, the Confederate sentinel atop the monument began his silent guard in the shadow of the First Baptist steeple, his back turned defiantly toward the North. After 1893, First Baptist parishioners traversed the steps of their church under the gaze of Orangeburg's memorial to the Lost Cause, a perpetual reminder that the purported righteousness of an unholy and defeated cause can live on as long as people keep it secure in their hearts and lives.⁶

Sixty-four years after the Confederate statue took up its post, the pastor of Orangeburg First Baptist Church across the street faced his own lost cause. The summer of 1957 marked Fred T. Laughon Jr.'s third anniversary in the First Baptist pulpit, but a happy celebration was not forthcoming. Instead, the forty-two-year-old Laughon found himself alone in his study on a June morning that year, pondering his future at the church. Inserting a clean sheet of letterhead into his typewriter, Laughon pecked out a confidential letter for Baptist headquarters in Tennessee to inquire about alternative employment options: "I will try so hard to live as the Lord wants me to do now, but I need a bit of extra strength. I hope I can achieve it. I also hope I won't have to live in it much longer," Laughon wrote. "The bad thing is that there are not many places to go to," the pastor continued. "If you get any ideas for a man like me I'm open to them. . . . Do you know a good college who wants a man without a doctorate who can teach Bible or sociology?"[7] The cause of Laughon's angst and the reason he was looking to exchange the pastorate for the professorate had begun the previous Sunday. As Laughon was making final preparations for worship on June 23, he was approached by Preston Cone, who requested the pastor call a business meeting after the morning service to hold a congregational vote on a resolution prepared by church members. Although two years Laughon's junior, Cone wielded authority in the church as a respected physician and leader of the Laymen's Sunday School class. To ensure Laughon understood that the young doctor's request was in truth a directive, Cone was accompanied by the chairman of the deacons, who also insisted that Laughon hold the congregational meeting after worship. Having no choice, Laughon conceded.[8]

Laughon had long dreaded this day. Over the previous year he had heard discontented rumblings among his parishioners about a growing emphasis on racial integration in Southern Baptist reports and literature, but thus far Laughon had managed to avoid addressing the issue directly with his congregation. But with Cone's request, such avoidance was no longer an option. Accordingly, Laughon preached his prepared sermon on forgiveness, but as the notes of the last hymn faded and the benediction was uttered, the congregation remained seated in the pews rather than filing out of the sanctuary. The time had come for the white members of Orangeburg First Baptist Church to take a stand for racial segregation.[9] Against Laughon's wishes that June Sunday, his congregation unanimously passed a resolution registering their disapproval of the "admission of negroes to any . . . institutions owned and controlled or contributed to by the Southern Baptist Convention." The resolution also threatened that if the Southern Baptist Convention (SBC) did not change course on racial issues, the time may come for Baptist churches in the South to withdraw from the convention and organize a new association of churches that would maintain proper fidelity to Jim Crow segregation.[10]

Laughon was deeply disappointed with his church's action. He personally agreed with the SBC's call for racial integration and believed he had failed to help his two thousand parishioners properly understand the issue.[11] As the summer wore on, Laughon's despondence grew. To his displeasure, the First Baptist deacons followed up their resolution by voting the next month to mail copies of the document to every Southern Baptist church in South Carolina, at which point Laughon began receiving congratulatory letters from Baptists across the state praising him for his fine leadership in taking a stand against race mixing.[12] By the end of July, Laughon decided the time for him to leave his Orangeburg church had arrived. Although his congregation had not asked for his resignation—"for this I am very grateful," Laughon confessed—he had concluded that "the best thing is for me to move on quietly out" at the end of the summer.[13] And so he did.

When Laughon exited First Baptist for the last time, the Confederate soldier the Orangeburg white women had erected the previous century was still standing guard on his pedestal across Russell Street. Though Laughon may not have realized it, his pastoral fate was sealed in part by the sentinel's presence. Laughon's inability to help his white parishioners harmonize their Christian faith with the idea of racial equality was related both consciously and unconsciously to the congregation's veneration of the Lost Cause. Just as James Armstrong had hoped at the monument's dedication in 1893, the Confederate statue had helped sustain notions about white supremacy and the supposed proper racial order in southern society. Such beliefs were essential for maintaining segregation and turning back attempts to foster racial equality in the twentieth century, even within the sacred space of southern churches. The Lost Cause, historians have argued, was tied "to the religion of southern churches. . . . On the racial question, indeed, the southern historical experience as embodied in the Lost Cause provided the model for segregation that southern churches accepted."[14] As Laughon learned in 1957, Confederate statues could wield more moral authority than pastors who were on the wrong side of the integration question. The Confederate soldier who watched over the First Baptist grounds was a constant reminder through the decades that the segregated all-white church meeting across the street did so in accordance with God's will. The white supremacy that the Lost Cause had intended to preserve through slavery lived on after the Civil War, now clothed in the garb of segregation. Segregated churches were included in this postbellum arrangement, and white congregations in the twentieth century intended on maintaining them.

Stories like Laughon's help provide an understanding of conservative white Christians' responses to black civil rights, revealing the disconnect between pronouncements about racial equality sounded by religious leaders and the reception of such pronouncements by local congregations. Laughon's story reminds us who held power in southern churches. Denominations could adopt positions, conventions could issue reports, and ministers could preach sermons, but ultimately the people in the pews decided the fate of platforms and pastors alike. Denominational leaders could espouse an idea, but no guarantee existed that congregations would follow suit. Southern pastors, meanwhile, who were out of step with their parishioners—especially on racial issues—risked losing their pulpits. Such was the case with Fred Laughon. In the end, the young pastor left his church, and his congregation did not mourn his departure. This chapter explains why.

At the very moment Laughon resigned his pulpit, white evangelicals throughout the South were beginning to recognize unwelcomed challenges to their way of life. The perceived threat in white Christians' minds in 1957 sprang not from an encroaching federal government or black demonstrators, though in time white Christians would denounce both. Instead, southern white Baptists and Methodists saw themselves endangered by heretics in their own denominations. The threat southern white churches foresaw came from a slow-burning fuse the Supreme Court had lit on May 17, 1954, declaring school segregation unconstitutional in its *Brown v. Topeka Board of Education* decision.

Southern historians have asserted that the civil rights era constituted a second Reconstruction for the region. In such a framing, the 1954 *Brown* ruling is the twentieth-century equivalent to Robert E. Lee's surrender at Appomattox in 1865, which helped inaugurate the South's first Reconstruction. In the same manner that Lee's surrender at the Virginia courthouse foretold the coming death of legalized slavery, so did *Brown* signal the beginning of the end for Jim Crow segregation. And just as white southern Christians in the nineteenth century had to grapple with abolishing an institution they believed God had ordained, so too did their twentieth-century descendants struggle after *Brown* with the reality that a social arrangement they believed God designed was suddenly unlawful.

A significant difference between 1865 and 1954, however, was the role denominational leaders played leading up to and following these watershed years in southern history. In the nineteenth century, proslavery theologians in southern denominations vigorously defended slavery as scripturally sanctioned in the years before the Civil War.[15] After the war, southern religious leaders recalibrated their proslavery ideas for a society that had seen its "peculiar institution" abolished, helping pave the way for state-sanctioned racial segregation throughout the South in the first six decades of the twentieth century.[16] But if white religious leadership made straight the path of Jim Crow in the 1800s, the same cannot be said of church leaders of the South's two largest religious bodies in the waning days of legal segregation the following century. By the midpoint of the twentieth century, the SBC and the Methodist Church alike stood against racial segregation, issuing statements that either condemned the practice or supported racial equality. In 1947 the SBC, for instance, adopted a race relations platform that included pledges to "teach our children that prejudice is un-Christian" and to "protest against injustice and indignities against Negroes, as we do in the case of people of our own race, whenever and wherever we meet them."[17] Likewise, in 1952, Methodists—who thirteen years earlier had repaired their antebellum split into northern and southern camps over the issue of slavery—declared that "no place for racial discrimination or racial segregation" existed in their churches.[18] Pronouncements like these did not necessarily reflect the thinking of the majority of southern white Christians, but as long as segregation remained the law of the land, such ideas were tolerated.

Following the United States' involvement in World War II, Southern Baptist and Methodist calls for racial equality mirrored a growing rhetoric of freedom and equal opportunity in broader American society. Such pronouncements from the denomination level before the *Brown* decision perhaps suggested that similar rhetoric represented the views of all Baptist and Methodist congregations.[19] Before this 1954 ruling, no widespread backlash in Baptist and Methodist churches in the South to the calls for equality and brotherhood reared its head. It is little surprise, then, that when the Supreme Court reversed the nearly sixty-year-old precedent of "separate but equal"—an arrangement voluntarily practiced in southern churches since the end of the Civil War—as unconstitutional, SBC messengers and Methodist bishops supported the ruling at their 1954 gatherings.

Yet the *Brown* decision changed the political calculus of the South in ways that would be replicated in Baptist and Methodist churches across the region. One prominent historian argues that rather than improving race relations or providing for substantive desegregation, the immediate effect of the 1954 *Brown* ruling was widespread backlash by southern whites, thereby effectively putting an end to racial moderation in the South for several years.

Movement toward ending state-sanctioned racial discrimination that had gathered momentum in the early years of the Cold War suffered a major setback after 1954 as southern politics veered hard to the right in reaction to *Brown*.[20] As it was in southern politics, so it was in southern churches. After the *Brown* decision, denominational calls for racial brotherhood and egalitarianism—which, prior to 1954, had received little comment from local churches—became anathema.

This change was not immediate. Meeting in St. Louis just two weeks after the Supreme Court issued its *Brown* ruling, the SBC adopted a report from the convention's Christian Live Commission (CLC) recognizing the ruling as being in "harmony with the constitutional guarantee of equal freedom to all citizens, and with the Christian principles of equal justice and love for all men."[21] The CLC report further reiterated the convention's support for the country's public schools, praised the court for suspending the implementation of its ruling until additional hearings could be had, and urged Baptists and all Christians "to conduct themselves in this period of adjustment in the spirit of Christ [and] pray that God may guide us in our thinking and our attitudes to the end that we may help and not hinder the progress of justice and brotherly love."[22] The resolution's adoption was overwhelming, nearly nine thousand to fifty, by some estimates.[23] But, before the messengers approved the resolution, signs emerged that *Brown* provoked rumblings of dissent that would, in time, erupt in churches across the South.

When the floor opened for discussion on the report's adoption, Pastor W. M. Nevins spoke first. "Brother moderator, brethren, for over 60 years I have been attending our convention. . . . I never expected to live to see the day when we would acknowledge we had been unchristian in our attitude toward the Negro race or any other race. I believe in emancipation; I believe in equality; I believe the Negro ought to have equal rights and all other citizens of our country ought to have constitutional rights," Nevins declared, "but I do not believe the Bible teaches and I do not believe that God approves amalgamation of the races." Nevins launched into a story to make his point:

> A short time ago I was visiting in a home in Lexington and the lady said she thought we had been very unfair to the Negroes, that we ought to take them into our homes, into our churches, into our schools, into our restaurants, into our hotels. I looked down and saw that she had two little girls that were growing up. I said, "Sister, when these girls get old enough to have company, how would you like for a Negro man to date them and come home

with them and sit in your parlor and court them and possibly marry them?"
And she said, "Oh, that's a different question." I said, "I beg your pardon, it's
exactly the same question." And brethren, that's what we're coming to if we
amalgamate these races. I don't believe the Bible endorses it; I don't believe
God approves it; if we're going to eat with them and go to school with them
and go to church with them, the time is going to come . . . when some of you
that sit in this audience today will have grand children with Negro blood.[24]

Nevins then urged his fellow messengers to eliminate support for the
Brown decision from the CLC report before yielding the floor to messenger
Arthur Hay from New Mexico. Hay lent support to Nevins's fears with
anecdotes of white women dating black men at a university near his home.
Hay concluded his comments by citing scripture that supposedly prohibited
interracial marriage and declaring, "Negroes are descendants of Ham [and]
we whites must keep our blood pure."[25]

Following Nevins's and Hay's diatribes, Jesse Weatherspoon, a prominent
member of the CLC, stepped in and effectively ended the debate over the
report: "The Supreme Court of the United States has made a decision. . . .
There is no immediate appeal from that." Weatherspoon continued, "We're
not going to shut our eyes to the fact that now in a critical period our nation
needs men of faith, men who believe in Jesus Christ, not to put our feet in
the mud, but we need to lift our hearts and to raise our minds to understand
as far as we can what is the Christian thing to do in a most difficult time."
The choice became clear. If the messengers followed the proposal of Nevins
and Hay and refused to show support for the *Brown* decision, Weatherspoon
argued, "we are saying to the United States of America 'Count Baptists out
in the matter of equal justice.'"[26] Moved by the passion of his appeal, SBC
messengers responded to Weatherspoon's earnest plea by adopting the CLC
report. But the arguments Nevins and Hay offered at the convention could
and would not be ignored. As the backlash to *Brown* grew, such arguments
found receptive audiences among southern white Christians, opening up
chasms between denominational positions and congregational beliefs. These
chasms existed on various levels in South Carolina: between state denominational bodies and their respective national counterparts; between the
state denominational bodies and local South Carolina churches; and, finally,
between ministers and parishioners within particular congregations themselves. Taken together, these conflicts illustrate that after *Brown*, conservative white Christians in the Palmetto State were no longer willing to abide

racial moderation in their church bodies. Ultimately, *Brown* became a line in the sand that conservative white South Carolina Christians would defend for nearly the next two decades.

South Carolina Baptists and *Brown*

In 1954, the South Carolina Baptist Convention occurred after the national SBC had already adopted the report endorsing the *Brown* ruling. At the state convention in November of that year, messengers meeting in Greenville asked church members to "earnestly and prayerfully" seek God's will on the issue of school desegregation, but these messengers did not take a position on what that will might be. They did, however, adopt a report from the convention's Social Service Commission that "urged an attitude of friendliness in race relations, [and] a general strengthening of public schools."[27] It was one thing to adopt a report encouraging racial harmony and egalitarianism at a national or state convention, but quite another to implement such ideas in local churches. Church laity was overwhelmingly against the idea of racial integration. Indeed, two years after *Brown*, 90 percent of the white population in South Carolina still opposed desegregation in schools. Thus, church laity found denominational sanctioning of such integration confusing.[28] Meanwhile, most Baptist pastors in the state tried to keep quiet on the issue rather than risk alienating their parishioners.[29]

As the CLC continued to produce pro-integrationist material in the years after 1954, lay Baptists' confusion turned increasingly to anger while Baptist ministers found it increasingly difficult to stay neutral. Such was the case in 1956 when the CLC disseminated theology professor's T. B. Maston's article supporting a Christian view of integration. Pastor Ralph Lattimore read Maston's article and then wrote to Baptist headquarters in Nashville to tell the author his errors. While Lattimore appreciated the effort Maston put into his writing, the South Carolina pastor found it "difficult to agree with [Maston's] conclusions when he does not have the complete picture of our problem in the South." According to Lattimore, "Much progress was being accomplished until the Supreme Court's decision regarding the public schools. Most of our citizens disagree with the decision and are dedicated to keep our schools separate. More help can be given our Negro friends if we follow the separate school and church plan."[30] As Lattimore viewed it, the SBC was causing harm by promoting articles that were "entirely contridictory [*sic*] to what they really believe" and suggested that the convention should focus on publishing materials that would "assist the pastor . . . and not harm his efforts" as Maston's article had so done.[31] Integrationist materials like Maston's, Lattimore informed SBC leaders, "will not help us here in the South. It will cause many pastors and laymen untold concern."[32]

Pastor C. Doyle Burgess of Paxvile, South Carolina, concurred that support for integration coming from SBC headquarters was causing unwanted stirs in Baptist churches. Writing to the CLC, Burgess suggested that white southerners when reading the commission's materials were bothered by "advocating [of] the mixing of the race[s] . . . into our churches." Burgess reported that after reading some of the CLC materials, his parishioners wondered, "Are the leaders of our denomination intimating, suggesting, or projecting the idea that we as Baptist Churches should open our doors to our colored brother and invite him to come and worship with us?"[33]

While Burgess harbored suspicions that the CLC was encouraging integration, others had no doubt. For example, Harry E. Dawkins from the First Baptist Church in Langley, South Carolina, was certain that the CLC had fallen prey to false teaching. When the commission published and distributed Pastor Avery Lee's pro-integration pamphlet, "Some Quiet Thoughts on a Turbulent Issue," Dawkins registered his disagreement with the author: "I must say that I am surprised [that] the Christian Life Commission has published this pamphlet at the expense of our Convention when certainly your views are not the views of all Southern Baptist Preachers," Dawkins wrote to his fellow minister. "In your reasoning you admit that you have not been preaching the true gospel until the Supreme Court opened your eyes," Dawkins continued. "I think Mr. Lee that you have been blind to many facts and you ought to re-examine your position. The ultimate goal of the NAACP in America is to bring about one race which of coarse [sic] will be a Mongoleon [sic] race. Do you have any children that you can encourage in an inter-marriage relationship?" Dawkins asked Lee. Dawkins ended his missive on a strident note, capturing the gulf between material published by the SBC and the reception such material found in local churches: "Preach, Sir, what you may in your own pulpit but do not have you views published and paid for out of cooperative program gifts to promote you own philosophy."[34]

After reading pro-integration material from the Christian Life Commission, Pastor George Lanier of the Beulah Baptist Church in Branchville, South Carolina, found irony in the commission's name: "You seem to be not so much concerned about 'The Christian Life' as that of using your offices and the money given to The Cooperative Program, etc., by our churches all over the [S]outh, to promote integration. What you are doing is quite alien to me as to what 'The Christian Life' really is," Lanier wrote.[35] On the issue of integration, Lanier believed "it is neither wise nor Christian for you to be so absurdly one-sided on this matter. Still more so for you to be calling those who do not agree with you un-Christian, ignorant and prjudiced [sic]."[36] Lanier ended his letter succinctly: "As for myself I do not care for your literature and I think that is true for thousands like me."[37] On this count, Lanier was correct.

Similarly, William Lancaster, the pastor of the First Baptist Church in Mullins, South Carolina, wrote to SBC leaders in Nashville to inform leaders there that the state convention was growing concerned with the material coming from headquarters supporting integration. "I take this opportunity to appeal to you, Sir, and to this Christian Life Commission, to go extremely slow in this matter," Lancaster wrote. In Lancaster's estimation, articles that supported racial integration "[have] not helped the christian [sic] cause in the deep South. To the contrary, it has hindered it. If the Commission will refrane [sic] from further declarations, publications and pronouncements . . . the cause of missions generally will be aided and abetted," Lancaster predicted.[38] Lancaster's warning to slow the tide of integrationist materials was indeed warranted. In South Carolina, discontent with the CLC boiled over after the 1957 SBC meeting in Chicago.

Because of the backlash in the years since 1954, members of the CLC had decided not to mention anything about race in their report to the convention in 1957. But for the sake of Baptist efforts evangelizing to nonwhite races around the globe, Baptist missionaries on furlough in the United States urged the CLC to include a strong statement against segregation in its report. Additionally, these missionaries requested that the commission put forward a pro-integration statement "that could be adopted by the official action of the Convention."[39] The CLC decided the racial climate was too volatile for the latter suggestion, but it did acquiesce to the missionaries by including a section against segregation in its 1957 report. Unfortunately, the speaker who submitted the report "took off into an extemporaneous discussion which placed both the Commission and its report in the wrong light," drawing perhaps unwanted attention to the CLC report.[40] In truth, the 1957 report was not much different from reports adopted in previous years. Nevertheless, perhaps being misled by the idealistic oratory proceeding the vote coupled with not understanding that actions of the SBC are never binding on individual churches, the

Associated Press (AP) reported that in adopting the CLC report, the SBC had endorsed racial integration and would open SBC churches to desegregation. As one South Carolina Baptist preacher wrote in the months that followed the erroneous AP story, there are three words "which makes folks in this state lose all objective reasoning power. They are: [f]raternities, dancing, and integration. The very mention of these words evokes an emotional episode among our people."[41] The preacher was not wrong. As the AP story circulated among South Carolina Baptists, churches in the state responded both quickly and emotionally indeed.

The congregation at the Edisto Baptist Church in Cope, South Carolina, passed a resolution declaring that "no Negroes [will] be allowed to attend a service or worship or any other meeting" at their church.[42] The Ebenezer Baptist Church in Cordova, South Carolina, declared that as a result of the CLC report, they would no longer send money to the convention's cooperative program, which funded the CLC. Instead, the church designated giving to "those institutions and causes that maintain segregation," believing this action "to be right in the sight of God and man for the best interest of the White and Negroe [*sic*] races."[43] In response to the alleged actions of the SBC in Chicago, the First Baptist Church of Denmark, South Carolina, voted unanimously at their quarterly church meeting "to go on record as opposing integration in any form" in their church.[44] The official newspaper of South Carolina Baptists, *The Baptist Courier*, was so inundated with angry letters and church resolutions protesting the CLC that the trustees allowed the paper to stop publishing them.[45]

In September 1957, tensions between South Carolina Baptists and the SBC grew when the Baptist seminary at Wake Forest in neighboring North Carolina agreed to allow qualified African American students to enroll at the school. For at least two Baptist churches in the Palmetto State, the decision by Wake Forest combined with the SBC's distribution of material they deemed integrationist meant that it was time to speak out. Both the Springfield Baptist Church in Orangeburg, South Carolina, and the Black Creek Baptist Church in Darlington County adopted resolutions that complained of the SBC's actions as being not "in accordance with the beliefs and desires of the churches of the Southland."[46] The Springfield congregation professed their belief "that the welfare of both races will be best served by having separate public schools, churches and Church Institutions," and they "[did] not intend to continue to support integrated Schools or Institutions." Furthermore, the Orangeburg congregation suggested that if the SBC continued endorsing integration, it might be necessary "to dissolve the so-called Southern Baptist Convention and reorganize, according to regions, different associations with Churches that share like beliefs and convictions."[47]

Baptist churches throughout South Carolina soon followed Springfield Baptist's lead, adopting resolutions denouncing the Southern Baptist Convention's pro-integrationist stance and suggesting it may be time to leave the convention altogether.[48] In October the Orangeburg Baptist Association, a voluntary organization of thirty-three Baptist churches in that city, adopted a resolution protesting integration in Baptist seminaries and colleges and alluded to "further action in protest thereof" if pro-integrationist practices continued.[49] The following month, the Santee Baptist Association followed suit, protesting the SBC's dissemination of "material encouraging integration of the races" and emphasizing that "the solution to the race problem is not to be found in . . . Supreme Court decisions."[50] By 1958, the antagonism between local churches and the SBC was so great that pastor Marion Woodson pleaded with the CLC to stop putting out material: "For God's sake and the sake of the Southern Baptist—and Cooperative Program, will you discontinue your obnoxious reference to integration and segregation? Please?"[51]

A degree of self-interest was embedded in Pastor Woodson's request. After 1954, the growing rift between the SBC and local congregations put clergy in uncomfortable positions. Southern ministers who were sympathetic to any degree of racial egalitarianism were often forced to avoid publicizing such views for fear of retribution from their parishioners. In particular, the vulnerability of Baptist pastors was acute because of the congregational polity in Baptist churches, which allowed the local congregation to replace its minister whenever it so desired. The son of a white Baptist minister in this period captured the reality of Baptist ministers' job security this way:

> If you are a Baptist preacher and want to be successful, you better size up the people quickly. If they want aqua carpet instead of the standard maroon, you'll take a sudden liking for the aqua. If they root for Ole Miss over the Crimson Tide, you'll not say too much about your fondness for the Bear. If they want you to keep quiet about Negroes, you'll put a lid on your uneasy conscience. No bishop or presbyter will come to your defense. The local

church is free to do its own thing, governed by the contingencies of race, class, and custom, by whatever idiosyncrasies prevail.[52]

As the backlash to *Brown* grew, so too did pressure on South Carolina pastors as the state's political leaders began to call into question clergy who refused to support segregation. Former governor James Byrnes cautioned clerics that "there is no better way for a minister to divide and destroy a congregation, than by entering the field of politics." Furthermore, Byrnes questioned the motives of pastors who did not toe the segregationist line: "While I do not question a Minister's right to oppose segregated schools for political reason, I do question his right now to declare 'unchristian' and 'sinful' the segregation laws that exist in almost half the states of the Union," Byrnes declared. "As a rule, the people of the South are Church-going people. They are familiar with the great preachers of the various Christian denominations who for the last century have supported segregated schools and Churches and have carried the Truths of Christianity to our people. They revere the memories of these good men who by their eloquent sermons and Saintly lies have influenced millions and inspired them to better lives," Byrnes chided. The governor was especially critical of pastors who had recently labeled segregation as contrary to the Christian faith. "These political preachers who declare segregation to be sinful should explain why through the years they have practiced segregation in their Churches. And when they indict all the great leaders of the Christian Churches for leading 'unChristian' lives, true Christians will ask God to have mercy on their souls."[53] For pastors who took the opposite side of the race issue than their congregation, their parishioners sought more than God's mercy; in some cases they forced pastors to abdicate pulpits, as illustrated in an incident from the Batesburg Baptist Church.

In the fall of 1955, Batesburg Baptist was pastored by George Jackson Stafford, a popular minister who during his tenure had grown the church membership rolls as well as its budget. Stafford favored school desegregation and as a delegate to the SBC in St. Louis the year before had voted to adopt the resolution supporting the *Brown* decision. Stafford knew not to be publicly vocal about his views on race; he preached no sermons on the topic and was not linked to any civil rights activities in the state. But in October 1955, Stafford was forced to resign his pastorate after his views on desegregation became known.[54] When a journalist reached out to Stafford to obtain his side of the story, the pastor cooperated. "My religious conviction on the subject of race relations is that a Christian should treat others as he would have them treat him, regardless of race," Stafford wrote. "In regard to the United States Supreme Court decision of May 17, 1954 declaring legally enforced segregation in the public schools un-constitutional," the minister continued, "I believe that the court decision is in keeping with the constitutional guarantee of equal freedom to all citizens, and also is in harmony with the Christian principle of equal justice and love for all men."[55]

Stafford made clear to the reporter that he had never publically expressed his views apart from a single vote he cast as a Baptist messenger in 1954. But he *had* privately expressed his views to the head of his church deacons, George Timmerman.[56] Timmerman was no common parishioner. Himself a federal judge, Timmerman's son and fellow Batesburg Baptist church member, George Timmerman Jr., was the South Carolina governor, having been elected in 1954. The younger Timmerman made his gubernatorial run on an anti-integration platform and could therefore hardly be expected to attend a church whose min-ister harbored feelings for segregation that were opposed to both his own and those of the majority of South Carolinians who had voted for him. In response to learning of his pastor's position on integration, the elder Timmerman sent Stafford a pamphlet arguing that Christianity and segregation were compat-ible. Stafford politely disagreed with the conclusions. "It is obvious that different people interpret the Bible differently as to what constitutes Christian race re-lations," Stafford wrote Judge Timmerman. "Since Godly and Christian men do have different interpretations of Christian race relations, I have taken the attitude that I will not exceed the limits of my position or responsibility in pro-moting my personal view on the subject. And I hope always to be motivated by the Christian virtues of humility, patience, courage, and love."[57]

Timmerman rejected Stafford's attempt to peacefully coexist in the same con-gregation. "I have definitely come to the conclusion—based on thoughts I have had for quite some time—that you and I do not belong in the same church," the judge wrote to his pastor. "Your letter in effect reaffirms what you told me some time ago about your attitude, viz.: that you favor not only the abolition of segre-gation in our public schools and churches, but also the integration of the negro and white races," Timmerman continued. "You claim Biblical support for your position. I am convinced that you have no such support and that, in practical effect, your position amounts to no more than a condemnation of God's act in creating the races of men. I am unwilling to support any movement in or out of church that has as an objective the abasement of mongrelization of my race."[58] Timmerman then informed Stafford he was going to make his concerns known at the next deacons' meeting.

When Stafford responded by asking Timmerman to put his concerns in writing, the judge was happy to do so. "I concede your right to believe in mixing the races in our public schools, but I do not concede you the right to represent to the world that our church joins you in that belief. . . . [I]t is . . . my opinion that you misrepresented the vast majority of [church members] when you voted in favor of racial integration [at the SBC in 1954]."[59] Timmerman repeated the charge that Stafford told him in Timmerman's home that the pastor favored mixing races in schools, churches, Sunday Schools, and the church playground and, most significantly, that Stafford had professed no objection to interracial marriage. With this in mind, Timmerman concluded, "I still believe that your position amounts to no more than a condemnation of God's act in creating the races of men. I know of nothing in the Bible that records Christ as having condemned segregation, although segregation was practiced while He was on earth, even in the synagogues."[60]

True to his word, Timmerman shared his concern with the other Batesburg deacons. When Stafford proffered his resignation after a drawn-out battle with the board of deacons, only a small minority of the church members voted to accept it; the others simply refrained from voting, a move Stafford no doubt appreciated but nonetheless did nothing to save his job.[61] As Stafford's case demonstrates, even privately held sentiments that deviated from the segregationist line could result in a minister's dismissal if such sentiments became known.

Reflecting on his experience months after his dismissal, Stafford surmised, "I do not think . . . the action of the deacons in forcing my resignation represented the attitude of the church members at large as much as it represented the prevailing political atmosphere of South Carolina."[62] In this respect, Stafford was likely correct. But as the political backlash to the *Brown* ruling gathered momentum in South Carolina, it became increasingly difficult to separate political views from religious belief, further exacerbating tensions between clergy and laity. Such was the situation among South Carolina Methodists in the aftermath of the *Brown* decision.

South Carolina Methodists and the Citizens' Councils

The rifts that appeared in South Carolina religious bodies after 1954 mirrored the growing backlash to the *Brown* decision that occurred throughout the state in the 1950s. Over a twelve-month period beginning in late 1954, reactionary responses to *Brown* surged in South Carolina in the form of white resistance groups organized to fight the integration of the state's schools. By November 1954, pro-segregation groups, such as the States Rights League, the Grass Roots League, and the National Association for the Advancement of White People, had formed in the rural eastern part of South Carolina. In addition to these groups, the powerful State Farm Bureau grew ever more vocal in its protest of *Brown*, arguing that segregating the races was a matter of local, rather than federal, concern. These efforts at local organizing and grassroots movements would later prove to be the scaffolding for the massive resistance bulwark that would culminate in the Citizens' Council movement in South Carolina beginning in the summer of 1955.[63]

Citizens' Councils had first formed in Mississippi less than two months after the *Brown* ruling in 1954. The idea behind the Citizens' Council movement was twofold. First, the councils were used to rally apathetic white southerners to the cause of segregation by educating them about the danger of racial integration. The second purpose of the councils—and the reason for the organization's notoriety—was to prevent desegregation by taking advantage of black economic dependence on the white power structure of southern society.[64] In this way, the councils could stave off attempts at school desegregation by using economic pressure. If black parents signed a petition requesting their child be transferred to an all-white school, for instance, the local Citizens' Council would spread this news through its network. As this information circulated, the black parents might suddenly find their credit cut off at a local grocery store or have their mortgage called in by the bank. Because the councils were composed of prominent members of southern society, they were able to exert pressure on anyone, white or black, who attempted to violate segregation.[65]

Having proven their effectiveness in preventing African Americans from integrating schools in Mississippi, council chapters sprang up in communities across the South. The first Citizens' Council in South Carolina organized in Orangeburg County in August 1955, after several black families petitioned local school boards for permission for their children to attend the now unconstitutional all-white schools.[66] When the council pressure successfully caused these families to rescind their petition, other councils began mobilizing throughout the state. For South Carolina whites opposed to desegregation, the Citizens' Councils' tactics of economic intimidation to keep local blacks in check were reassuring.[67] By October 1955, the council movement had become so popular among white South Carolinians that they formed at a rate of one per week in the state for the next year.[68] Almost immediately, the councils flexed their political muscle, writing to senators and congressmen to express their disappointment that national leaders were not doing more to protect their way of life and demanding that their elected officials state on the record what efforts they were taking to preserve segregation.[69]

The councils quickly caught the attention of South Carolina leaders. Senator Strom Thurmond began appearing at council rallies in December 1955 to speak about the importance of segregation in schools, earning high praise from councilors for doing so. "YOU are a great American, and should RIGHT NOW 'throw your hat in the ring' for the presidency," a satisfied constituent wrote to Thurmond after hearing the senator defend segregation at a Citizens' Council meeting.[70] As the movement grew, so did Thurmond's support of it, with the senator frequently returning to attend organizing rallies for the councils throughout 1956.[71] "Rest assured," Thurmond informed the Florence Citizens' Council, "I shall do everything possible to help maintain segregation in our schools."[72]

Thurmond was not the only politician supportive of the councils. At a rally in Kingstree in early 1956, over 1,300 people packed a local auditorium for a Citizens' Council rally featuring Congressman Mendel Rivers. People had to be turned away at the door as white South Carolinians from around the state came to hear the congressman defend segregation.[73] Councils, meanwhile, distributed pamphlets across South Carolina denouncing integration with titles like "The Ugly Truth about the NAACP" and "Conflicting Views on Segregation." Such pamphlet dissemination was a service the councils performed well into 1960s, eventually registering an extensive list of pro-segregationist titles that sympathetic parties could consult in defense of white supremacy.[74]

By January 1957, the Association of Citizens' Councils in South Carolina had grown to nearly sixty local chapters and initiated a drive to increase that number.[75] In addition, by 1958 an effort was put forward to organize a state-wide Citizens' Council. Apprising Strom Thurmond of these efforts, Pastor Marion Woodson—who weeks earlier had scolded the Southern Baptist CLC for disseminating integrationist literature—informed the senator that his fellow Southern Baptists "appreciate your fight for our rights and [hoped Thurmond would] never grow discouraged in this continued fight for our great Republic. The south is praying for you and supporting you I am sure." Woodson further encouraged Thurmond that his efforts were not in vain, saying, "Southern Baptists are beginning to rally to the side of segregation more and more. Keep up the good work."[76]

The statewide Citizens' Council became active in supporting causes beyond school desegregation, such as petitioning the federal government to keep Veterans Affairs hospitals segregated, claiming "the humiliation of integration causes deep phychological [sic] reactions on physically helpless war veterans which could greatly injure their health and well being in a way likely never to be undone."[77] The South Carolina Citizens' Councils also passed resolutions denouncing the end to an investigation of black New York congressman Adam Clayton Powell that did not lead to prosecution and condemning the appointment of Wilson White as assistant attorney general of civil rights. But the issue of school desegregation was always paramount. In a letter to Thurmond a local council wrote, "We would like to state to you that . . . we are back of you 100 percent in your fight for state's rights and keeping our schools segregated in South Carolina; and at any time that we can be of service to you in your work, please feel free to call upon us."[78] With the *Brown* decision threatening to end their segregated way of life, white southerners clung to the councils for hope in troubled times. Discussing the council movement's promise, a former South Carolina state senator in 1956 confessed that the councils could possibly achieve what the state could not, saying, "Naturally the state will use every legal means to head off destruction of constitutional rights, but in the final analysis, the Citizens' Council movement stands between segregation and integration."[79]

The Citizens' Council movement's growth in South Carolina paralleled the rising intolerance white Christians had for pronouncements from church leaders calling for more moderate race relations. In some instances, the councils even nurtured potential rifts between the laity and clergy by sending out questionnaires to South Carolina ministers to gauge their feelings on integration. These questionnaires included such queries as "Do you think it is a Christian attitude to integrate people against their will?" and "Do you think segregated schools are best for both races?" In explaining the reason for the surveys, J. A. Shuler, the chairman of the Charleston, South Carolina, Citizens' Council, reported, "We are not trying to put pressure on any minister. We are only trying to get information that we may find the understanding to make a better community in which to live. We hope that each minister will cooperate in answering these questions that we might keep our Council on a Christian basis."[80] The councils may have denied attempts to pressure ministers, but given the organization's widespread popularity among white South Carolinians, any church leader who crossed the Citizens' Councils risked retaliation, as two Methodist ministers learned in 1955. Their story reveals how the power of white laity in southern churches could be wielded in defense of racial segregation in the 1950s.

Like other national denominations, the Methodist Church supported the *Brown* ruling at an early date. Six months after the Supreme Court's decision, the church's Council of Bishops issued a statement making explicit the Methodist denomination's official position on the ruling: "The declaration of the [*Brown*] decision was made in the magnificent home of the Supreme Court in Washington, but the ultimate success of the ruling will be determined in the hearts of the people of the nation," intoned the bishops. "We accept this responsibility," the bishops declared, "for one of the foundation stones of our faith is the belief that all men are brothers, equal in the sight of God. In that faith, we declare our support of the ruling of the Supreme Court."[81] Of course, unwavering support of this type for *Brown* could hardly be expected at the state level in the South. And indeed, a month before the bishops met in Chicago and issued their statement in support of *Brown*, white South Carolina Methodist delegates at their annual conference served notice of their opposition to the "mandatory mixing of the races."[82] This opposition to integration passed unnoticed in 1954, but the following year it resulted in upheaval in the state.

The white annual conference meeting of the Methodist Church in South Carolina coincided in 1955 with the arrival of the first Citizens' Councils in the state. As delegates gathered in Florence that year, the councils were already showing their ability to stop racial integration, thereby drawing the attention of several Methodist clergy who were concerned about the group's tactics of economic and political intimidation. These ministers decided their denomination should say something about such abusive practices. Late Saturday afternoon, the day before the conference meeting was to conclude, two young ministers brought a hastily drafted resolution before the assembled group of Methodists for its consideration. The resolution's authors, A. McKay Brabham Jr. and John V. Murray, thought it necessary to take a stand against the Citizens' Councils use of economic coercion to maintain segregation. Their resolution in part read as follows:

Whereas, it has been brought to our attention through the public press that various communities in our state are in the process of organizing groups commonly titled Citizens' Councils . . . and whereas it is popularly supposed

that these councils are being formed for the express purpose of exerting economic pressure upon a portion of our citizenry to prevent the exercise and
development of their moral conscience and their civil rights according to
the dictates of their conscience, now therefore be it RESOLVED, that we
the members of the South Carolina Conference here assembled do hereby
affirm our belief in the Sermon on the Mount as the basic expression of
Christian philosophy of behavior toward others and do further declare our
belief that any action which seeks to strip a person of his means of liveli-
hood in violation of his conscience is a contradiction of the basic teachings
of our Lord and Master.[83]

It was a short statement—less than two hundred words in total—and was
passed without much fanfare. But in the ensuing weeks and months after
its adoption, Brabham and Murray's resolution resulted in a firestorm of
protest from Methodists across the state and exposed in clear ways the
fault lines between white Christians and church leaders over the issue of
racial equality.

Days after its passage, Brabham denied that his resolution explicitly
condemned the Citizens' Councils movement in South Carolina, a position supported by a close reading of the resolution. "The resolution did not
discuss segregation, for or against. It neither condemned nor commended
the 'Citizens' Councils,'" Brabham wrote in a letter to his local newspaper.[84]
Instead, Brabham and Murray's resolution condemned using economic pressure against a person simply for pursuing their constitutional rights. Another
minister wrote to the pro-segregationist *Charleston News and Courier*
attempting to make this same distinction. "Now the Methodist Conference
did not oppose the Citizens' Council movement, but simply disapproved as
unchristian talk of coercion," wrote Reverend Albert Betts, attempting to
quell the growing backlash to the resolution. "The Citizens' Council movement may yet prove to be a very constructive step forward, probably settling
many questions out of court with justice, goodwill and cooperation among
all concerned," Betts predicted.[85] The *Methodist Advocate*, the official organ
of South Carolina Methodism, likewise tried to clear up the "misunderstanding" about Brabham and Murray's resolution. In an editorial, the paper
reported, "There was nothing in the resolution criticizing the Councils as
such. The Conference was not asked to evaluate the Council movement as a
whole, nor did it do so. The resolution said nothing for or against segregation

itself."[86] In the ensuing uproar about the resolution, nuances of this variety went unappreciated. For the majority of white South Carolina Methodists, any threat—be they real or imagined—to the racial status quo could not be countenanced. And by clearing the way for black South Carolinians to exercise their civil rights, the resolution seemed a challenge to Jim Crow.

The *South Carolina Methodist Advocate* portrayed Brabham and Murray's resolution in a positive light. A week after the annual conference ended in Florence, the *Advocate* ran an editorial titled "A Conference to Be Proud Of . . . ," which listed various achievements that came out of the Florence meeting. "The Conference pointed up the lack of Christian insight in the actions of those Citizens' Councils in the state that are using or plan to use economic pressure upon minority groups," the editorial reported, concluding that "this was a much-needed statement for an age in need of religious guidance in controversial areas."[87] Such words supporting Brabham and Murray's resolution proved too much for Carol Ervin of Dillon, who wrote the *Methodist Advocate* to register her complaint about the journal's endorsement. "I wonder how many members of the membership in general of The Methodist Church in South Carolina are proud of what happened in regard to race relations at the Conference in Florence," Ervin asked. Displeased that her denomination was spending time dealing with an issue "so foreign to the question of Christianity," Ervin placed the blame squarely at the feet of the clergy. "It is unfortunate for us that we have leaders in our Church who receive such satisfaction and sublimity from breaching this isolation," Ervin wrote. In concluding her letter, Ervin captured the divisions that would grow in southern churches as the civil rights movement progressed: "We are seriously opposed to *a certain few* expressing such a viewpoint as coming from The Methodist Church which we love and of which we are a part."[88] Ervin's letter reflects the lines that began to harden between South Carolina Methodists over racial issues in the mid-1950s.

The *Charleston News and Courier* noted such lines and ran several editorials highlighting the tension between the small number of church leaders desiring racial change and the majority of the denomination who found the idea of desegregation reprehensible. Referring to Brabham and Murray's purported anti–Citizens' Council resolution, the newspaper speculated that its passage was not in accordance with the "sentiments of most churchmen in South Carolina." In support of this claim, the paper reported that at an organizing rally for a Citizens' Council chapter in Orangeburg, the most prolonged applause of the evening was drawn by a man who lambasted " 'so-called Christian leaders' for calling separation of the races 'un-Christian.' "[89] After local Methodist congregations began to make known their disagreement with Brabham and Murray's resolution, the *News and Courier* returned to the cleavage between church leaders and the laity, suggesting:

> Church leaders may find their spiritual influence does not extend to matters which are essentially social. If they insist on pressing social theories unacceptable to the majority of people, these people may withdraw support from churches or change their leaders. Of the two courses, we believe a change of leadership would cause less damage. The fundamental beliefs of religion do not change with fashions of social thinking or even with the personalities of churchmen. As more congregations and individual members make known their feelings on the great social and political issues of the day, we believe that officials of the denomination will heed them.[90]

Whether responding to the *News and Courier*'s editorial or acting on their own accord, South Carolina Methodists did make known their support of segregation. Across the state, South Carolina Methodists responded to Brabham and Murray's resolution with resolutions of their own in *support* of the Citizens' Councils. For example, the Asbury Memorial Methodist men's club endorsed organizing the councils "to preserve control in the hands of law-abiding, right thinking Christian people and insure the continuation of separation of the races in accordance with the will of God in creating different races," and sent their resolution to the bishop and conference superintendent.[91] Similarly, the official board of the Elloree-Jerusalem Charge Methodist Church unanimously voiced their opposition to the annual conference's Citizens' Councils resolution. The church board "hereby goes on record as condemning the action of the South Carolina Methodist Conference in adopting the said resolution and respectfully requests that the action of said Conference be rescinded as soon as possible."[92] Methodists in Norway, South Carolina, adopted almost word for word the same resolution as their brethren in the Elloree-Jerusalem church, but they also noted why they disagreed with Brabham and Murray. Regardless of their tactics, the Norway church reasoned that the Citizens' Councils were doing invaluable work "for the purpose of protecting and fighting integration in our public schools." Along these lines, the Brabham and Murray resolution "does not express the views of the members of the Norway Methodist Charge," who "strenuously oppose any form of co-mingling of the white and colored races in any of [the denomination's] churches, colleges and assemblies."[93]

In adopting their resolution against Brabham and Murray, the official board of the Kingstree Methodist Church emphasized that racial integration was a political issue, and thus church leaders had no business trying to in-fluence thinking on the subject, although the church held its own opinions. The Kingstree church declared, "Too many leaders and ministers in our Methodist Church have been saturated with propaganda and even made to have a guilt complex with reference to the question of integration of the races." In response, the Kingstree official board resolved to stand behind the Citizens' Councils and any other individuals or organizations whose purpose was to "maintain segregation in our schools, churches, or other institutions where it is traditionally felt that to do otherwise would be harmful to the races."[94] At the Hemingway Methodist church, the issue of racial integration was concerning enough that both the church's official board and its Women's Society of Christian Service adopted resolutions opposing action by the denomination that would mix the races, with the women's society plainly stating, "We are definitely in favor of racial segregation."[95]

Individual Methodists also wrote letters registering their disagreement with church leaders over the Citizens' Council resolution. "The Citizens' Councils are everything we could have hoped for: community organizations, with almost unanimous support, led by the natural leaders of the commu-nity (not politicians), by the lay leaders of the Methodist Church," declared Thomas Traywick in a letter to the *Methodist Advocate*.[96] Another layman, Robert Rowell, from Trio, articulated his personal ideas about responding to the growing rift between the laity and clergy over desegregation. "We . . . ought to refuse to receive or support any minister who believes in the false doctrine of mixing the races. We ought to have all Methodists who be-lieve in segregation to organize to this end. We ought to make it our business to find out what our ministers believe before next Annual Conference."[97] And Charles Haigh of Florence hoped that the events that transpired at the annual conference would "awaken some of these complacent church members who need a jolt." Chastising his denomination's leaders, Haigh wrote, "You people should be attending Citizens' Councils and lending your moral and physical support to the same instead of trying to break them up."[98]

No doubt to Haigh's pleasure, some Methodist ministers came out in support of the Citizens' Councils after the 1955 annual conference. One dis-
placed northern minister who chose to settle in South Carolina because of
his preference for the state's "people, climate, and conditions" wrote to the
Methodist Advocate that in his judgment, "the formation of Citizen's [*sic*]
Councils and other organizations seems to me perfectly proper."[99] Likewise,
Reverend E. S. Jones of St. Paul's Methodist Church in Orangeburg also
offered support for racial segregation a week after the annual conference
passed Brabham and Murray's resolution. In a written statement to his
congregation, Jones noted, "A number of people have asked that I make a
statement concerning the question of races in the public schools. I have
from the beginning felt that it was unwise for the races to be thrown together in the public schools and I have not changed from that position."[100]
Some lay Methodists believed it necessary to defend their beleaguered ministers in the aftermath of the Citizens' Council resolution. Speaking of the
many ministers he had encountered, one Methodist layman stated, "Most
of those I know deplore the sinful intermixing of the races . . .[and] about
97 percent of the ministers come from the same backgrounds as the laymen.
I have heard of no plan to put anything over on the laymen."[101] Yet many lay
Methodists suspected such a plan existed, questioning how the resolution
could have otherwise passed.

Indeed, exactly how the resolution garnered the necessary votes for passage became a contested point in the aftermath of the resolution's adoption.
In its initial reporting on the affair, the *News and Courier* noted that Brabham
and Murray's resolution only "drew some scattered negative votes" before
being passed without discussion.[102] After the *Methodist Advocate* put the
estimated margin of victory for Brabham and Murray's resolution at 150 to
12, a delegate who had opposed the resolution took issue with the journal's
numbers. "I made it a point to look around [to] see just how many voted
against the resolution," layman David McLeod wrote. "There were very few
present at this session and an estimate of 150 'yea' votes in my opinion, was
extremely excessive." In McLeod's estimation, the only reason the resolution
passed was because it was "sprung" on the conference members late Saturday
afternoon after many lay delegates had already left.[103] Had the laity known
it was coming, McLeod suggested, the resolution would have never passed.
Disproportionate representation of clergy members became a popular explanation for the resolution's adoption. The *News and Courier* cited a source who
confirmed that the Citizens' Councils resolution was "passed after . . . most

lay delegates had left."[104] The Asbury Memorial Methodist Church's men's club adopted a resolution of their own specifically condemning the procedure that, in their view, made the Citizens' Council resolution passage possible, charging, "The annual conference of the Methodist Church of South Carolina did at an inopportune moment late on the afternoon of August 27, 1955, pass a resolution that condemns the organization of Citizens' Councils, which could not have been passed at a scheduled time."[105] To avoid another situation of having a resolution foisted on them, E. Robert Rowell admonished his fellow Methodists that "all lay delegates should **go** and **stay** until the Annual Conference is over."[106] Lay Methodists claiming they were not properly represented when the vote occurred on the Citizens' Council resolution heightened the divide between the clergy and laity. "Rules, policies, etc., may be made by church officials but the laymen will carry the final vote in his or her support of the church," wrote Cohen Davis of Charleston Heights.[107] Highlighting the validity of Davis's assertion of lay authority is the case of Reverend John Murray, the coauthor of the Citizens' Council resolution whose career was suddenly altered by his resolution's passage.

Murray was the minister for four small churches in Orangeburg County, none of which were pleased with their minister's newfound fame as cosponsor of the Citizens' Council resolution. Representatives of the board of stewards from each of Murray's churches met with Orangeburg district superintendent Pierce E. Cook and asked that Murray be relieved of his duties at their churches, "due to his being co-author of a resolution passed at the recent South Carolina Methodist Conference."[108] In turn, the superintendent conferred with the bishop over South Carolina, with both men determining that the best course of action was to transfer Reverend Murray to a different charge. The whole affair took place so quickly that within a month of his resolution's passage, Murray had been relieved of his duties in Orangeburg and transferred to the Gilbert charge in Lexington County, a location where racial tensions were less pronounced.[109]

Murray continued pastoring his four congregations until his replacement could be found. In the bulletins for his churches the Sunday after his fate had been decided, Murray included a short letter informing his congregations of his imminent transfer due to "the misunderstanding arising from the resolution, of which I was the coordinator, passed by the South Carolina Conference." Until a new pastor could be found, the embattled Murray offered to continue his ministerial duties, telling his congregations, "If I can render pastoral service to the churches during this period, I shall be happy to do so."[110]

Murray's transfer was met with approval from advocates of the South
Carolina Citizens' Councils. "We congratulate the church on its courageous
action in asking that the preacher be relieved of his duties and removed from
the charge who offered the resolution in Florence," a Methodist from Beaufort
wrote, adding, "the pity of it all is that he [Murray] was pushed off on some other
charge."[111] But for Methodist ministers, the action taken against Murray sent
a distressing signal. Unlike Baptist churches, church polity in the Methodist
structure did not grant authority to the local congregation on matters concerning ministerial appointment. Transferring a minister who did not cater to
the views of his congregation set a dangerous precedent, wrote one minister,
because "such action makes the position of the minister mighty hazardous not
only with reference to the racial issue but any other issue where laymen may
disagree with the clergy. . . . We are not a called ministry, and laymen must be
taught again, if our system is to survive, that they **will take** the minister assigned
to them," declared Reverend James M. Copeland.[112] In the mid-1950s, however, issues of race in South Carolina were volatile enough that even a Methodist
minister—one ostensibly protected from lay backlash by the bishop—could be
dismissed for offending his parishioners' racial sensibilities.

The tensions that arose in South Carolina churches in the wake of the *Brown*
decision in the mid-1950s reveal several important points for understanding
how conservative southern white Christians responded to black civil rights.
First, these tensions demonstrate that there was a significant divergence between
official denominational pronouncements and the accepted beliefs of the majority of lay members within those denominations on the issue of racial equality.
The progressive, even moderate, reports and resolutions that Southern Baptists
and Methodists adopted both before and immediately following the 1954 *Brown*
decision had no discernable impact on altering the racial perspectives most
white Christians held during this period. As the laity proved in both words and
deeds, they alone were the true arbiters of the position southern white churches
would take on the issue of segregation, regardless of church polity.

Second, because the laity held the balance of power in southern churches,
ministers were often ineffectual agents in leading their congregations into
positions of harmony with denominational calls for racial equality. From
secure positions in seminaries, future clergy of more progressive theological persuasions occasionally boasted about their ability to enact changes in
southern churches. For instance, in protest of John Murray's transfer and the
entrenched racism such a move reflected, seminarian Mason Stapleton Jr.

wrote to the *Methodist Advocate*, predicting, "I think it must also be said that I am not a voice crying in the wilderness. The chorus is swelling. I am one of a group who will soon be leaving the walls of seminary to take upon ourselves the frightful task of ministering in the Church of Christ. If I know us all aright, we shall come, if necessary, in the name of him who said, 'I come not to bring peace, but a sword.'"[113] Such words proved almost impossible to practice in the 1950s. White southern Christians atop the racial hierarchy were not prepared to question their racial beliefs. Any minister attempting to prompt a re-examination of these beliefs did so at the risk of his job security. During this period, southern ministers quickly learned that speaking out for racial reform came at a high cost.[114]

Four months after their Citizens' Council resolution passed, as Methodists were still decrying it in publications around the state, a journalist wrote to Brabham and Murray to obtain their views on school integration. Fearful that his remarks would be misrepresented, Brabham responded, "I have given a good deal of thought to this matter and have come to the conclusion that I have nothing to say at this time. . . . If I could write the headline which would accompany the article, I might find I have something to say."[115] Brabham eventually left the pulpit for a more secure position editing the *South Carolina Methodist Advocate*, where he raised the ire of conservative Methodists in the state for years to come.[116]

In his circumspect response to the journalist, Murray demonstrated he had learned an important lesson in the wake of his transfer. Although he demurred to publishing his views, Murray responded confidentially that "[a] pastor, in a new field of work, can very easily be misunderstood, especially when he speaks on controversial social issues. Since I have been in my present pastorate less than six months you can understand why I do not wish to make a statement."[117] Respecting Murray's position, the journalist did not publish the pastor's reply. "The pulpit is ever this earth's foremost part; all the rest comes in its rear; the pulpit leads the world," novelist Herman Melville accurately wrote in the nineteenth century.[118] But in the following century the arrangement had switched; Melville's aphorism regarding clerical leadership was turned on its head in southern white churches on the issue of race. As the examples of Fred Laughon, George Jackson Stafford, and John Murray demonstrate, southern pulpits were unable to lead their people anywhere other than where the pews wanted to go.

Finally, because the power of southern churches resided in the laity, the true position of southern churches on racial questions is best understood at the grassroots level. From this vantage point, we can begin to understand how southern white Christians sought and were often able to maintain segregation of the races in their churches, schools, and homes in the years after 1954. But before examining how white Christians carried out these battles, we must understand why they did so. The theological basis for white Christians' defense of Jim Crow is where we turn next.

2

The Bounds of Their Habitation

The Theological Foundation of Segregationist Christianity

When the First Baptist Church in Camden, South Carolina, held its inaugural worship service in 1810, black and white Christians alike were numbered among the faithful. The congregation met in a simple, wooden-frame structure congruous with the town in which it stood, a small community situated along the banks of the Wateree River. In the decades after First Baptist's founding, African Americans were a contributing and valued part of the church body. Church records from the antebellum period include both free blacks and slaves on membership rolls, describe various leadership positions blacks held in the church, and record the dates of African American baptisms. Inclusion of black parishioners at First Baptist did not imply racial equality existed in congregational life or, for that matter, even within the sacred space of a baptismal service. After all, the same records documenting a slave's new birth in the waters of baptism also noted the permission granted by white enslavers to receive this ordinance—a stark reminder of white supremacy's prevalence and the enslaved's status as "property" even within the church.[1] Nonetheless, in the decades before the Civil War, First Baptist Church of Camden fit the model identified by historians as spaces where blacks and whites had interracial exchange on ground more level than perhaps any other part of southern society.[2]

This biracial arrangement abruptly ended. In the first weeks of 1866, less than a year after the guns of the American Civil War had fallen silent, attendance in the First Baptist pews thinned. On the morning of January 22 of that year, the black members of First Baptist gathered for a day-long meeting to consider their future in the Camden congregation. At the end of a day of deliberations, the black assembly adopted a resolution declaring that "the time has come when our religious interests and the wants of our people demand that we form ourselves into a separate church." First Baptist's white deacons readily agreed, providing letters of dismissal to all 104 of their black

The Bible Told Them So. J. Russell Hawkins, Oxford University Press. © Oxford University Press 2021.
DOI: 10.1093/oso/9780197571064.003.0003

parishioners that same day. Wasting no time, the dismissed members called a pastor and established a church of their own the next morning. This all-black congregation met just down the road from their former church and called themselves Mount Moriah Baptist. With Mount Moriah's founding, white-only worship commenced at First Baptist for the first time in the church's history. What slavery joined together, freedom had put asunder.[3]

The actions of the founding members of Mount Moriah Baptist Church anticipated conclusions the South Carolina Baptist Convention published only weeks later regarding new churches for recently freed slaves. "There is reason to believe that in certain localities, and under certain circumstances, [black Baptists] will prefer to be organized into separate churches," the convention stated. In such cases, the convention recommended that black parishioners be given letters of dismissal and allowed to establish their own congregations. The state convention, however, cautioned that black members should remain at their current church "until such time as they themselves shall of their own accord seek separation and a distinct organization."[4] From the state convention's perspective, the separation of churches along racial lines after emancipation was inevitable. It was not a question of if black parishioners would seek their own vine and fig tree, but when. Undoubtedly, churches like Mount Moriah helped shaped the state convention's assumptions while also proving them true.

Ninety-one years after Camden's First Baptist Church agreeably dismissed its black members, its congregation took steps to ensure they would not return. On a Sunday morning in November 1957, after the hymns had been sung, offering collected, sermon preached, and altar call given, Pastor Floyd Montgomery convened the First Baptist members in a business session to address a crisis: black Americans shaking off the shackles of second-class citizenship. The signs of a coming revolution were becoming difficult to ignore in the fall of 1957. The previous year, African Americans—under the leadership of a black Baptist minister—captured national attention in waging a successful boycott in Montgomery, Alabama, to desegregate the city's buses. Earlier that same fall, President Dwight Eisenhower had dispatched bayonet-wielding soldiers of the United States Army to Little Rock, Arkansas, to assist black students in their integration of Central High School. This action in Arkansas came on the heels of the federal government bowing to years of pressure from black Americans by passing the first civil rights legislation since Reconstruction. For the white parishioners gathered in the First Baptist pews that late fall morning in 1957, the racial integration of southern society and perhaps even of their own church likely seemed a real possibility for the first time in their collective memories, a possibility these white Christians could not accept. A century earlier, black and white Christians had lifted their hands and bowed their heads together in worship in the sanctuary of the First Baptist Church. But those days were no more. So it was on that autumn Sunday in 1957 that when the board of deacons presented a resolution making clear First Baptist's "unalterable opposition" to the "integration of the white and colored races in either the schools or Baptist churches of the South," the all-white congregation adopted the resolution as stated and mailed it directly to the Southern Baptist Convention headquarters to register their beliefs.[5] In the minds of the white parishioners of the First Baptist Church, segregated Sundays were not merely the result of human preference, but the manifestation of divine will.

First Baptist Church's theological logic was more fully articulated in a resolution passed at a church up the road from Camden by the Clarendon Baptist Church in Alcolu, South Carolina. When adopting their resolution denouncing integration in October 1957, the white parishioners of Clarendon Baptist included additional rationale that revealed the theological convictions from which such resolutions emerged:

> We believe that integration is contrary to God's purposes for the races, because: (1) God made men different races and ordained the basic differences between races; (2) Race has a purpose in the Divine plan, each race having a unique purpose and distinctive mission in God's plan; (3) God meant for people of different races to maintain their race purity and racial indentity [sic] and seek the highest development of their racial group. God has determined "the bounds of their habitation" (Last part of Acts 17:26).[6]

This resolution explicitly stated what Camden First Baptist's had only implied: God had segregated the races for his own purposes, given this arrangement divine sanction, and instructed the faithful through scripture not to pursue racial integration. What began as a voluntary separation between Christians of different races in the nineteenth century had, by the midpoint of the twentieth, become a holy command in the minds of many white southerners.

As the push for civil rights began in earnest throughout the South in the 1950s, white Christians—both clergy and laity alike—turned to their faith to mount a defense. These white Christians preached sermons, published pamphlets, and authored articles and books that mined both nature and scripture for supposed evidence of God's support of Jim Crow segregation. Taken together, these sources constitute a theology of segregation that helped shaped the Christian imaginations of white southerners and served as the foundation for Christian resistance to racial equality in the middle decades of the twentieth century. When competing theological interpretations called into question the legitimacy of segregationist Christianity, few Jim Crow apostles were persuaded. Instead, segregationist Christians waged a defense of their hermeneutics on democratic grounds by pointing to such theology's popular support. Segregationist Christians were ultimately outflanked in the public sphere by both civil rights activists and federal legislation that brought *de jure* segregation to an end in the South. But white Christians did not surrender the belief that God had ordained segregation. Even as civil rights advanced through the South, some Christians implored elected officials to maintain Jim Crow as an act of obedience to God.

Developing a Theology of Segregation

Christians who understood God to be the author of racial segregation predictably derived their theological position from the Bible. But scripture was never the lone rallying cry of those who interpreted Jim Crow as God's will. Instead, before they ever cracked the cover of the Good Book, Christian segregationists saw divine sanction for segregation manifested in the book of nature. As a theological principle, general revelation suggests that humanity can learn about God through observation of the natural world; for many white southerners in the mid-twentieth century, nature revealed God to be a segregationist. "The heavens declare the glory of God and the firmament sheweth his handywork," a segregationist minister quoted from the nineteenth Psalm. "The corollary of the above passage," continued Pastor W. C. George, "is that since nature is God's handywork, it reveals his laws to those who have the diligence and the insight to discover them."[7] Following George's line of thought, white Christians found in nature divine justification for Jim Crow.

While employing both scripture and general revelation in their defense of Jim Crow, Christian segregationists such as Festus F. Windham challenged anyone to prove that segregation was sinful. "I am referring to *voluntary* segregation," Windham clarified, the kind he believed existed between southern whites and their black neighbors. "We find much voluntary segregation even in nature," the Alabama Sunday School teacher continued. "Hordes of black ants several times larger than the little red ants do not integrate with any other ants, though they may live not too far apart in their ground tunnels."[8] When Dr. Mack P. Stewart Jr. similarly explained to his congregation of nearly a thousand why he believed in segregation, the Louisiana Baptist minister said, "I am a segregationist because God ordained it. It is true with plants and animal life. . . . If you leave plants and animals alone, they will stay separated. Animals will not mix. Birds will not mix. Plants do mix if left alone. God intended it that way."[9] In like vein, the Reverend William Talley Jr., a Methodist preacher in Florida and Alabama, affirmed this interpretation of general revelation, writing, "Birds, fish, and any animal you care to name is separated according to 'kind' in keeping with the primary creative formula by God Himself."[10] And in one of the most widely circulated defenses of segregation in the 1950s, Reverend G. T. Gillespie insisted that God built racial separation into nature. "The fact that man . . . is a gregarious animal and that human beings everywhere and under all conditions of life tend to segregate themselves into families, tribes, national or racial groups," Gillespie told his audience of white Presbyterians, "only goes to prove that all human relations are regulated by this universal law of nature."[11]

Carey Daniel, the pastor of First Baptist Church in West Dallas and vice chairman of the local Citizens' Council chapter, suggested that the earth's geographical features further demonstrated God's intent to keep the races apart. "Mother Nature, with her huge geographic barriers of oceans, deserts, and gigantic mountain ranges, clearly confirms that [God prohibited the mixing of the races]," Daniel proclaimed the Sunday following the *Brown* ruling in 1954.[12] *The Councilor*, a segregationist newspaper in Louisiana whose circulation reached a reported quarter-million readers, reprinted an article by the Reverend A. C. Lawton that echoed Daniel's perspective: "God originally separated his five races by mountains, oceans, continents, language and colors. God does not change and his color scheme should never be obliterated as world powers are trying to do today."[13] In like manner, H. C. McGowan, a self-described "servant of God," perceived segregation in the heavens predating even the creation of humanity: "After God had created the heavens, He made the other worlds, stars, suns, moons, and all the other wonders that are in the heavens; and God created them, He separated them from each other, and set each one in his individual place with perfect balance and commanded them, 'Hitherto shalt thou come, but no further.' "[14]

Believing that God separated each created entity, many southern white ministers, Sunday School teachers, and evangelists declared that the integration of blacks and whites violated God's plan since God himself had created the different races and endowed them with the desire to remain distinct. Even a cursory observation of the natural world, they believed, revealed this truth. Birds of a feather, in fact, flocked together. But if evidence from nature was not enough, white Christians also posited that the South's flourishing and, indeed, the shedding of God's grace on the entire nation under Jim Crow further indicated God's segregationist preferences. After all, these men supposed that if God desired integration, why would he have so generously lavished favor—and in these white Christians' minds, God clearly had—on a region that practiced racial separation. Apologists of this stripe could not comprehend why segregation would now come under attack by some in the church and wondered why the South had enjoyed God's blessing if the separation of the races was contrary to Christian teaching.[15] As one Baptist church group wondered, "If segregation became wrong in 1954 [with the *Brown* decision] why was it not wrong before that year? And, if it is wrong, why has the God of both races so wonderfully blessed the area . . . where total segregation has been practiced?"[16] To express belief that the South's blessings and divine favor had come because of segregation, Methodist pastor Medford Evans quoted from the New Testament book of Matthew: "By their fruits ye shall know them." With all the blessings the South enjoyed, Evans succinctly concluded, "The system of segregation has worked."[17] In similar fashion, Reverend Maylon D. Watkins interpreted God's favor as extending beyond even the boundaries of the South, writing, "For over 150 years our nation has prospered under the practice of separation of the white and negro races. With this practice our nation has built the most churches, the best schools, and has become the wealthiest nation with the highest standard of living for all people of any nation of earth."[18] If God was intolerant of segregation, why were his blessings so abundant, pondered white Christians.

Although southern white Christians utilized the natural world and their region's perceived flourishing to build their case against racial integration, they derived the majority of their arguments for divine segregation from the pages of the Bible. "Who wants desegregation?" C. W. Howell asked in the pro-segregation pamphlet he published for fellow Christians. "I am going to say first the Devil wants it. Because his desire is to oppose the teachings of God's Word and God's Word plainly teaches **separation** which is **segregation**."[19] In agreement with Howell, countless white Christian clergy and laity throughout the South understood the Bible to be a segregationist text and combed through scripture to prove it.

A common starting point in such efforts was the Genesis story of the Tower of Babel. In the Babel account, "the whole earth was of one language and of one speech" until all humanity decided to build a city with a tower reaching to heaven. With their work progressing, God intervened. "Behold, the people is one, and they have all one language . . . and now nothing will be restrained from them, which they have imagined to do." At the story's end, God confounded humanity's language and "scattered them abroad from thence upon the face of all the earth."[20] Segregationist Christians read the Tower of Babel story as the point when God separated people groups and placed them where he wanted. According to this narrative, southern whites and blacks are segregated races placed exactly where they are by God's hand. They thus viewed the federal government's attempt to hoist integration upon the South as a plan contrary to God's clear intent as established in the Babel story. Calling attention to some religious leaders' support for racial integration in the 1950s, one segregationist Christian sarcastically declared, "The good church people of the United States want to rebuild the Tower of Babel." After writing a twenty-four-page pamphlet to protest church leaders' involvement in anti-segregation causes, the New Orleans businessman-turned-segregationist publisher Stuart Landry concluded, "Let it [the church] not try to rebuild the Tower of Babel, and to attempt to bring together in concordance, discordant and disintegrating elements of the great human family, separated by God thousands of years ago."[21]

Beginning with the premise that God had separated people at the Tower of Babel, segregationist Christians asserted that maintaining segregation was essential to God's plan for humanity. Reverend Montague Cook unpacked this perspective in a sermon series he preached to his congregation in Georgia in the fall of 1963. According to Cook, God created his chosen people by calling the Jews to be set apart from other groups. The Baptist preacher deduced from his reading of scripture that "one of the basic requirements God set up for his 'holy' people, and which was reaffirmed by the prophets and a thousand years of Jewish history was **racial segregation**."[22] Other segregationist Christians shared Cook's interpretation, culling from their Bibles examples of God's desire for races to remain apart. Most of these citations were Old Testament passages that spoke of God's prohibition of or punishment for intermarriage between Jews and those outside of Israel. From Abraham's desire to find a wife for his son Isaac from his own people rather than the surrounding Canaanites to Ezra's command that returning Jewish exiles from Babylon "put aside" their foreign wives, segregationist Christians pointed to a host of biblical figures whose actions purportedly demonstrated God's desire for racial separation. Meanwhile, stories such as Sampson's illicit liaisons with the Philistine Delilah and Solomon's marriage to hundreds of foreign wives supposedly revealed that God punished disobedience in the area of racial purity with death and destruction. In these stories and others, white Christians saw examples of divine endorsement of Jim Crow and cited passages ranging from Genesis to Jeremiah in support of these separatist interpretations.[23]

Having established that racial segregation was an acceptable and indeed necessary part of the biblical narrative, segregationist Christians extrapolated the importance of Jim Crow for their contemporary society. "As the Jew was the instrument of God's purpose in the development of monotheistic religion, which in turn produced a Messiah, so the white man is God's instrument in the development of modern civilization," Montague Cook told his congregation. The Georgia minister continued, "As racial segregation was vital in maintaining the racial quality that made the Jew serviceable, so racial segregation is now necessary to maintain in the white race those qualities which can control and advance the civilization which the white race has produced."[24] Following such logic, southern Christians applied the set-apartness of the biblical Israel to the racial separateness of white Americans. Seemingly, both groups were God's agents of civilization and redemption for the rest of the world.

Those who espoused such a Christian defense of segregation in their arguments often conflated social integration and racial intermarriage. "The enemies of God, who would destroy Christianity, know that they must turn the white race into a 'coffee-colored race,' if they are to succeed," A. C. Lawton cautioned his readers.[25] In the view of Georgia pastor "Parson Jack" Johnston, more than just Christianity was at stake in the issue of intermarriage: the fate of the world was also in question. After all, Johnston reasoned, the sin that led God to destroy the earth with Noah's flood was "mongrelization." Johnston quoted from Genesis to support this assertion: "And it came to pass when men began to multiply on the face of the earth, and daughters were born unto them, that the sons of God saw the daughters of men that they were fair: and they took them wives of all which they chose."[26] Although God had promised not to destroy the earth again in a flood, his wrath could still be poured out in other ways.

The ubiquity of sentiments similar to Lawton's and Johnston's reveals that a fear of miscegenation lay at the heart of segregationist theology and was foundational to Christian support of Jim Crow.[27] But interracial sex was not the beginning and end of all biblical interpretations fashioned in service of segregation. Instead, Christians buttressed biblical proscriptions against interracial marriage with additional scriptural proofs that had nothing to do with the marriage bed. In such passages, these Christian believers found additional evidence to demonstrate that God's desire for segregation extended beyond his apparent disapproval of interracial sex.

C. H. Hardin, for instance, pointed to God's response to history's first murder as proof of God's segregationist leanings. As punishment for killing his brother, Abel, God put a mark on Cain and made him wander the earth. As Hardin interpreted the story, God's marking of Cain was the first instance in which God enacted segregation.[28] As Christian defenders of Jim Crow continually pointed out, God's support of segregation occurred regularly in scripture, even appearing in the more esoteric parts of Levitical law: "Thou shalt not let thy cattle gender with a diverse kind: thou shalt not sow thy fields with mingled seed: neither shall a garment mingled of linen and woolen come upon thee." From these divine decrees, southern white Christians extrapolated God's detestation of mixing races.[29] Should anyone object to their appeal to Old Testament laws as a valid defense of segregation, Christian segregationists noted that in the Sermon on the Mount, Jesus himself declared that he came not to abolish the law but to fulfill it and that "one jot or one tittle shall in no wise pass from the law, till all be fulfilled."[30]

The biblical defense of segregation, however, was not limited to passages from the Old Testament, though explicit verses in support of Jim Crow from the New Testament were more difficult for segregationist Christians to come by. According to C. R. Dickey, the reason for this difficulty was quite natural: "New Testament writers said little or nothing about the law of segregation because it never occurred to them that Christians would question or repudiate any fundamental law in the Old Testament," Dickey explained.[31] Undeterred by the challenge of finding explicit material supporting segregation in the New Testament, segregationist Christians combed through the gospels and epistles for evidence that God maintained his desire for segregation even after the Word became flesh. Such efforts turned even the most seemingly irrelevant New Testament passage into a segregationist proof. According to Marvin Brooks Norfleet, for instance, Jesus was a segregationist as evidenced by the fact that upon his return all nations will be gathered before him, "and he shall separate them one from another."[32] William F. Johnson, meanwhile, noted that in the book of Acts, Philip the evangelist and the Ethiopian eunuch met together only briefly in a chariot until the Holy Spirit "immediately . . . restored segregation" when Philip was supernaturally spirited away.[33] Using Paul's letters to the Corinthians and to Timothy in which the apostle discussed women's submission to men, Reverend J. U. Teague concluded that "the modern teaching that God created all people equal in every respect is not substantiated by the Scriptures."[34] Teague therefore reasoned that the racial equality civil rights activists were attempting to impose upon the South opposed biblical precepts.

Maylon D. Watkins also made use of the apostle Paul's first letter to the Corinthians to find justification for segregation. Quoting Paul's instruction to "let all things be done decently and in order," Watkins concluded, "To mix the races is not only unscriptural and unChristian, it is indecent, disgraceful, and completely and altogether out of order."[35] In addition to using Paul's epistles to support their cause, segregationist Christians also drew defenses of Jim Crow from the apostle's life. For instance, citing the example of Paul and fellow missionary Barnabas's decision to separate in the wake of a disagreement, E. Earle Ellis reasoned that "even within the church the differences between individuals and/or groups are not done away. Paul and Barnabas came to the conclusion that in certain circumstances their best unity lay in separation." Employing this interpretation as a response to other Christians' call for unity on racial issues, Ellis declared, "The unity of Christians does not necessarily mean a physical 'togetherness' or organizational conformity; the Kingdom in the church does not negate the church's relation to the social customs of the world."[36]

Without question, the biblical verse cited most often by white Christians in the twentieth century to defend segregation came from another of Paul's actions. As recounted in the book of Acts, during Paul's visit to Athens, the apostle gave an impromptu sermon before the philosophers of the city in which he declared that God "hath made of one blood all the nations of men for to dwell on all the face of the earth and hath determined the times before appointed, and the bounds of their habitation."[37] Using this scripture verse, segregationists read Paul's words to mean that God had drawn limits between the physical space of people groups. Acts 17:26 then became a favorite among segregationist Christians. For example, Henry W. Fancher's thirty-one-page booklet "Segregation: God's Plan and God's Purpose" was said to be inspired by the Alabaman pastor's reading of this single verse, and few segregationist pamphleteers failed to utilize the verse at some point in their Jim Crow defenses.[38] Being so widely cited, Acts 17:26 was for twentieth-century segregationist Christians what the Curse of Ham account had been for nineteenth-century proslavery Christians: the foundational scriptural passage from which much of their hermeneutic sprang.[39]

Interestingly, integrationists often appealed to the first half of Acts 17:26—the idea that God had made all the peoples of the earth from one person—as evidence that all humanity shared a common ancestry before God and could therefore lay claim to the equality that Jim Crow denied. Christian segregationists rejected this interpretation as biblical proof-texting. "One of the worst things any preacher and any Bible teacher can do is take a piece of Scripture out of its context," J. Elwood Welsh told his Baptist congregation in Columbia, South Carolina, before launching into a sermon defending segregation as Christian. "For many good people in our denomination and many in other denominations, both clerical and lay, who entertain opposite opinions on this great matter as voiced this morning, I have only the profoundest respect. . . . But having said all this, I cannot suppress expressing my surprise at some of the conclusions many of these good people come to," said Welsh, drawing his sermon to a close. "I cannot concur in their conclusions. I am baffled to understand their refusal to face many self evident facts. I am stunned at their urging mixed membership in our churches."[40]

Reverend Welsh was not alone in his confusion over calls for racial equality and integration by some in southern churches. For segregationist Christians like Welsh, the idea of racial integration ran counter to everything they had observed in the church or heard from the pulpit. As some religious bodies began calling for moderation on racial matters in the wake of the 1954 *Brown* decision, Christian defenders of segregation were forced to respond to their fellow Christians' biblically based calls for integration. Religious leaders who called for racial equality, for example, cited the apostle Paul's declaration that "There is neither Jew nor Greek, there is neither bond nor free, there is neither male nor female: for ye all are one in Christ Jesus."[41] W. Clyde Odeneal's response to "those who advocate the violation of God's law" in citing this passage from Galatians mirrored the usual rejoinders segregationists gave when confronted with these supposedly biblical calls for racial equality. To segregationists like Odeneal, Paul was not speaking literally about there being no distinction between the races for those in Christ. After all, Odeneal reasoned, Christians retained their differences in sex as "conversion to the Christian faith neither destroys nor changes the sex of the convert. With both sex and race the lack of distinction is spiritual, not physical or racial."[42] The emphasis on the spiritual rather than the physical was a crucial distinction for Christian segregationists. "When I was living in China as the son of a missionary," Pastor Carey Daniel explained, "I was one in spirit with every born-again Christian in my native homeland, even though we were separated physically by the widest ocean in the world."[43] According to Daniel's logic, spiritual unity should not be confused with physical proximity. It was possible for black and white Christians to be one in spirit and still respect Jim Crow's customs. Indeed, black churches and white churches could exist—and in fact, *should* exist—and God's law be honored.

As the civil rights movement effectively highlighted the incompatibility of racial segregation with the ideals of a liberal democracy, many southern white Christians remained unmoved, demonstrating the possibility of deriving a defense of segregation from a particular reading of the Bible. In response to these segregationist interpretations, the *South Carolina Methodist Advocate* as early as 1954 offered advice to those turning to scripture to deny black gains in civil rights. "A lot of people these days are saying that segregation has divine sanction. Sometimes they even go so far as to say that segregation is supported by the Bible. Therefore, so the argument goes, segregation is in accord with God's will, for the Bible says so. Christians need to be careful here," the editors cautioned. "What is happening is that many people have already made up their minds about segregation, and then go back to the Bible to find 'proof' texts to support their view. This is not good exegesis, nor the proper way to use the Bible."[44] The newspaper's warnings largely went ignored. Good or proper exegesis has never been a prerequisite for constructing a usable theology, a fact southern white Christians would continually demonstrate in the years to come.

Defending Segregationist Theology

When the States' Rights Council of Georgia formed in 1954 as an organization that "supports wholeheartedly the system of racial segregation," the group moved quickly to address a point of concern for segregationist

Christians. In the South, the council noted, there exists "some agitation for the mixing of the races in churches and schools on the false premise that 'segregation is unChristian.'" The States' Rights Council called upon Methodist minister J. Paul Barrett to bring some clarity to the dispute. In his sermon, "The Church and Segregation"—later published by the States' Rights Council and circulated throughout the South—Barrett rehearsed the standard arguments many white Christians employed to demonstrate that God's word supported the segregation the Creator designed. But Barrett also assured his audience that they need not be overly concerned about fellow Christians who saw the issue differently: "I am aware that some churches and church leaders have followed strange ideas and strange voices. But because some are misled does not mean that all are misled. There was a Judas Iscariot among the twelve apostles but they were not all traitors." "There are some," Barrett allowed, "who sincerely believe that segregation is wrong. But they are in the minority."[45]

Reverend Barrett's assertion that only a minority of Christians supported racial integration was significant for legitimizing segregationist Christianity. Historians have long noted the democratic nature of American Christianity in which "it is the *people* who are custodians of orthodoxy."[46] Orthodoxy, in other words, is determined in the United States by majority rule. For segregationist Christians, then, the legitimacy of their biblical hermeneutic was predicated not on "sound" exegesis but on popular opinion. For this reason, it became imperative for segregationist Christians to demonstrate that while some of their fellow believers may have been led astray by the false teachings of integrationists, the majority of Christians maintained that God demanded racial segregation. In the eyes of segregationist Christians like Paul Barrett, there would always be those within the church who erred in their biblical understanding, a situation as unavoidable as it was unfortunate. But as long as the many—either in actual numbers or simply perception—accepted segregation as biblical, it mattered little that the few did not. Segregationist Christianity was rendered true by popular belief, not by the standard of proper exegesis. On these grounds, Christian segregationists as well as their opponents sought to cast themselves as the majority during the civil rights years.

The battle to claim the majority position was highlighted in a 1959 incident in South Carolina. In April of that year, newly elected governor Fritz Hollings publicly stated that integration would never come to the South. In response to the governor's statement, Methodist minister James Copeland wrote a letter to the Charleston *News and Courier* questioning Hollings's prediction. The governor, Copeland wrote, "should realize that the Christian Church and its leadership are almost solidly behind the doctrine of the brotherhood and equality of all races of men." Copeland conceded that there were some ministers "here and there" who might speak out against integration, but these ecclesiastical leaders by no means represented the majority of white pastors.[47]

Copeland's letter reverberated throughout South Carolina, generating dozens of replies that took issue with the Methodist minister's premise that only a few church leaders defended segregation. Some South Carolinians were upset enough with Copeland that they registered their disagreement in state newspapers *other* than the *News and Courier*, which had published Copeland's letter.[48] When the *News and Courier* declined to print Copeland's response to one of these letters, the Methodist minister and the paper's editor, Thomas R. Waring Jr., the latter a staunch segregationist, exchanged heated missives: "I can understand your refusal to print my letter. . . . [T]he truth hurts, doesn't it? In fact, I can well understand why you do not wish to start another round," Copeland wrote to Waring. "Segregationists really hate the light."[49]

For his part, Waring did not let Copeland's charges go unanswered. "You say that you understand our refusal to print your second letter, but in the next sentence you show that you have chosen to misunderstand," the newspaper editor responded. "Your generalization that 'segregationists really hate the light' is an enlightening reflection on your own thinking. My acquaintance with other Methodist ministers leads me to believe that in this respect you do not represent their customary approach to these grave matters," Waring wrote in closing.[50]

One of the other ministers to whom Waring referred was William C. Stackhouse, pastor of Trinity Methodist Church in Charleston, South Carolina. Waring had passed along his correspondence with Copeland to Reverend Stackhouse for the Charleston minister's thoughts. "I feel that you have made a wise decision not to print further letters from Mr. Copeland," Stackhouse confided to Waring. "Anything further that he might have to say on the subject could only lead to further misunderstanding on the part of the general public as his views relate to the clergy in general. While I cannot deny that some of the brethren are too far to the left," Stackhouse continued, "by and large his view represents only the fringe minority, the less notice we can give to such the better off all concerned will be. Unfortunately, there are many people who will accept [Copeland's] view as being typical of the clergy in general."[51]

As the letters exchanged between Waring, Copeland, and Stackhouse reveal, integrationist and segregationist clergy alike were eager to claim the mantel of the majority. For every James Copeland who claimed that the majority of southern clergy stood solidly behind integration, there was a William Stackhouse who said otherwise. "Most Southern Pastors Favor Obeying the Court," blared the headline of a 1958 newspaper story about a survey finding that the majority of southern ministers supported the Supreme Court's edict to integrate public schools. The accompanying article, however, clarified that, in point of fact, only a majority of ministers who *responded* to mailed questionnaires favored integration. Perhaps appropriately, given the exchange between Copeland and Waring, the responses from South Carolina ministers to the poll were evenly split between clergy who favored and opposed segregation.[52] And so, the debate raged on.

When the Southern Baptist Convention (SBC) published a pamphlet endorsing integration as Christian, Texas pastor Carey Daniel wrote to Baptist headquarters to register his disagreement, tellingly using numbers rather than scripture in his dissent. "Southern Baptists are the largest church body represented among Southerners who in those recent state referendums voted over 4 to 1 for continued segregation," Daniel noted. The Dallas minister continued, "At least nine-tenths of the Baptist Preachers and laymen whose opinions I have asked on this subject (without any previous effort to prejudice them one way or the other) have assured me that they were in wholehearted agreement" that God desired segregation. With these figures on his side, Daniel confidently pronounced that the SBC's booklet endorsing integration "does NOT speak for Southern Baptists generally nor for their pastors (many of whom are militant members of our Citizens' Councils, as they all should be)."[53]

While it is impossible to know their actual number, segregationist ministers in the South indisputably played a significant part in giving divine sanction to Jim Crow. As Carey Daniel referenced in his letter to SBC headquarters, clerical aid was particularly instrumental in legitimizing Citizens' Councils, the most important anti–civil rights groups in the South. In the council meetings, carefully crafted liturgies forged connections between the segregationist organization and the Christian faith. The official newspaper of the Citizens' Councils of America, for instance, noted that "every [Citizen's Council] session is opened with fervent prayer to God for guidance, leadership, and protection in these times when the devil is shaking the very foundations of our land."[54] The same local pastors who opened the meetings with these prayers remained on hand to close the gatherings with benedictions, the pastors' mere presence lending tacit credence to the reputed righteousness of the segregationist cause.

As the Citizens' Councils movement grew, so too did ministerial support of the organization. White ministers frequented local chapters of the Citizens' Councils in such increasing numbers that the men drew praise in council pamphlets: "We are proud of the growing numbers of Christian clergy who have joined in the great Council movement, and who are lending their support and influence in the fight for our people—both Negro and Caucasian," the Incorporated Association of Citizens' Councils of Louisiana admiringly proclaimed. "Our churches and our ministers are bulwarks of strength in our Christian world," the association continued. "Without their uplifting influence, our lives would present a confused pattern of spiritually weak and troubled people."[55] Such strong clerical participation in local council chapters is unsurprising, considering the positions pastors held in the national and statewide Citizens' Council movement. In 1961, a quarter of the editorial board for the nationally distributed *Citizens' Council* newspaper was made up of clergymen, while white ministers were either the president or executive secretary of the statewide Citizens' Councils in Arkansas, Florida, Georgia, North Carolina, South Carolina, and Virginia between 1955 and 1958.[56]

In the 1950s, ministerial endorsement of the Citizens' Council movement was especially strong in South Carolina. Newspaper articles printed the talks that pastors gave at local council meetings, such as Reverend J. S. Meggs's, the featured speaker at the Hartsville, South Carolina, meeting in November 1958. "Segregation is not the least bit sinful," Meggs told the councilors. "Many churches and preachers are taking the wrong stand or no stand at all. Many young people are being taught the wrong thing. We should be kind to and helpful to all men, but that does not mean we have to socialize with other races," the Baptist preacher told his listeners.[57]

For their part, the Citizens' Councils welcomed the Christianizing legitimacy that came through associations with local ministers. "On behalf of our Citizens' Council, I want to take this opportunity to express our deep appreciation for your coming to speak to us this past Thursday evening," the chairman of the North Charleston Citizens' Council wrote to Pastor Marion Woodson. "The Citizens' Councils of South Carolina should be very greatful [sic] to God for such men as you. . . . The burden of work on the leadership of the Citizens' Council would be greatly reduced if all our spiritual leaders would give us this kind of support," continued Chairman Ed Roberts. "I feel confident that the majority of the ministers in the Charleston area know that integration and mixing of the races is wrong, and that it is harmful morally and spiritually. . . . May God continue to bless you as you do this fine work for the State Association of Citizens' Councils," Roberts closed.[58]

Roberts may have been confident that most ministers supported Jim Crow, but orthodoxy via majority continued to gnaw at other Christian segregationists. When George Bell Timmerman, the US district judge who had been instrumental in dismissing his own minister over the latter's integrationist leanings, was mailed a complimentary copy of a book advocating for a moderate position on race relations, Timmerman initiated a letter exchange between himself and the book's author, John B. Morris. Especially galling to the segregationist Timmerman was that Morris was an Episcopal priest. In Timmerman's view, Morris's call for moderation on the race issue put the priest in the category of "churchmen and public officials [who] have been carried to the mountain top and have been tempted, and have succumbed." In Timmerman's estimation, "There is no middle ground on the issue of racial integration. It cannot be both right and wrong," thereby rendering Morris's moderate position untenable. "I believe that God knew what He was doing when He created the races and separated them, just as I believe He knew what He was doing when He created the beasts of the fields and the birds and gave them the instincts to live apart," Timmerman instructed Morris. Judge Timmerman grounded his argument in the assurance that "there are millions of white citizens . . . who are firmly convinced that, if God made a mistake in creating the races and separating them, Christ knew about it and would have corrected it while He was on earth; that so important a matter would not have been left for the infiltrators of our seminaries to discover and correct."[59]

Responding to Timmerman, Morris pointed out that he was not calling for complete integration of the races and reiterated his call for moderation: "I beg, sir, if we would preserve the good qualities of Southern living, not to require that all Southerners be totally 'with' you or, if not, thereby 'against' you. There is a 'respectable middle ground,' I believe, and I have talked with hundreds of leading South Carolinians who stand there."[60] Timmerman, however, refused to budge. In his reply, the judge made clear his view that " 'massive resistance' is proper in fighting any evil, none more so than the God defying racial mongrelization movement; and . . . where the choice is between right and wrong, between condemning God and praising Him, there is no respectable middle ground."[61] Timmerman ended his exchange with Reverend Morris by returning to the question of whose views enjoyed the most popular support. In an earlier letter, Morris had noted that he had spoken to hundreds of South Carolinians who shared his view. Timmerman was unimpressed, and in his final rejoinder to Morris, he inadvertently inflated the priest's claim: "I note you say you have talked to thousands," Timmerman wrote. "You should talk to the tens of thousands that you have missed."[62] Morris may not have spoken to the silent majority in South Carolina who, Timmerman claimed, supported segregation as a Christian truth, but that was no matter. As the civil rights movement unfolded, this silent majority spoke for themselves.

Deploying Segregationist Theology

In late December 1955, Mrs. T. E. Wilburn of Union, South Carolina, penned a letter to Strom Thurmond to wish the senator "a very merry Christmas and a happy prosperous New Year." But yuletide greetings were not the only thing on Wilburn's mind that winter. The upcountry woman was also concerned about the growing threat to Jim Crow, and she included in her Christmas card to Thurmond a reminder that defending segregation was imperative: "God in his infinite wisdom divided the races, making them of different interests, inteligence [sic], character and colors. He set His mark on them as well as he did different classes of birds. These birds do not ever break over into the others and begin a new group. If man is so wise, why isn't he wise enough to keep his race pure and be proud of it? Negroes have no morals."[63] Wilburn's letter to her senator was not exceptional. The sermons, booklets, pamphlets, and articles promoting racial segregation as consistent with Christianity often circulated throughout the South in rhythm with the struggle for racial equality in the region. Each gain won by civil rights activists in dismantling segregation—be it in the courts, the legislature, or the streets—prompted another round of sermons and pamphlets denouncing the victory. White segregationist Christians refused to remain silent as the civil rights movement undermined what they saw as a fundamental component of the society God ordained. Instead, these Christians marshalled the arguments gleaned from pulpits and pamphlets—or from their own reading of scripture—and presented them as weapons to their elected officials in the fight to preserve segregation. As can be seen in using South Carolina as a case study, segregationist theology helped feed the public backlash to integration even as Christians in the Palmetto State urged their political leaders to maintain the state's racial caste system. Each time Jim Crow came under attack, white South Carolinians reminded their elected officials of the institution's divine status.

The Supreme Court's decision in *Brown v. Board of Education* was the first event that caused widespread petitioning of elected officials by segregationist Christians. In the days following the 1954 ruling, South Carolinians flooded Senator Olin Johnston's office with letters urging him to fight *Brown* and maintain the South's tradition of racial segregation. In many of these letters, the segregationist theology long taught in churches was now brought to bear on the political question of Jim Crow: "I am a southern born man and firmly believe in segregation from both a moral and Christian standpoint of view and I believe I am right in my conviction," wrote one constituent.[64] He was not alone. I. D. and Marion Yonce wrote Johnston to ask if the senator thought "white and colored children could go to school day in and day out together without leading to intermarriage?" Their fear, the Yonces told Johnston, was that school desegregation "would mix the races and we as Christians, do not believe that God intends this."[65] Thomas Howe of Spartanburg shared the Yonces' conviction. "My God said to love every body but he don't want negroes and white people mixing this way," wrote Howe. "He made the white man and he made the negro. If God would[n't have] wanted it this way he [would have] made us all alike. I am a Christian and I believe in the right thing. We should take our troubles to God. The South doesn't want this. God loves a peace maker not a trouble maker."[66] Similarly, in Jan Revill's letter to Olin Johnston, the Sumter woman declared that "segregation is a perfectly proper social order, or situation, and is fully upheld by the teachings of the Bible." These sentiments were echoed by James B. Davis, who cited the story of the Tower of Babel in Genesis and the apostle Paul's teaching on the "bounds of habitation" in Acts 17 to bolster his claim to Johnston that segregation was biblically sanctioned.[67]

In 1954 and the years that followed, biblical arguments denouncing the *Brown* decision also consistently appeared in newspaper articles and letters to the editor. When a *News and Courier* reader wanted to know the source of the South's adamant defense of segregation, J. J. Patrick responded in a letter to the paper claiming, "God created the different races and set their bounds and habitation. God commanded, demanded, and taught segregation from the Flood, right on down until the Bible was written and said that

Heaven and earth shall pass away but My word shall never pass away."[68] More than a year later, Mrs. B. E. Clarkson of Kingstree was still aggrieved by the *Brown* decision, writing to the *State* newspaper in Columbia that "had God meant the races to mix He would have made all one color. Had God meant the races to mix He would not have placed the Negro in Africa to themselves when He created them." Clarkson confessed bewilderment that the Supreme Court would suddenly find God's plan for segregation problematic in 1954. "If it is unconstitutional, it's strange it took them so many years to find it out," Clarkson wrote.[69]

Former South Carolina governor James F. Byrnes, a retired Supreme Court justice himself, shared Clarkson's suspicion about the late date of the court's awakening and suggested the decision was negatively influencing American churches: "For more than a century, in churches North and South, preachers have led their flocks in segregated congregations. The people have looked to the church for theological guidance," Byrnes told the Georgia Bar Association. "If a preacher honestly believed segregation was un-Christian, it was his duty as a Christian leader to make known his views. However, I do not recall ever hearing this 'un-Christian' charge until after the segregation decision of the Supreme Court on May 17, 1954."[70] R. K. Wallace shared Byrnes's views and wrote to Senator Strom Thurmond to complain about "those preachers who are running up and down the road to the Supreme Court to get their religion." Wallace urged Thurmond to do his best to "stop this folishiness [*sic*] about Civil Rights" and reminded the senator that "if it was not God's plan to separate the races socially it would not have taken him two thousand years to let it be known, but when he separated the races at the building of the tower of babel he established the laws of segregation."[71]

The response to the *Brown* decision began a pattern that segregationist Christians repeated over the subsequent decade with the advancement of civil rights. When black Americans procured their constitutional freedoms, white Christians reacted by writing their elected officials to remind them that these changes violated God's plan for humanity. As the South's representatives, these white Christians also insisted the region's politicians had a Christian duty to fight for segregation. In such respects, segregationist theology proved not to be hollow rhetoric, for it guided the way these Christians saw the world and shaped the expectations they put on their elected representatives.

Occasionally the mere appearance of advancing civil rights for black Americans was enough to prompt letters from concerned white Christians.

For instance, when a black orderly at a hospital in Georgia was accused of raping a restrained psychiatric patient in 1955, city officials refused to release the orderly's name and, according to the *Augusta Herald*, they tried to "keep the case under cover."[72] Protecting the identity of the accused was too much for E. A. Wilder of Belvedere, South Carolina, who wrote to Thurmond to express his belief that sensible people would understand that the black hospital orderly "ought to be hung or something else." But Wilder was not surprised. After all, he wrote, these incidents should be expected when the "scalawags and carpet baggers . . . throw them [black Americans] down our throat and put them on equal with white people." To Wilder, society was obviously trying to upend the hierarchy that God's word made clear: "The Bible tells us that they are and [*sic*] inferior race to the white and a curse was put on them and they would know their color. They was turned black and cast out into the wilderness to find his wife." Wilder acknowledged that Thurmond was "fighting and doing all you can to keep them out of our schools," and he encouraged the senator to "keep on fighting to the end."[73]

Most often public officials received letters from their constituents when the existing racial order seemed imperiled by the actions of civil rights demonstrators or agents of the federal government. In early 1956, for example, Ann White—a self-described "housewife, mother, and Bible reader"—wrote to Attorney General Hebert Brownell to protest the Eisenhower administration's complicity in school desegregation. "You are trying to take away God's prerogative in the matter of segregation," White wrote. "If you will refer to your Bible, in particular to the Book of Genesis Chapter 1, vs. 26-28, after God created Adam (a white man) He gave him AUTHORITY over everything that He (God) had created." White quoted additional passages from Leviticus, Deuteronomy, and I Peter before concluding, "We can deduce from this that ALL men were not created equal, and if He had intended anything different, He would have changed His plans long before now."[74]

After President Dwight Eisenhower used his State of the Union address in 1956 to propose a Civil Rights Commission, South Carolina officials received letters from constituents like N. Y. Mathis of Sumter. Mathis wrote to both Strom Thurmond and Olin Johnston to remind the senators that "God made this world according to his own plans. He created everything of a kind exactly the way he intended them to be. As we all know, this world belongs to God, the fullness thereof, and they that dwell therein. . . . No man or men on God's earth have the power to integrate God's people of His races." Mathis encouraged Johnston and Thurmond to fight the proposed Civil Rights

Commission and continue the work of keeping the races segregated in accordance with God's plan. In turn, Mathis would continue to ask God to "add his blessing unto you and all who join with you in your efforts to make this world a better place to live."[75]

The 1957 integration of Central High School in Little Rock, Arkansas, brought more letters from Christian segregationists. When Senator Paul H. Douglas of Illinois expressed his disappointment that Ike was not doing all he could to support school desegregation after Little Rock, William Simpson of Greenville was dismayed that a Christian politician would support integration. "If you profess to be a Christian and believe in the New Testament, please look up St. Mark, Chapter 9; Verse 42, and see if that verse does not apply to supporters [of school desegregation]," Simpson admonished the northern senator. From Simpson's perspective, Douglas's criticisms of Eisenhower were causing only trouble for Christians in the South: "I just wanted to write you one more letter as you are a professing Christian, to urge that you do not continue to engender hatred and strife, as you are doing in many church and civil groups," the South Carolinian concluded.[76]

While Senator Douglas may have thought President Eisenhower was not doing enough to support school desegregation, some southern Christians could not believe the damage Ike's tepid support had already wrought. In the wake of the Little Rock crisis, Mabel Harvey of Columbia wrote to Senator Thurmond to express her bewilderment that "our President or the Supreme Court believ[e] that the white race and black be on equal standards. God did not intend for this to be," Harvey wrote. "In the New Testament Christ came to give us the . . . laws to live by. He did not select a negro for His deciples [sic] or did He at any time appoint a negro for any mission. . . . I am sure God doesn't want His people to become a mongrel race when he definitely created the various nations for a purpose just as he created the various birds of their kind." Harvey closed her letter by observing that "this integration problem is very much misconstrued by our President and Supreme Court. I shall pray that men like you will correct some of the chaos."[77] R. T. Mathews of Summerville went a step further than just praying for his senator. In 1959, he sent Thurmond evidence drawn from the books of Ezra and Nehemiah that showed God supported segregation, with the hope that the senator could use the information to stem the tide of the growing civil rights movement. Should Thurmond cite these biblical materials publicly, Mathews asked not to be given credit, requesting that Thurmond "please do not use my name as hundreds of negroes pass my house going to school."[78]

As much as some white southerners may have been disappointed with Eisenhower's record on race, the president's successor in the Oval Office promised even dimmer prospects for Christian segregationists. Shortly before John F. Kennedy's inauguration, Mrs. A. B. Conolly of Greenwood wrote to the National Council of Churches (NCC) to protest the group's integrationist stance: "Am I to understand your Church Council (against God's Laws) want to immerge the Negro into the white race?" Conolly asked. Incredulous as she was with the NCC, Conolly saw the group's stance as symptomatic of a larger problem represented in Kennedy's election: "Our Nation has ceased to seek God for guidance. . . . [W]e would have peace if we had Christian leaders." In Conolly's mind, that even church organizations had gone astray was evidence that the country's leaders had stopped doing God's will. The Bible taught that "if you obey my laws I will be your God and you will be My people," Conolly reminded the NCC. As Conolly saw it, the country was abandoning God's law as it pertained to race. "The Negro has his churches and his schools, God means for His people to show the minority races how to live, but not mix with His People that must remain as created to carry on His work," the South Carolina woman wrote.[79]

As the 1960s progressed, civil rights activism gained momentum. In 1961, black and white passengers boarded Greyhound buses and rode through the South to protest the persistence of segregation in interstate travel despite the Supreme Court having ruled such segregationist practices unconstitutional. In response to the freedom riders, southern Christians pointed out that although the court may have changed its mind, integration still violated God's law. "It is an undeniable fact that God Himself is the author of segregation," Reverend Gary C. Posey wrote in a letter that he asked Thurmond to pass along to John and Robert Kennedy in hopes that the president and attorney general would bring the freedom riders to heel. Posey cited half a dozen passages from the Old and New Testaments to support his claim before concluding that "If God was so careful with the Israelites that he did not permit them to mix themselves with the white gentiles, there is no reason to believe he would endorse our white gentile race to mix with the colored or black race." Thurmond dutifully forwarded the letter to both Kennedy brothers, fulfilling Posey's request.[80]

When civil rights protests moved from bus depots to street demonstrations, segregationist Christians continued their campaign to remind representatives that such protests countered God's will. In the spring of 1963, black activists in Birmingham, Alabama, captured national attention by marching and being beaten in the streets to protest Jim Crow. These demonstrations also caught the eye of James T. Bowen, a South Carolina man who wrote to Strom Thurmond with "the scriptural answer to the question that we as Christians face today concerning racial demonstrations." In his letter, Bowen cited and explicated various gospel passages, concluding that "the racial demonstrations of today are in direct opposition to the teachings of Christ, and they are a mockery to the very name of Christ."[81]

In Bowen's opinion, the civil rights demonstrations in Birmingham may have mocked the name of Christ, but they were nonetheless effective in bringing about changes to the law. In the wake of the Alabama demonstrations, President Kennedy put forth civil rights legislation that would effectively end Jim Crow segregation in the United States. As southern congressmen and senators strategized how to defeat Kennedy's proposed civil rights bill, southern Christians contributed to the cause by reminding their representatives that their legislators were doing God's work. Boyd Hall of Rock Hill, for instance, wrote to Strom Thurmond to remind him of the abundant ways God had made his segregationist desires clear in nature. After an exhaustive exploration of segregation in animals and geography, Hall definitively concluded that "it is right in the eyes of God to separate the races."[82] Thurmond agreed, thanking Hall for the letter that "may come in handy during the 'civil rights' debate."[83]

As Kennedy's civil rights bill hung in the balance, white Christians continued to register their opposition. "We all admit that God has not told us that because we are white we are 'better' than the Negro," wrote Percy and Margretta Nauglie of Moncks Corner. "However, even the Negro must admit that God has made the white and the Negro different to each other." Further, the Nauglies did not think "that the average Negro actually wants to sit in church with the white— neither does he wish his offspring to produce half-white offspring, and that is what forced integration will eventually bring." The couple signed their letter to Strom Thurmond with "sincere admiration for you in your strong, unyielding stand. May God give you strength."[84] Despite all the God-given strength he and other segregationists in Congress could muster, Thurmond could not stop the passage of the Civil Rights Act of 1964. Nor were segregationist legislators successful the following year in thwarting the Voting Rights Act of 1965. The best efforts of segregationists to maintain Jim Crow's place in southern society failed, and the institution fell with remarkable speed in the second half of the 1960s.

With segregation's legal demise, the theological defense of the practice underwent a transformation. By the middle of the 1960s, explicit segregationist theology that cited chapter and verse for the biblical support for racial separation grew sparse in public discourse. The segregationist message so commonly heralded in pulpits and pamphlets across the South in the previous decade became muted as the civil rights movement successfully transformed southern culture. This transformation of a culture that had nourished and fed segregationist theology in white churches had obvious implications for Christian segregationists. As public espousals of racist views grew infrequent as the 1960s progressed, so too did public statements from southerners expressing their belief in divinely mandated segregation.

As the 1960s reached their midpoint, a southern minister or layman would occasionally make news by publicly expressing the segregationist theology that was becoming increasingly limited to private correspondence by that time. Such was the case of Presbyterian minister and Clarendon County, South Carolina, school district superintendent L. B. McCord in May 1964. In a speech that month before a Citizens' Council meeting in Mississippi, McCord told the crowd of segregationists that "there is no such thing as equality. Read your Bible. We're everything but equal. God was a segregationist."[85] Though white southerners continued to express such ideas behind closed doors and in private letters, public pronouncements like McCord's grew scarce in the public record in the second half of the 1960s. But ideas do not die simply because they are no longer openly spoken, nor does a change in law lead seamlessly to a change of minds. No paradigm shift in the thought of Christian segregationists occurred merely because polite society dictated that they not express their beliefs in such blunt fashion.

Segregationist Christians were never absent from the mainstream battles of the traditional civil rights struggle. The crowds howling outside Central High School for the heads of the nine black students inside, the mobs at bus depots in Alabama waiting to attack the freedom riders on their arrival, the state troopers beating back peaceful marchers on the Edmund Pettus Bridge—Christians could be counted among them all. At lunch counters in Nashville, in schoolhouse doors in Tuscaloosa, and in the streets of Birmingham, white Christians were there, fighting to maintain segregation, confident of God's blessing. But the full impact and lasting power of white theological beliefs about segregation were most clearly revealed not in these flashpoints of the civil rights struggle, but in lesser-known intramural conflicts that unfolded later in the 1960s: the desegregation of church colleges, the integration of denominational structures, and the establishment of private Christian schools. With the faith of true believers, segregationist Christians battled in these arenas as well and entered the fray certain they were doing God's work. After all, the Bible told them so.

3

Jim Crow on Christian Campuses

The Desegregation of Furman and Wofford

As the clock struck twelve on the afternoon of December 17, 1860, Dr. J. C. M. Breaker, pastor of the First Baptist Church in Columbia, South Carolina, stood in his church sanctuary, head bowed, asking for wisdom and discernment for the individuals seated in the pews before him. While praying at the front of his church was routine for Breaker, the practice on this particular day was unusual. To begin, December 17 was a Monday, not typically the day of the week that Christian ministers beseeched the Almighty from their pulpits at noontime. Adding to the unconventional scene in the First Baptist sanctuary, the men occupying Breaker's pews were not the minister's parishioners. Instead, the congregation assembled at First Baptist on that chilly and overcast December day were delegates to the state's Secession Convention. Abraham Lincoln had been elected president only weeks before this gathering, and with the Republican's ascension to the White House, fear was rampant throughout the South that slavery's days were numbered. Nowhere was that fear more strongly felt than in South Carolina. Upon hearing the news of Lincoln's election, a South Carolina woman, reflecting the feelings of many in the state, recorded in her diary that "The die is cast. 'Caesar' has past the Rubicon.' We now have to act. God be with us is my prayer and let us all be willing to die rather than free our slaves."[1] State political leaders agreed with such sentiments. The day after Lincoln's election, the entire South Carolina federal congressional delegation resigned their positions in Washington, DC, and returned home. That same day, South Carolina's General Assembly called for a state convention to consider its next steps.[2] The delegates who assembled in the First Baptist Church—the men for whom Dr. Breaker was now seeking divine aid—were the answer to the General Assembly's call. Determined to keep their enslaved populace, the delegates began debating whether their state could remain in a country they saw growing ever more hostile to their peculiar institution.

The Bible Told Them So. J. Russell Hawkins, Oxford University Press. © Oxford University Press 2021.
DOI: 10.1093/oso/9780197571064.003.0004

Given the magnitude of the issue before the delegates, First Baptist was a fitting locale for the Secession Convention. In 1860, the church was the newest in Columbia, boasting a massive brick-columned portico and a nine-hundred-person seating capacity, the largest of any building in the capital city. Its size made the church's selection for the convention site an easy one. The church sanctuary also had the city's largest balcony, a necessary accommodation for the large number of enslaved parishioners who attended First Baptist and dutifully sat each Sunday in this segregated section.[3]

As the temperature outside continued to drop throughout the December afternoon in 1860, the delegates in the First Baptist sanctuary wrestled with the question of leaving the Union. With a heavy fog adding to the darkness at nightfall, gas chandeliers illuminated the sanctuary by the time convention-eers arrived at the question that had brought the men together: should South Carolina leave the Union to protect their slave interests? Casting their ballots in the First Baptist Church that December night, the delegates answered unanimously in the affirmative, moving their state toward seceding from the United States of America. Three days later, the state formally did so.[4]

Four years of war and 750,000 deaths were the cost of bringing South Carolina and the ten other slave states that seceded back into the Union. As punishment for the death and untold destruction that had followed South Carolina's secession, William Sherman's army intended to destroy First Baptist as the origin site of southern secession when the troops entered Columbia in February 1865. Union soldiers ultimately put torches to six churches in the capital city, but First Baptist was curiously not among them. For reasons that remain unclear, First Baptist somehow avoided Sherman's punitive measure and escaped the flames that consumed so much else during the final months of the general's march.[5]

Whatever the cause of First Baptist's sparing, the same brick-columned portico and spacious sanctuary that had housed the Secession Convention were still standing a century later when, in 1964, delegates once again gathered in the church's pews for a convention that held echoes of 1860. The enslaved parishioners had long abandoned the church where they had once been forced to worship, but their spirit nonetheless hung over the proceedings of the 1964 South Carolina Baptist Convention. This convention in Columbia was the culminating episode of a thirteen-month process to determine whether Furman University, the flagship Baptist college in South Carolina, would open its doors to black students. With the former slave balcony as a backdrop, white Baptist messengers at the 1964 convention debated whether the descendants of those who a century before had occupied that balcony should be allowed to attend Baptist colleges. The same sanctuary that 104 years earlier had seen a Baptist pastor bless southern secessionists now witnessed a Baptist minister call for a vote to support racial segregation on the campuses of Baptist universities throughout South Carolina. Sitting in the same straight-back wooden pews of their antebellum predecessors, white Baptists in 1964 voted to deny black students' entry to their church schools, preferring instead to keep their colleges for white students only.[6] Although a century separated the two votes in the First Baptist Church, both were connected across time and space by a perceived threat to an established racial order. The nineteenth-century secession vote was cast by a group of white Christians determined to maintain white supremacy in the face of a changing social order. So too the vote at the 1964 state Baptist convention was the act of white Christians seeking to preserve a racial hierarchy they saw slipping away.

As the calendar approached the midpoint of the 1960s, a revolution in social attitudes and practices toward race in the United States marched on, and with it black and white southerners alike witnessed their society transform. While not a cause for celebration for a majority of white southerners, the group nonetheless foresaw the revolution's coming. For instance, an opinion poll conducted early in the 1960s found that over three-quarters of white southerners believed integration would one day come to the South. But expecting change and welcoming it were not the same. Other opinion polls taken in the early 1960s found that 71 percent of white southerners disapproved of the racial integration that three-quarters saw as inevitable.[7] Despite knowing that it was coming, desegregation occurred sooner than most white southerners could have imagined.[8] By 1964, all state universities throughout the South had desegregated, and the region's public elementary and secondary schools were slowly beginning to do the same. Similarly, municipalities had integrated public parks and beaches throughout the South, and a sweeping civil rights bill all but eliminated legal discrimination in public accommodations such as retail businesses, hotels, and restaurants.[9] After seven decades, Jim Crow was seemingly on his deathbed.

These changes to the racial social order provoked the ire of the majority of white southerners, but they were especially worrisome to those white

Christians in the South who had prayed for and pleaded with their elected officials to do God's will and preserve racial segregation. Their politicians had failed them; the public sphere was lost. But within their own churches and institutions, segregationist Christians found arenas in which to carry on the fight. Christian colleges and universities now became the first battlegrounds in an ecclesiastical struggle to keep Jim Crow alive and demonstrated that segregationist theology continued to call white Christians to arms even as the world around them changed.

In 1960, debating the desegregation of a Christian university would have been unthinkable in most parts of the South. Indeed, if visitors were to tour *any* school—private or public, elementary or college—in the Deep South in the early 1960s, they would find school integration almost nonexistent and little indication that significant desegregation would occur in the foreseeable future. Resistance to school integration was especially fierce in South Carolina, where not a single crack in Jim Crow's bulwark had emerged. In fact, at the start of the 1961 academic year, South Carolina joined Alabama and Mississippi as the only three states left in the country that maintained complete segregation at all levels of their public education system.[10] In the fall of 1961, classrooms from kindergartens to colleges remained strictly segregated along racial lines in the Palmetto State, the seventh year since the Supreme Court had declared such arrangements unconstitutional. Even though government officials in South Carolina seemed in no rush to integrate public institutions, private religious colleges could integrate their classrooms and dormitories overnight if they so desired. Desegregating these institutions, however, was perhaps even more unlikely than integration in their public counterparts, given the influence of segregationist theology in Christian circles in the state. The effects of this theology meant that, in the words of one contemporary observer, Protestant schools in the South "clung to segregated patterns more tenaciously" than their secular counterparts.[11] Desegregation in South Carolina's Protestant colleges and universities in the early 1960s would represent a significant break with both the patterns of segregation and the theological beliefs of many white Christians.

Nonetheless, there were some in South Carolina who hoped such a break would come soon and called for the state's Baptist and Methodist colleges to lead the change. Reverend James Copeland, the same Methodist minister who had raised segregationists' hackles two years earlier by claiming that a majority of South Carolina clergy members opposed segregation, caused a new row in the autumn of 1961 when, in the pages of the *Greenville News*, he called for an end to segregation in the state's Christian colleges:

> The great majority of church bodies, including the Southern Baptist Convention and the Methodist Church, have declared themselves unequivocally in favor of the integration of the races. Thunderous pronouncements by these and other church bodies have sounded the death knell to antiquated ideas and concepts of race. From the standpoint of official pronouncements, the churches on the whole have been gloriously progressive and have shown a desire to point the way, at last, for those who name the Name of Christ. It is in the realm of practice that the churches have been painfully derelict. Like the Pharisees of old, they have said, but they have not acted. The churches have spoken the truth, but they have failed in the practical application of the truth. Every church worthy of the name Christian and every church related college should, not only in theory but in practice throw their doors open to receive all of any race who love God and seek to learn about and lead a better life. . . . The churches and church related colleges must get their frightened heads out of the sand and begin at once to face up to life as we find it crowding in upon us now. If we fail, we will deserve the just and certain condemnation of God and an enlightened world. Wake up, churches! Wake up, church related colleges![12]

Copeland's prediction that denominational pronouncements had served a "death knell" to "antiquated ideas" about race was premature. Far more than by church statements, the vitality of segregationist theology was best measured by the actions of southern Christians themselves. And by such a standard, segregationist Christianity appeared hale and hearty.

Just weeks after Copeland's letter appeared in the *Greenville News*, Baptists from across the state gathered in the upcountry city for the 1961 South Carolina Baptist Convention. The messengers met that year on the campus of Furman University, a Baptist institution that only enrolled white students per the school's racially exclusive admissions policy. Unforeseen by the messengers, this policy would soon become a point of contention during the convention. On the convention's second afternoon, the messengers debated banning fraternities at Furman and the other Baptist-supported schools in the state. Outlawing Greek life was indeed a complicated matter. To be sure, the majority of Baptist messengers believed fraternities to be detrimental to students and campus culture, but no consensus existed for taking action against the social clubs. At question was whether the state convention had the authority to instruct college trustees—essentially to dictate—on matters of school policy. After a lengthy discussion, the messengers voted to request the trustees at every Baptist-controlled college and university in South Carolina to end fraternities on their campuses beginning in 1962. Whether trustees were actually bound to follow this request remained unclear among the messengers.

Immediately following this vote, and just as the tired messengers were preparing to break for dinner, a pastor named David Wells approached the convention stage with a surprise motion. Gaining the attention of his fellow messengers from the podium microphone, Wells moved that "since we are so determined to be Christian . . . we instruct all our institutions to receive students irrespective of race, color, or creed." Without saying another word, Wells descended the platform steps and walked back up the aisle as the messengers sat in stunned silence. What had started as a debate about fraternities had unexpectedly become an issue about integration. Taken aback, none in the crowd offered a motion to discuss Wells's impromptu resolution, causing convention president John C. Murdoch to call for a voice vote on Wells's motion to desegregate Baptist colleges. As the *Greenville News* reported, "There was a weak 'aye' vote from perhaps 50 to 75 persons. Then many hundreds voted 'no' in a loud and definite manner," thereby rejecting the idea that Furman should admit nonwhite students. The same men that sought to outlaw Greek letter fraternities on Baptist campuses in 1961 because of the organizations' perceived damaging effects on students found no such threat by Jim Crow's presence at their Christian colleges.[13]

A month after the messengers' stand against integration at Furman, some students and faculty at the Baptist school expressed alternative feelings on the matter. In an unofficial vote conducted at a campus chapel service in early December 1961, Furman students, by a narrow majority (512 to 432), voted in favor of considering "all properly qualified applicants regardless of race or color" for admission.[14] News of this vote made its way into newspapers and radio editorials around the state, raising eyebrows about the beliefs of the student body. Students, though, could be excused for their youthful ignorance. What did ignite a backlash across South Carolina was the news that the Furman faculty, voting on the same statement as their students, affirmed that the school should do away with its racially restrictive admissions policy by a count of 68 to 12.[15] "I read with amazement the vote of students and faculty of Furman relative to admission of all qualified students," one Furman alumna wrote to the school's president, John Plyer. "Every local alumni of Furman with whom I have talked was 100 percent against such action. While we might understand such a vote from the students, we do not understand the faculty vote. Apparently the leadership, which the faculty should offer, is not what we would in South Carolina expect."[16] Another letter writer agreed that the faculty position ran counter to South Carolina sentiments and suspected that the Furman faculty had been infiltrated with carpetbaggers, asking Plyer, "Just how many of your faculty are from this state or border state[s]?"[17] That so many professors endorsed admitting black students indicated "a thorough brain washing by the members of the faculty and bear out that most colleges and universities are full of socialistic idealists."[18] Noting the number of faculty who supported enrolling nonwhite students at Furman, one parent wrote to Plyer that "there are definitely sixty-eight faculty members who should be fired forthwith."[19]

As the news of the faculty and student votes spread throughout South Carolina, more parents and alumni wrote to President Plyer to register their displeasure. "Both as a parent of a student at Furman University and as President of the Tri-County Chapter of the Alumni Association, I am amazed and alarmed by the action taken on the campus by the student body and faculty relative to the admission of Negroes to the University," wrote one concerned mother who worried that the vote reflected "an extreme liberal element" at her child's school.[20] Another alumnus wrote to Plyer asking, "How any person could be prevailed upon to betray the traditions, thinking and conscience of at least ninety percent of the white people of the South. Nor can I understand how this sort of thing could take place on the campus of my beloved university."[21] Equally perplexing to this same alumnus was why any Furman faculty or student would *want* nonwhite students admitted to their campus: "So far as I am concerned, I have yet to hear one good argument for this thing. It certainly violates every lesson of history. There is no sound biological argument for it. I think it is un-Christian and basically atheistic," he wrote to Plyer.[22] The outcry over the 1961 integration vote grew loud enough that the university put out a statement defending the rights of its students and faculty to vote their conscience: "It has always been in the best tradition of Baptists to permit each individual to seek the truth and to express his opinions and convictions in democratic fashion. Any attempts to stifle freedom of speech and expression would be counter to time-honored Baptist policies of democratic conduct," declared Furman's official statement concerning the integration vote.[23]

Democratic principles were well and good, but there was a higher law at stake for some white Christians concerned about the Furman vote. "The indelible laws of creation cannot be altered by the Supreme Court or anybody else," wrote Winfield Martins to Plyer in response to the vote. "Red birds do not mix their flights with the bluebirds, nor did God choose to create any purple birds! I realize that it is much more popular to please man than to please God, to 'conform' rather than 'be transformed,'" Martins concluded, but he nonetheless urged the school to follow God's plan to keep the races apart.[24]

Theological concerns aside, several Furman supporters wrote to Plyer questioning why the faculty would support voluntary integration at a moment when other schools in the state could soon be made to do so against their will. "I am the chairman of our local school board and am interested in education," one alumnus wrote to Plyer. "We in the schools may be forced to integrate by the courts. Furman is in the enviable position of being a privately supported school, and not subject to court ruling[s]. What can they gain by integration?"[25] Other graduates expressed similar perspectives. "Many of us among the alumni have felt that the efforts to force the integration of negroes in the public tax-supported schools gave to Furman and other like universities their opportunity to serve as a refuge of higher education for their children, free from race pollution and the inevitable dilution of standards."[26] From such views, the faculty vote made no sense. Not only did segregation violate God's intent but also it violated sound business practices. When the state universities integrated, parents would be looking for safe havens for their children. Segregated Christian colleges like Furman were uniquely positioned to meet that need, provided they kept black students from enrolling. At any rate, Furman reassured parents and supporters that they should not read too much into the 1961 faculty and student votes. One Furman insider wrote to a concerned alumnus that "whatever the students and faculty may think, only the Board of Trustees can make basic policy decisions" and assured him that "there is no agitation or move of any sort under way to bring about integration at our University."[27]

Despite attempts to calm worried supporters, the sizeable number of faculty who voted to admit black students to Furman was a potential problem for school administrators. After all, the faculty vote to support integration came on the heels of the state Baptist convention expressly voicing its desire to keep Furman segregated. If pro-integration attitudes grew on campus, conflict with the state Baptist convention would be hard to avoid. To determine where the university legally stood in case of such a conflict, a Furman trustee asked a US circuit judge to review the school's charter to clarify the relationship between Furman and the state Baptist convention. In May 1962, the school received assurance that the convention's control over the Furman trustees ended with their appointment. While convention messengers nominated and elected trustees, it could neither replace those trustees nor exercise any managerial authority over them. If Furman University chose to abide by the wishes of the state convention, it was out of courtesy rather than obligation.[28]

The prediction that Christian colleges would soon be the last option for segregated higher education in South Carolina proved true. In the summer of 1962, a young black man named Harvey Gantt started the process that would desegregate the state's public colleges and universities when he attempted to enroll at Clemson College. Gantt's enrollment efforts brought him to the Clemson campus on a June afternoon where he was greeted by Reverend Charles A. Webster. Webster was a white pastor in his late twenties who, as director of student work at Clemson First Baptist Church, also ministered on the college campus. Webster directed Gantt—the latter also a Baptist—to the office of the registrar "as a gesture of Christian courtesy" from one believer to another.[29]

Webster's "Christian courtesy" was interpreted differently by Clemson officials who, rather than noting benevolence in the young minister's action, saw a "subversive plot to integrate the college."[30] The day after Gantt's first visit to Clemson, two members of the college's administration contacted Webster's church and suggested First Baptist investigate to determine "if the Baptist church has been used to integrate the college."[31] It would take until January 1963 for a federal court to decree that Harvey Gantt could start classes at Clemson College, but no court order could save the white minister who had assisted Gantt. The First Baptist deacon board followed the advice of the college administrators and looked into Webster's interactions with Gantt. By the time Gantt officially enrolled in classes at Clemson in January 1963, Charles Webster was no longer ministering on campus, having been ousted from his position at First Baptist when church deacons recommended it was time for the white minister to find another church. Webster took the deacons' suggestion and tendered his resignation, which the First Baptist congregation "voted overwhelmingly to accept." Not surprisingly, he never ministered in another Baptist church.[32]

Webster's dismissal from the Clemson First Baptist Church on suspicion that he was using his ministerial position to integrate Clemson became a bell-wether for the battle ahead over desegregating Christian colleges. If Webster could be dismissed for doing little more than befriending a black student who was seeking his constitutional right to attend a public college, how much more would the resistance be to Baptists who voluntarily chose to do what no court had ordered. That challenge soon presented itself.

Ten months after Harvey Gantt integrated the first public university in South Carolina, private Christian institutions began to follow suit. In the fall of 1963, the board of trustees at Furman University held a three-and-a-half-hour meeting during which they voted to drop the school's racially exclusive standard and adopted a resolution allowing Furman for the first time to "con-sider applications for admissions from all qualified applicants."[33] Newspaper accounts noted that the length of the meeting was a testament to how dif-ficult the decision was for the Furman board, but ultimately all but one of the trustees voted to allow African American students to enroll. The lone holdout among the trustees pounded the table with his fists and declared that the day Furman admitted a black student "was the day he ended all associ-ations with the university."[34]

The reaction by the trustee was not unique among South Carolina Baptists. When the news reached local Baptist churches that Furman trustees had cleared the way for black students to enroll in their university, denunciation of the school was swift and decisive. Cameron Baptist Church, for example, called a business meeting after Sunday worship soon after the trustees' deci-sion to register their disagreement: "We, the members of Cameron Baptist Church wish to go on record as opposing this planned racial integration of Furman University or any other of our Baptist schools and institutions at this time, or at any time in the future," the congregation wrote. They made their reason for their opposition clear: "We feel that segregation of the races is a plan set up by God for the ultimate good of all men, not to promote the superiority of any race, but to maintain and develop the inherent worth of each individual race." Keeping with traditional segregationist theology, the Cameron congregation cited verses from Genesis, Deuteronomy, and Acts to support their belief that "God segregated the races of man" and claimed that racial integration in schools was the equivalent of "changing God's plan and destroying His handiwork." The congregation further recommended that "all messengers to the Association and to the State Convention be instructed to vote 'no' to any and all proposals to open the doors of any Baptist schools or institutions to all races, at any time."[35] The only two members of the all-white church who voted against the Cameron Baptist resolution were the pastor and his wife.[36]

As intimated in the Cameron church resolution, the South Carolina state Baptist convention was set to meet a month after the Furman trustees voted to change their admission policies. In the wake of receiving resolutions from around the state like Cameron Baptist's, South Carolina Baptist leaders moved to limit the controversy of the Furman desegregation debate at the state convention with a preemptive strike. When the executive committee met to finalize the agenda for the state convention in Charleston, it requested that Furman "defer any action based on its recently announced racial policy" for twelve months until the state convention could adopt a policy for all Baptist schools the next year.[37] In the meantime, the executive committee tried to limit the debate at the 1963 convention by asking messengers to approve a year of study on integration at Baptist schools rather than debating the issue of integration at their meeting. Such a move, the executive committee hoped, would minimize divisiveness among messengers at the convention.

Despite the executive committee's desire to maintain as much unity as possible, Baptists across South Carolina were eager to argue the larger implications of the Furman situation, and by this time they had already divided into two camps. The first camp was composed of Baptists like Reverend R. C. Johnson Jr., of Early Branch, South Carolina, who stated, "When the state convention meets . . . , I am sure the people of this state will see the South Carolina Baptists go on record as favoring segregated schools for their children by overwhelmingly reversing the action taken by the [Furman] trustees." Opposing such forthright calls for maintaining segregated schools were Baptists in the second camp who expressed concerns about the precedent of the state convention overruling the university trustees. "We Baptists must learn the meaning of trusteeship," remarked Reverend L. D. Johnson in response to the segregationists. "A trustee is named upon the presumption of his competence in the area in which he is made a trustee. The wisdom of directing the destiny of a church-related college through trusteeship is confirmed when one observes it being done on the floor of a convention meeting," Johnson continued. Johnson warned his fellow messengers what might happen if the state convention could dictate trustee actions, suggesting that "under such conditions the institutions may become the pawn of politically inspired denominational forces."[38] The opposing views espoused by both Reverend Johnsons revealed the conflict facing the messengers when they gathered in Charleston in 1963 for their convention. Should religious belief trump church polity? Such indeed was the pressing question to be answered in Charleston.

When convention business took up the executive committee's resolution requesting Furman to delay its open admission policy for a year of study on integration, the ensuing debate reflected the concerns of the two camps. The first messenger to speak to the issue reminded his fellow Baptists that "we are messengers which means we are not bound by our churches, neither are our churches bound by any action we take." The issue in question, messenger Edward Byrd argued, was if the state convention was going to remain true to Baptist polity of local autonomy. If local Baptist churches were not required to abide by the pronouncements of the state convention, why should a different standard hold for trustees of a Baptist college? "Let the trustees of each institution determine their own course," Byrd reasoned with his fellow Baptists. Before returning to his seat, Byrd moved to amend the original motion for a year of study as follows: "We leave to the trustees of each college the policy on which students are accepted." Reverend Julian Cave immediately challenged Byrd's substitute amendment and spoke out against the action of the Furman trustees. Cave proposed an alternative motion of his own, suggesting "that the 1963 South Carolina Baptist Convention disapprove of integration in its colleges."[39] Cave conceded that Baptist missionary efforts overseas could *possibly* suffer by maintaining segregated church-related schools, but he believed missionary endeavors would *certainly* be thwarted "by creating a colossal problem in [our] church and denomination. Integration will not bring the millennium," Reverend Cave concluded. Delegates broke into applause for Cave's adamancy, causing the convention president to call the messengers back to order.[40]

With the lines now drawn by the Byrd and Cave substitute amendments, a lengthy debate followed. Proponents of the Cave amendment appealed to traditional segregationist theology, claiming that desegregation at Furman would result in mixed-race marriages that were scripturally prohibited by God. These arguments prompted a call from A. A. Lawson to his fellow messengers to reread the ninth and tenth chapters of Ezra in hopes of correcting their misunderstanding of God's view of mixed marriages.[41] Following Lawson's plea for a re-examination of the last two chapters of the book of Ezra—perhaps because of it—Julian Cave withdrew his substitute motion, which ensured that the 1963 convention would not officially condemn integration. Other messengers, however, refused to surrender on

integration and continued to speak out against it even after the Cave amendment had been withdrawn.

Eventually, the messengers returned to considering the Byrd amendment,
which would entrust full authority on matters of desegregation at Baptist-
sponsored universities to the trustees of those schools. After continued
debate, the messengers voted this amendment down, returning, finally,
to the original resolution requesting a year's postponement on desegregation at Furman. When this motion carried by an overwhelming majority, a
segregationist-minded messenger quickly moved that the language of the
resolution be altered so that the convention would "instruct" rather than
"request" that Furman trustees wait a year until implementing their new
admissions policy. This motion was defeated.[42]

The state convention's request that Furman delay its open admission policy
put the school's trustees in a difficult position. While most stakeholders at the
university had accepted the idea of an integrated campus, the convention debate indicated that most white Baptists in the state had not. The issue even
made its way into state politics, with state legislators crafting a bill to remove
trustees from religious colleges at the request of a majority of the institutions'
beneficiaries.[43] At the same time that political forces were aligning themselves with those desiring to exercise control over school trustees, a critical mass of Furman students clamored for school officials to ignore the
convention's resolution and enact the new admissions policy immediately.
Caught in this divide, Furman trustees granted the state convention's request
and agreed not to change the university's admissions policy until the denomination had studied the situation for a year.

After passing the resolution to study integration in Baptist schools,
the state convention created a nine-member committee to carry out this
mandate. The committee's task was not an easy one. The 1963 convention
showed that segregationist theology was alive and well in Baptist churches
even as southern society as a whole inched closer to a forced abandonment
of Jim Crow segregation due to a pending civil rights bill in Congress. To
better understand where Baptists stood on racial issues, the committee convened a one-day conference on race relations in Columbia at the end of
April and invited all interested Baptist church members in South Carolina
to participate. Over a thousand people accepted the invitation.[44] The conference organizers stressed that the purpose was not for debate or to conduct business; rather, it was to simply have a conversation about the state
of race relations. Conference organizers arranged for the state convention's

Christian Life and Public Affairs Committee to give formal presentations in the morning before opening the floor to comments from the public in the afternoon.[45]

During the afternoon session, H. K. Whetsall was one of the first to speak, declaring that, while the state convention and committees might be nudging Baptists toward integration, the Bible did not. "There is scriptural basis for White supremacy," Whetsall asserted, and he reminded those in attendance that the Bible "condemns racial intermarriage."[46] Robert Head followed Whetsall at the microphone and scolded the state convention "for 'brainwashing us' about integration." Head's comment drew agreeable laughter and applause from those in attendance.[47] R. V. King suggested that Furman should delay integrating until a majority of South Carolina Baptist churches had themselves integrated and could prove such action could be done peacefully. King cautioned, however, that each church should first vote whether they would even be willing to admit black Christians to join their congregation.[48] W. A. Barnett claimed that "integration alters that basic principles of our doctrine. This fanatic infatuation with another race leads only to pagan idolatry."[49] Other conference attendees went on record with their beliefs that racial segregation was in line with Christianity; that Furman trustees should be prevented from integrating the university; and that if the Baptist school integrated, it would "violate the will of a majority of South Carolina Baptists."[50] When the afternoon session ended, forty-four Baptist ministers and laymen had publically spoken out against integration and requested that all Baptist-related schools remain segregated; only nine individuals expressed public support for desegregating the schools.[51]

Despite the strong opposition to racial integration that many white Baptists voiced during the twelve-month period of study, it became apparent that Furman officials intended to desegregate regardless. In the summer of 1964, Furman hired a new president who accepted the position on the condition that the school desegregate. Additionally, the school was trying to secure federal funds in 1964 for the construction of a new science building and needed to comply with new federal nondiscrimination policies to qualify for government money to assist with the project.[52] By the time the South Carolina Baptists convened their annual convention in the fall of 1964, the end of segregation at Furman was a foregone conclusion for university administrators. Baptist messengers at the convention thought otherwise.

Just before the 1964 convention began in Columbia, the study committee submitted its final report to the denomination's general board for

consideration. The committee's findings read in part: "We consider it imprac-
tical, at this time to adopt a uniform admissions policy for all our colleges.
Therefore, we approve the policy of allowing each college to deal with student admissions in whatever way the Trustees feel is best for that particular
institution and the South Carolina Baptist Convention." By appealing to the
traditional Baptist polity of local autonomy, the committee hoped to thread
the needle between the two groups. The segregationists who constituted a
majority of the state convention could be appeased in that the committee had
not endorsed integration, while Furman gained permission to pursue the
policy to which it had already committed. The committee's suggested path
forward also conveniently avoided the looming question of segregationist
theology's biblical perspicuity. Satisfied with this arrangement, the Baptist
general board adopted the proposal and passed it on for the consideration
of the assembled Baptist messengers at the state convention in November.[53]
One newspaper editorial predicted that at the 1964 convention South
Carolina Baptists "would have one of their characteristic battle royals with
much furor and the outward appearance of deep cleavage and harsh feelings.
But in the process, they will do much soul-searching and they usually come
up with the right answer."[54]

As noted at the outset of this chapter, the 1964 South Carolina Baptist
Convention conducted its proceedings in the sanctuary of the First Baptist
Church of Columbia, the same sanctuary in which South Carolinians a
century before had cast their votes to secede from the Union. More than
two thousand Baptist messengers were crowded into the church when
Dr. George Lovell introduced the proposal to allow admission policies at the
denomination's colleges and universities to be determined by the institutions
themselves. The proposal, Lovell told his fellow Baptists, had been "prepared in agonizing prayer," and he urged respect from those gathered before
moving on with the proceedings. Surprisingly, the convention chose not to
debate the resolution and instead put the proposal allowing for institutional
autonomy regarding integration to an immediate vote by secret ballot. The
proposal lost by a margin of 28 votes—943 to 915—demonstrating that the
continued segregation of their schools was important enough to a majority
of these white Baptists that they were willing to abandon traditional Baptist
principles to exercise authority over Furman trustees.[55]

Having asserted its desire to have a say about the integration of its
denomination's schools, the South Carolina Baptist Convention now acted
to make its beliefs about integration known. Reverend Julian Cave, who a

year earlier had proposed a segregation amendment at the convention only to withdraw it, now rose again to ask the messengers to take a stand on the integration question. Saying that the trustees of Baptist colleges needed to know what the convention thought about racial integration, Cave moved that "the messengers of this convention vote direct 'yes' or 'no' as to whether they favor or disfavor, approve or disapprove integration in the schools owned and promoted by this body." Confusion reigned throughout the sanctuary as shouts of "define integration" rang out amid attempts to table Cave's motion. With order restored and ballots distributed, South Carolina Baptists, sitting in the same pews their forbearers had occupied when deciding to leave the Union, overwhelmingly voted against the idea of racial integration in church schools, 905 to 575.[56]

The decisive vote margin against integration caught the attention of the editorial page of the *Charleston News and Courier*. The vote, according to the newspaper, highlighted "the unwillingness of the state's most numerous denomination to integrate the races in colleges that it supports. Despite pressures—religious, social and political—for change, these Christian people are not ready to go along with new notions of a multiracial society."[57] As the newspaper noted, the society around them was surely changing, but these white Christians remained steadfast in their commitment to the idea that God called them to a different standard.

With the state Baptist convention opposed to the idea of racial integration and unwilling to yield control over admission procedures to the college, Furman trustees were stuck. On one hand, the school was not bound legally to follow the convention's directives, and Baptist polity always favored local autonomy over outside control. On the other hand, the state convention had elected the Furman trustees, so a sense of obligation to the group likely existed to some degree among the trustees. Meanwhile, Furman's president-elect, Gordon Blackwell, still several months from taking office, wrote to the trustees reminding them that he had accepted the job with the understanding that the school would be desegregated. Blackwell's letter helped tip the scales toward integration. In a meeting in early December 1964, Furman's trustees cast their lots with President-Elect Blackwell—as well as the significant federal funds for which the nonracially exclusive stance would make the school eligible—voting to defy the South Carolina Baptist Convention and implement their previous decision to admit any qualified student regardless of race.[58]

Baptists across the state expressed disbelief over the Furman decision. The president of the state Baptist convention, R. W. Major, was restrained in his reaction, saying, "I'm a little surprised to hear the news. I thought they would have gone along with the convention." Ben E. Manley, the chairman of the South Carolina Baptist Laymen's Association, was less guarded with his disappointment: "I had no idea they would do anything like this in the face of the decision of the convention. It's a tragedy. It is my opinion that 80 to 90 percent of the church members in the state oppose this decision. We recognize the school as being ours and not the private domain of school officials. If they integrate it, our objective will be to disintegrate it." Manley called for "a study of the charter of Furman and of the Baptist Convention to see what can be done with the democratic process." Another Baptist lay leader similarly promised, "We church members are not going to let a minority tell us what to do. We must maintain the democratic principle of the rule of the majority."[59] With their interest in vigilantly abiding by the convention's wishes, these lay Baptist leaders were actually departing from Baptist governing procedures, which granted little authority to the state Baptist convention.

Ultimately, Furman's autonomy from the South Carolina Baptist Convention shielded the institution from the denominational backlash threatened by lay leaders. The only recourse Baptist churches in South Carolina had against Furman was to withhold their funding of the university through the convention. Such an act might achieve a symbolic victory but would do little to hinder school operations since convention money made up only 6 percent of the Furman budget.[60] Angry though they may have been, segregationist Baptists could legally do nothing to prevent Joe Vaughn from enrolling at Furman in January 1965, becoming the first black student in the school's 139-year history.[61]

Upon reading the news of Furman's desegregation, James M. Copeland publicly congratulated the Baptist school. The Methodist minister who had chided segregated church schools in an editorial letter three years earlier at last had reason to celebrate: "May I say a hearty congratulations to Furman University trustees for their progressive move in agreeing to admit all qualified students to the university," wrote Copeland. "It must be, and rightly so," he continued, "a great satisfaction to the Baptists of South Carolina that Furman University has read the signs of the times so well that they have been able to pave the way for the other church related colleges."[62] Copeland undoubtedly had his own denominational schools in mind. South Carolina Baptists, after all, were not alone in grappling with integration at their denomination-affiliated colleges in the mid-1960s; Methodists were struggling with the same issue. Ground zero in the Methodist battle over integration was Wofford College in Spartanburg. As with Furman, the question of desegregation at Wofford—a small, all-male, liberal arts institution in the South Carolina upcountry—involved disputes over school trustees setting Wofford's admissions policy. And like the Baptist row, the fight over integration at Wofford revealed the persistence of segregationist theology among white Bible-believing Christians in South Carolina.

Signs of trouble around desegregation at Wofford began as early as 1960 when a member of the college's board of trustees became concerned that a professor at the school was "an integrationist, if not an outright believer in mongrelism."[63] Board member Edgar Brown complained that he was "getting tired of being a Methodist, supporting Wofford and hearing such a fellow as this [professor] holler. The ministers aren't going to do anything," Brown continued, "most of them being fooled on this subject [of integration] and, if some red-blooded South Carolinian . . . does not up the situation at Wofford and other Methodist Schools, it's going to be too bad."[64] Two years passed before the trouble Edgar Brown predicted came to Wofford, and, as Brown had foretold, the trouble arose from an integrationist minister.

The 1962 annual conference meeting of South Carolina Methodists took place in Spartanburg. After the report of the Board of Christian Social Concerns had been read that year, Reverend James Copeland took the floor to call "attention to the position of the Methodist Church in the matter of race, and urg[e] more action in this matter." To this end, Copeland made a motion that the report of the Board of Christian Social Concerns include the following statement: "We recommend that the doors of admission to Wofford and Columbia College [the men's and women's Methodist colleges in South Carolina, respectively] be open to receive all qualified students irrespective of race or national origin and that this action become effective September of 1963."[65] After making his motion, Copeland lectured his fellow delegates: "We ought to be ashamed of ourselves for our reticence," Copeland told the assembled Methodists. "The Methodist Church ought to be in the forefront of this very great issue. Most ministers of South Carolina believe as I do and so do many of our laymen. It is time for the Church of Jesus Christ to speak out."[66]

Copeland's proposal and remarks irritated his fellow Methodists with alternative views on race relations in the church. Reverend W. R. Kinnett, for instance, disagreed with Copeland's claims and took the floor to dispute them. "I resent the overtones that to disagree [with Copeland] is to divide those who are Christian on this issue from those who are not," Kinnett told the delegates. Another minister, R. C. O'Donnell, similarly challenged the claim that a majority of Methodist clergy and laity agreed with Copeland's thinking on issues of racial equality, charging that desegregating Methodist colleges "is too far down the road for our people to accept at this time."[67] The vote on Copeland's motion confirmed O'Donnell's suspicions. The official denominational record did not record the vote tally, noting only that Copeland's amendment was "defeated by a large majority." A reporter covering the 1962 annual conference, however, estimated that fewer than twenty of the more than a thousand Methodist delegates rose in support of Copeland's call to desegregate church colleges, a resounding denouncement of integration by white South Carolina Methodists.[68]

The next year in June 1963, South Carolina Methodists gathered again for their annual conference, and again James Copeland proposed integrating the denomination's colleges. Copeland's proposal at the 1963 conference was almost identical to his defeated motion the previous year, coming as a proposed amendment to the report of the Commission on Christian Social Concerns that read, "The South Carolina Methodist Conference go[es] on record as approving enrollment of all qualified students to Wofford and Columbia Colleges irrespective of race, color, or national origin and that this action become effective September 1963."[69] Recognizing that an amendment so similar to the one that had failed the year before had little chance for success twelve months later, Claude Evans, the long-time editor of the *South Carolina Methodist Advocate* who shared Copeland's views on integration, suggested an alternative. Evans proposed that the conference endorse racial integration in its colleges but that the "time and date of this change be left to the discretion and wisdom of the respective Boards of Trustees."[70]

After heated debate, the delegates adopted an amendment that made no endorsement of racial integration. Instead, it put the South Carolina annual conference on record as wishing "to express our confidence in our trustees of our colleges, both as regards their spiritual dedication and their administrative wisdom. Therefore we wish to declare that we place no restraints on them in their policy-making activities in regard to the racial or other composition of the student bodies of our colleges."[71] Although the adopted amendment was significantly weaker than Copeland's original version, it nonetheless was a step toward the desegregation of Methodist colleges in South Carolina.

Leaving the 1963 annual conference, some segregationist Christians saw clouds gathering on the horizon and started preparing for the coming storm. The Moncks Corner Methodist Church, for example, was among the first to react to the adopted amendment, and its response foreshadowed the battle ahead. In June, the official board of Moncks Corner Methodist took up at its monthly meeting the issue of the possibility that denominational colleges might integrate. Troubled that the annual conference had placed admitting students at Methodist schools "solely within the discretion of the board of trustees . . . with no restriction being placed on admittance of Negro students," the official board moved to make their support for segregation known. Moncks Corner wrote to President Charles Marsh at Wofford, informing him that "in the event that a member of the Negro race is voluntarily admitted as a student" at Wofford, "all funds allocated in the Unified Budget of The Moncks Corner Methodist Church . . . shall immediately cease to be paid . . . with any pledge . . . to cease and terminate immediately."[72] Such threats would become a pattern in the years ahead.

For his part, President Marsh was conflicted about desegregating his school, despite the path to integration the annual conference had provided for Wofford. In a confidential statement four months after the Methodist conference put the integration decision in school trustees' hands, Marsh told the group that he had "no personal objection" to admitting black students and saw "strong moral and ethical reasons why they should be granted this opportunity." However, as a long-time resident of the South, Marsh was "sympathetically aware of the strong personal feelings of some members of this Board and many other constituents of the College against the admission of Negroes to Wofford."[73] In his statement to the Wofford trustees, Marsh listed adverse effects for both rejecting and admitting qualified black students. Of the ten negative outcomes Marsh imagined would result from preserving segregation, economic reprisal—in the form of either denial of federal grants or reduction in donor giving—was the main concern of eight of them. In addition to potential monetary consequences for maintaining segregation, Marsh believed Wofford would have difficulty recruiting faculty and students and would grow increasingly isolated "from the main currents of educational and religious policy and practice." As Marsh reasoned, "Most of the national educational associations and religious bodies have taken strong positions in favor of integrated admissions policies at colleges and universities."[74] Marsh may have been sympathetic to the hesitations his fellow white southerners had toward integration, but a mix of economic pragmatism and enrollment concerns ultimately caused the Wofford president to push his school toward desegregation.

Before going to the board of trustees for a vote on admitting black students, Marsh solicited feedback on this issue from the Wofford faculty and staff. The responses Marsh received varied, but most seemed to accept desegregation as inevitable. Religion professor C. F. Nesbitt, for example, told Marsh that he hoped Wofford would open its admission policy immediately. "Since the pronouncement of the Supreme Court about racial equality in education, I have been personally much concerned over the silence of the churches and their institutions, and their lagging behind the state institutions in complying with the stated law of the land," Nesbitt wrote. "It seems to me high time we took some specific step forward in the name of Methodism."[75] But Marsh also received less-than-enthusiastic responses from other college stakeholders. The director of college athletics, Conley Snidow, told the Wofford president that it was his "personal preference that Wofford have no negroes in the student body." Snidow acknowledged that while he had "no aversion to working with them as athletes, I would not recruit negroes unless directed to do so." The athletic director did concede that he thought "there would be very little problem in acceptance of the negro in our student body."[76] Faculty member C. E. Cauthen, meanwhile, told Marsh that "although I must confess that I can not escape completely southern prejudices, it seems to me that both ethical and the more mundane financial aspects of the question require that Wofford liberalize admission policies in regard to Negro applications."[77] Similarly, Professor Howard Pegram admitted that he "would definitely prefer to see Wofford remain all-white," but he had "no serious objection to the admission of qualified students of any race." Pegram did caution that in the long run admitting black students might hinder the college's reputation. "Suppose we admitted one or several negro students," Pegram wrote to Marsh. "Since some of our students have always flunked out, it would be evident that some of the colored ones might well do the same. Then, because it seems to seize upon any pretext to build propaganda, wouldn't the NAACP immediately make a big noise saying, in effect, 'Yes, Wofford admitted them, but of course they were discriminated against—they got rid of them by giving them F's.' The general publicity would not be good," Pegram concluded.[78] Overall, the response by the faculty and staff to an integrated Wofford ranged from enthusiastic support to begrudging acceptance, but none of the feedback Marsh received from his internal constituents was adamantly opposed to black students enrolling at the college.

In January 1964, Marsh then created a special committee to explore the logistics of desegregating Wofford. Taking Marsh's and the faculty's perspectives into consideration, the committee unanimously recommended that "no qualified student be barred from Wofford college on the account of race or creed" and advised the board of trustees to act accordingly.[79] When word of the committee's recommendation became public, the Methodist church in Bamberg wrote to Wofford to plead that the school not follow such a course. The Bamberg Methodists acknowledged that "the social and economic customs of years past are in a state of flux," but for these Christians the changing social mores of southern society were all the more reason to hold fast to traditional practices. According to their understanding, following tradition meant that segregation at Christian colleges was not "wrong or unchristian" and integration was "not necessary or desirable."[80] In May 1964, Wofford trustees, "after months of study and careful and prayerful consideration," ignored requests like the one from the Bamberg Methodist Church, choosing instead to open the doors of the Methodist college to any qualified applicant, irrespective of race.[81]

Some of the Wofford faculty had recommended that if the school decided to open its admissions policy, it should not widely publicize the fact. Colonel Marcus Griffin of Wofford's Military Science division suggested to President Marsh that the school make "a simple statement to the South Carolina Methodist Conference" that Wofford had changed its admissions policy. Griffin feared that Wofford would attract unwanted attention from segregationists in the state and urged Marsh to keep the news quiet.[82] But the possibility of a Christian institution desegregating was too significant a news story to go unnoticed in South Carolina in 1964, and press coverage proved impossible to avoid. With the coverage came the backlash Griffin had feared, the first of which came from a trustee on the Wofford board responding to an erroneous report that the trustees' decision had been unanimous. "I wish to say that I *was* and *still am* very definitely opposed to the motion passed by the Board changing the admissions policy," trustee W. Cantey Sprott wrote to the editor of the *Methodist Advocate*. "I was one of those voting with the minority against the motion and I make no apologies to *anyone* for this stand."[83] For many white Methodists, Sprott's actions required no apology. These Christians instead saw Sprott's stand against integration as admirable and praiseworthy, and in the months after Wofford opened its doors to black students, these Christians made their feelings known.

Only days after the Wofford decision, the Official Board of Trinity Methodist Church in Sumter called an emergency meeting, voted to end the church's financial support of the college, and divided the roughly $2,500 in annually allocated funds between other Methodist schools in the state.[84] The Sumter church was the first of several congregations that took immediate steps to punish Wofford and set the stage for a confrontation at the upcoming annual conference meeting. Just two weeks after his school announced its new racially inclusive policy, President Marsh traveled to the annual conference and tried to counter the growing segregationist tide. Addressing the delegates, Marsh appealed to the better angels of their nature, saying, "We at Wofford humbly believe that this step we have taken to open the doors of your college to future Negro leaders of our state will help to release from this reservoir the streams of Christian love needed to ensure the kind of South Carolina all of us want."[85] Despite Marsh's efforts, the clamor against the Wofford action grew louder. For many delegates, Marsh's sentiments of Christian love directly contradicted their long-standing beliefs about Christianity and race relations, turning the annual conference in the summer of 1964 into a battleground.

More than a dozen churches sent resolutions to the annual conference announcing that they were cutting off funds to Wofford and would send the money to the state's other two Methodist schools, provided these schools maintained racial segregation.[86] One delegate made a motion that the Wofford College Board of Trustees "be requested to restudy their new admissions policy, and that in so doing, they consider opinions of Wofford men and South Carolina Methodists." After much deliberation, this motion was narrowly defeated 272 to 250.[87] On the heels of this defeated motion, another delegate moved that the Wofford trustees "rescind their recent action to integrate Negroes into the College, and that the Board of Trustees of Columbia College and Spartanburg Junior College [the other two Methodist schools in the state] not take any action in the future to integrate their respective institutions." After sharp deliberations, this motion was also defeated.[88] The decision to integrate Wofford had emerged from the annual conference intact.

If segregationist Methodists were unable to get the annual conference to support their efforts, they nonetheless made sure their opinions on racial integration were known in the wake of the Wofford decision. Letters flooded Charles Marsh's office protesting the school's admission policy. E. B. Woodward wrote Marsh and requested that he be removed from the school's mailing list while arguing that as God is unchanging, so too should ideas about racial segregation remain static. "If you think integration is right," Woodward asked Marsh, "please explain why you have made no move in that direction long, long ago; or was it wrong then and now it is right?"[89] Other Methodists opposed to integration were more explicit in wielding their theological arguments. "I am still opposed to mixing of races and base my stand on the Holy Bible which clearly teaches separation. . . . Mixing of races brings not racial peace but the exact opposite as clearly proved by examples in other countries. Let us return to the Scriptures," Paul Harless wrote to Marsh.[90]

The Official Board of the Manning Methodist Church published an extended letter in the *Methodist Advocate* reaffirming their belief that "segregation of the races is best for the white people and the colored people of our state" and suggested that the decision of Wofford "makes one wonder who is calling the signals—is it our God who thought it best to create man with different colors and characteristics and none of us equal? Or is it our leaders in government and church who think that He made a mistake? To our knowledge Christ never preached equality nor did He preach integration."[91] The segregationist theology so prevalent during the racial uproar of the 1950s proved to have currency with white Christians as the calendars reached the mid-1960s.

The majority of letters Charles Marsh received opposing Wofford's integration omitted explicit theological arguments for their position. Nevertheless, segregationist theology was a latent influence for many writers. For instance, dozens of Methodist churches across South Carolina informed Marsh via letters that they would no longer be financially supporting Wofford in light of its racially inclusive stance. If these congregations believed God favored racial integration—or was even neutral—they would not adopt formal resolutions condemning Wofford's move toward integration and redirect their financial contributions to the two Methodist schools in the state that continued to practice segregation. Yet, official boards and Sunday School classes in Methodist churches across the Palmetto State condemned Wofford and reallocated their contributions in response to the school's desegregation. The Young Adults Sunday School Class at the Bethlehem Methodist Church in Bishopsville, South Carolina, for example, wrote Marsh to "go on record as being fervently opposed to the recent decision of the Board of Trustees of Wofford College concerning the lowering of racial barriers. There are twenty-six members of our Sunday School class, and in the not-too-distant future our children will be ready to attend Wofford and Columbia College.

They, and we, have been betrayed by this infamous action, and we cannot under any circumstance condone it," wrote Dan McDaniel on behalf of the Young Adults Sunday School Class.[92] Such letters portended difficulties for Wofford enrollment in the years ahead, but of more immediate concern for Wofford officials were churches who severed their financial ties to the college. Throughout 1964, Marsh received word from the official boards of Methodist churches from all corners of South Carolina that Wofford would no longer receive their annual contributions. Often, such correspondence included the resolution church members had adopted to voice their displeasure over Wofford's integrationist stance. In almost all cases, the resolutions reallocated funds originally designated for Wofford to Columbia College and Spartanburg Junior College, the two Methodist colleges in South Carolina that retained segregated admissions policies in 1964. In several instances, the church resolutions stipulated that support of these two latter institutions was conditional upon the schools' retaining their racially segregated charters.

Church contributions to Wofford in 1963 had made up nearly 13 percent of the school's operating budget, a percentage significantly higher than the South Carolina Baptist Convention's support of Furman.[93] Throughout the spring and summer of 1964, Marsh received notice on an almost daily basis from churches that had decided to pull their support for Wofford. By September of that year, eighty-six Methodist churches in South Carolina reported they had ended financial contributions to Wofford as a response to the school's integration.[94]

Individual contributors also joined the churches in withdrawing their money from the Wofford coffers. Kenneth Suggs wrote Marsh to express his "shock" that "without any vote being taken on the subject by the membership of the alumni or the churches which are affected, the Trustees, had . . . opened the doors of Wofford to the mixing of races. While my contribution has not been much in the past, I have no further interest in making contributions to the college for any purpose."[95] Similarly, upon hearing about his alma mater's integration, W. W. Alman was upset enough to cancel his membership in an alumni association and inform school officials that he had rewritten his will "and Wofford is no longer mentioned—a rather nice legacy gone."[96] Despite the loss of financial support from churches and individuals throughout the state, Wofford moved forward with its plan to consider any qualified applicant regardless of race. In the fall of 1964, Albert W. Gray became the first African American student to attend Wofford College.

Wofford officials remained concerned about giving levels throughout the 1964–1965 school year. In May 1965, however, Roger Milliken, a wealthy textile executive from Spartanburg and long-time friend of Wofford, discreetly donated one million dollars to the college to establish a "Gift Stabilization Fund," which school officials could tap if donations continued to shrink.[97] Although many of the churches who withdrew support were numerically small, the cumulative effect of their actions forced Wofford officials to dip into Milliken's fund. While accessed only once, the Milliken fund assuaged the concerns of Wofford's administrators and was a welcomed insurance policy against the backlash to Wofford's desegregation.[98]

While the doors of Furman and Wofford were ostensibly freely open to black students by 1964, integration required that students of color actually walk through them; for many years, small numbers at either school did so. Four years after Furman dropped its white-only policy, only 8 of the school's 1,728 students were African American and reported feeling alone and excluded in an "atmosphere of unfamiliarity."[99] Meanwhile, at Wofford, over 96 percent of the student body remained white nine years after desegregating.[100] Thirty years after desegregating, nine out of ten Wofford students were white. Similarly, three decades after desegregation came to Furman, 93 percent of its student body was white.[101] For at least one astute observer in 1964, the lack of latter-day integration at the schools would have been unsurprising. On the eve of the school's desegregation in 1964, Wofford professor R. A. Patterson wrote to President Marsh to express his belief that the school's integration would likely have less impact than many of its white Christian constituents feared: "I believe that the number of qualified negroes applying will be few and those admitted, even though scholastically capable, would not be very happy at Wofford due to the great diversity of class associates. In all probability they would withdraw and seek a more congenial atmosphere. In other words, they would voluntarily segregate themselves, and Wofford would have no problems. Twenty years from now we will look back with utter amazement that we were so wrought up over this question. Perhaps we are making a mountain out of a mole hill."[102] Patterson proved to be prescient. As the statistics and stories from the years after 1964 bore out, Furman and Wofford continued to function as what sociologists would come to call "white institutional spaces," wherein the schools' segregationist history continued to exert influence on the campuses even after the schools' policies changed.[103] These white institutional spaces meant that, although black students could legally attend the schools, the institutions themselves did not make it easy for students of color to do so—psychologically, culturally, or otherwise. Black students who attended both Furman and Wofford in the early years of desegregation would later recall their time on campus as "lonely, frightening days" when they regularly needed to "flee the campus on weekends to find companionship and the strength to forge ahead."[104] The inertia of white institutional spaces ultimately yielded for many years after integration what so many segregationist Christians desired but feared they could not maintain: racially homogenous church-related colleges.

Examining the fallout from Furman's and Wofford's decision to integrate reveals important aspects about segregationist Christianity in the mid-1960s. The controversy surrounding the desegregation of Furman and Wofford demonstrates that segregation theology maintained viability in the eyes of conservative white Christians into the mid-1960s. As shown in both the state's Baptist convention debate over Furman and the letters Methodists sent to Charles Marsh protesting Wofford's admission policy, some white Christians in South Carolina continued to make overt appeals to segregationist theology in justifying their desire for racially segregated church schools. Only a minority of segregationist Methodist letter writers and Baptist messengers, however, explicitly invoked theological arguments in public debates. Yet, by a huge majority, Baptist messengers in 1964 rejected the idea of integrating Furman, while Methodist delegates overwhelmingly voted down a plan to integrate their denominational colleges in 1962. And when Wofford did desegregate in 1964, Methodists throughout South Carolina withdrew their financial support to the point that the school had to utilize an emergency fund to meet its budget. In this respect, conservative Baptists and Methodists still practiced the belief that racial integration violated God's will, even as they grew reticent in publicly vocalizing such ideas by the mid-1960s. While public articulations of segregationist theology diminished as the 1960s progressed, such theology retained currency for the segregationist Christianity that many conservative white Christians in South Carolina sought and practiced.

The quieting of explicit segregationist theology is accounted for by examining the cultural context of racial equality in the mid-1960s. Indeed, the controversy surrounding the desegregation of Furman and Wofford provides the opportunity to view the social forces that prevented South Carolina Baptists and Methodists from freely espousing their religiously motivated segregationist beliefs even as they continued to be influenced by them. It is clear that the desegregation of Furman and Wofford did not occur in a cultural vacuum, or that cultural isolation was even possible by the time the schools desegregated in 1964. One Southern Baptist seminary suggested that "the South could once ostracize and silence those who spoke out against its cultural way of life. No longer, in the days of Interstate highway, the movement of people between states, and the appearance of television is this possible."[105] This assessment was accurate. The motivations for the decision to integrate both Furman and Wofford, after all, came from outside forces. At Furman, the goal was to raise the university's reputation by recruiting a top-level president and faculty, which school officials discovered was impossible as long as Jim Crow resided on campus. At the same time, Wofford desegregated in large part to qualify for federal funds while Wofford faculty repeatedly noted that they would have preferred to remain all white and/or held traditional southern prejudices against the mixing of the races. But these same faculty also recognized that times were changing. Ultimately, school officials at both Furman and Wofford were able to gauge those shifting tides of public opinion and federal policy against discriminatory practices and accordingly made accommodations at their respective institutions.

Not only did university bureaucrats sense the shifting tides on issues of race, but also average white southerners by the 1960s increasingly felt the changes that had occurred around them even as they braced for more to come.[106] Such changes were hard for white South Carolinians to miss as they emanated largely from the efforts of their black neighbors. The civil rights demonstrations in the South that had done so much to effect changes in the racial climate of the region by the mid-1960s had also occurred with regularity in South Carolina. Nonviolent direct action protests in the state began in February 1960 in Rock Hill, when African American college students sat down and asked to be served at the "white only" lunch counters in several of the city's drug stores. Although the South Carolina legislature moved almost immediately to enact measures making it more difficult for activists to carry out protests, African American demonstrations against discrimination and segregation continued unabated for the next decade.[107] As white Baptists and Methodists considered ending segregation in their denominational colleges, they did so in the midst of African American protests over the practice.

Civil rights demonstrations coupled with reform brought on by federal economic pressure had created an environment in the South where open and blatant displays of racial antagonism and discrimination were becoming less socially acceptable. The impact of this change in southern culture on a religion predicated on cultural accommodations was telling. By the mid-1960s, it was an affront to polite social customs to talk about God's desire and plan for racial segregation even while the belief of God as a segregationist maintained significant motivating power. Sociological research on the accommodationist tendency in conservative Christianity helps explain the incongruence between social conduct and doctrinal belief. Such research asserts that "cultural pluralism places pressure on the adherents of a particular belief system to be accepting of those from other traditions. [Conservative Christianity] has resisted accommodating to this pressure at the doctrinal level; it has made certain concessions at the level of social demeanor and social discourse."[108] In other words, when conservative Christians hold beliefs that run contrary to the broader culture, they have historically stopped publicly *espousing* these beliefs for the sake of social civility. But they do not stop believing them.

The accommodationist trend within conservative Christianity was on full display in the backlash to the Furman and Wofford desegregation decisions. While only a minority of South Carolina Baptists and Methodists publicly vocalized their opposition to racially integrating their denominations' colleges in explicit theological terms, by their deeds a majority of the state's Baptists and Methodists at the state conventions and conferences demonstrated they continued to hold to the doctrine that God desired racial segregation.

Additionally, by voting against the desegregation of their denominational colleges and withdrawing financial support when those institutions did finally desegregate, the Furman and Wofford incidents reveal that the divisions within religious denominations over racial issues continued into the 1960s, with the laity often diverging from the broader denomination's institutional positions. It is worth noting that it was the chairman of the South Carolina Baptist Laymen's Association who publicly announced his intent to disintegrate Furman should the school desegregate. Similarly, it is telling that it was Methodist ministers in 1962 and 1963 who proposed the resolutions that ultimately paved the way for Wofford's desegregation. It was one of these ministers that J. C. Hubbard took to task in an angry letter to Charles Marsh a month after Wofford announced it was opening its doors to any qualified applicant regardless of race. Hubbard singled out J. Claude Evans for purportedly saying that "no respected Bible scholar in America today will say that racial segregation is Biblically based. Why is today different from any other day?" Hubbard rhetorically asked Marsh. "I do not know just who he [Evans] classifies as a Biblical scholar. I am at least glad he did not say 'respected Methodist.' Can he point out in the Bible where integration is Biblically based?"[109]

Like Hubbard, Climent J. Mint was also distressed about the direction Methodist bishops and liberal clergymen were taking the denomination. "It is evident that some of our Bishops and Superintendents have forgotten that the Laymen pay the bills," Mint wrote in a letter to the *Methodist Advocate* responding to the changes at Wofford College. "We are looking to the day when the great Methodist Church again will feel the heart beat of the Local Church. When the dead branches are trimmed off, the pulse of Methodism can be felt again in America. . . . The Conference and the Institutions, with all its leaders, including the Bishop and the District Superintendents, have forgotten that they need the local church and its support."[110] The sentiments expressed by Hubbard and Mint spoke for countless other laymen throughout South Carolina in 1964. Church colleges may have desegregated. Liberal clergy and denominational boards might speak out for racial equality. But for the majority of white churchgoers who filled South Carolina pews in the mid-1960s, their version of Christianity continued to hold that segregation was part of God's plan, and they would continue to fight for this divinely mandated social arrangement even in the face of societal change.

Nonetheless, the integration of Baptist and Methodist colleges in South Carolina illuminated a transformation occurring within segregationist Christianity. By 1964, it was becoming difficult to avoid the conclusion that, in addition to losing its cultural currency in the broader societal sphere, the rhetoric of segregationist theology might soon have difficulty even carrying the day in church institutions where a majority of adherents still held it as truth. If Baptist and Methodist schools could be made to integrate, were their churches next? Would their homes follow? It was becoming clear by the mid-1960s that if white Christians were to maintain segregation in the realms they could still control—which had diminished to churches and homes—they would need to change the way they marshalled their defense. Traditional understandings of segregationist theology still motivated these white Christians, but the cultural transformation occurring around them dictated that public appeals to such theology would no longer suffice. As the battle of racial inclusion expanded into the churches themselves by the late 1960s, segregationist Christians needed new language. A fight over integration in the Methodist church provided the arena to craft such language and showed the way forward for Christians who believed God was against racial mixing but required new ways of expressing such truth. Segregationist Christians proved up for the challenge.

4

Embracing Colorblindness

The Methodist Merger and the Transformation of Segregationist Christianity

On a Monday morning in May 1896, eight Supreme Court justices slipped on their black robes and took their seats on the bench of the highest court in the land. They convened that spring morning to issue rulings on nearly three dozen cases they had heard over the previous months, including one from Louisiana involving a law requiring racially segregated passenger cars for trains operating in the state. The case centered on a mixed-race passenger named Homer Plessy who, in coordination with a train company that wished to avoid the cost of additional cars on its lines, had violated the statute by taking a seat in a coach designated solely for white passengers. Plessy's fare was for a short ride—only about thirty miles from New Orleans to Covington, Louisiana, on the other side of Lake Pontchartrain—but the twenty-nine-year-old shoemaker never left the station. Instead, a waiting detective immediately arrested Plessy after he refused to follow the conductor's orders to move to the colored passengers' car. Plessy's train ride ended before it started, but the legal challenge to segregation that his actions sparked began a long, slow journey through the courts.[1]

Four years after Homer Plessy intentionally broke Louisiana's segregation law, the Supreme Court justices were prepared to declare if he had constitutional protection to do so. Plessy's lawyers had argued before the justices that the segregation statute denied their client's privileges, immunities, and equal protection under the law granted by the Fourteenth Amendment, effectively rendering Homer Plessy a second-class citizen. In a seven-to-one decision, the justices disagreed. "The object of the [Fourteenth] amendment," Justice Henry Billings Brown wrote for the court's majority, "was undoubtedly to enforce the absolute equality of the two races before the law, but in the nature of things it could not have been intended to abolish distinctions based upon color, or to enforce, as distinguished from political equality, or a commingling of the two races upon terms unsatisfactory to either." In other words,

The Bible Told Them So. J. Russell Hawkins, Oxford University Press. © Oxford University Press 2021.
DOI: 10.1093/oso/9780197571064.003.0005

from the majority's perspective, the Louisiana law treated blacks and whites equally insofar as both races were provided train cars. Feelings of social inferiority resulting from the segregation statute, meanwhile, were hardly the legislation's fault. "We consider the underlying fallacy of the plaintiff's argument to consist in the assumption that the enforced separation of the two races stamps the colored race with a badge of inferiority," Brown wrote. "If this be so," the justice continued, "it is not by reason of anything found in the act, but solely because the colored race chooses to put that construction upon it." Rejecting Plessy's argument, Brown continued his dismissal: "The argument also assumes that social prejudices may be overcome by legislation, and that equal rights cannot be secured to the negro except by an enforced commingling of the two races," Brown wrote. "We cannot accept this proposition. If the two races are to meet upon terms of social equality, it must be the result of natural affinities, a mutual appreciation of each other's merits, and a voluntary consent of individuals."[2] The Plessy *decision came at the close of the century that had seen slavery legally abolished in the United States and, for a time, political equality extended to former slaves and their descendants. But that equality was fleeting. The involuntary servitude that perished by the swords of Civil War soldiers gave way to forced segregation nourished by the pens of Supreme Court justices. With his decision in 1896, Justice Brown ensured the following century would be marked by a color line upheld by force of law. The Jim Crow era had begun.[3]*

By the opening years of the twentieth century, racial segregation was a way of life throughout the nation, but especially in the South, the region that nine in ten black Americans called home at that time. Southerners of both races in the twentieth century navigated a world created and sustained by the logic of Justice Brown's ruling, in which segregation began in the cradles of Jim Crow delivery rooms and ended in the graves of Jim Crow cemeteries. Lives between these births and deaths were likewise marked by segregation, which existed in southern schools and workplaces, hotels and restaurants, parks and beaches. For southerners, segregation became all-encompassing, at times bordering on the absurd. Some locales outlawed interracial games of checkers, while others applied segregation to phone booths. Atlanta kept different sets of Bibles in its courtrooms so testifying witnesses could take oaths using scripture untouched by someone of a different race. In New Orleans, even prostitutes were required to abide by segregation statutes.[4] The world Justice Brown's ruling brought about was totalizing, shaping the way that white and black southerners alike understood their place in society.

> *What Frederick Douglass had decried about slavery's impact in antebellum America was no less true for Jim Crow segregation after the war: it had the power to "make and unmake Presidents, to construe the law, dictate the policy, set the fashion in national manners and customs, interpret the Bible, and control the church."[5] And for seven decades, so it did.*

Despite the inferior station to which Justice Brown's ruling rendered black Americans, they refused to accept their status as second-class citizens under segregation, ceaselessly pointing out the hypocrisy of racial segregation in a land that espoused equality for all. By the mid-1960s, these tireless advocates for civil rights had won over the support of all branches of the federal government, and, marshalling this federal power on their behalf, black Americans undid the world of *Plessy*. Seventy years after Henry Billings Brown's ruling had helped give Jim Crow life, legal segregation was dead.

But in one realm of southern life, segregation lived on, supported by custom rather than law. As Jim Crow crumbled around southern churches in the 1960s, these churches remained starkly segregated, protected by the First Amendment's guaranteed religious liberty from governmental intervention. This arrangement suited white segregationist Christians, but it was far from perfect. After all, calls to desegregate southern churches could always come from within the church bodies themselves, and as the 1960s progressed, such calls increasingly came. In 1964, a group of Methodist laymen in South Carolina created the "Methodist Bulletin," a newsletter for conservative Methodists concerned by efforts to make their denomination more racially inclusive. Earlier that same year, Wofford College had desegregated and the "Methodist Bulletin" now identified a new threat on the horizon: "There should be no doubt that the present leadership of the Methodist Church has adopted the goal of integration—the absence of all racial distinctions," the editors of the "Methodist Bulletin" warned their readers.[6] These segregationist Christians were right to be concerned. A battle was indeed brewing in the Methodist denomination in late 1964 as church leaders considered ending the racial segregation embedded in the denomination's structure since 1939, and for segregationist Christians this battle required new rhetorical weapons. Appeals to scripture in the 1950s had not stopped the broader southern society from falling to integration. Meanwhile, the fight over desegregating their Christian colleges and universities revealed that while segregationist theology still motived white Christians, their position could be dismissed as out of step with the times even if it was in the majority. If churches were to remain free of the evils of integration, these segregationist Christians understood they needed new tactics. The ordeal of desegregating the Methodist Church in the South served as a useful proving ground for segregationist Christians testing these new strategies.

Seven years after the "Methodist Bulletin" first sounded the alarm about integration in their church, segregationist Christians had developed an effective response to the threat. In a 1971 letter to the leaders of the integration effort, a well-respected South Carolina journalist, prominent Methodist layman, and ardent segregationist named William Workman deployed the new rhetorical device white Christians had fashioned in their efforts to avoid integration.[7] Workman was part of a new organization of conservative evangelical Christians in South Carolina called the Methodist Christian Fellowship (MCF), whose purpose was preventing the integration of the Methodist Church in the state. As a spokesman for the MCF, Workman eschewed the explicit appeals to segregationist theology of previous generations that cited chapter and verse how God deplored racial integration, adopting instead new language better suited for a post–Civil Rights Act South. The fallacy in pursuing a racially inclusive church, Workman wrote for the MCF in 1971, is that it "is likely to produce continuing friction and would perpetuate and emphasize race consciousness, since race would become a critical factor in determining church assignments and associations."[8] The problem, Workman argued, was the persistent discussion of race among Christians. What the church needed was simply to "eliminate racial distinctions or discriminations in the conduct of Methodist affairs." In other words, Workman was calling for ending the *problem* of race by ending *attention* to race. Rather than focusing on race itself, Workman insisted on behalf of the MCF that Christians should adopt colorblindness, by which racial inequalities would disappear as individuals no longer gave race consideration. While this MCF position seemed benign, perhaps even magnanimous for its time, it had indisputable ties to a less benign era, ties Workman explicitly revealed in his letter. Christians, Workman wrote in drawing his letter to a close, should promote an "atmosphere in which 'natural affinities, a mutual appreciation of each other's merits, and a voluntary consent of individuals' may contribute to the ultimate elimination of emotional as well as structural barriers between the races."[9]

The phrases "natural affinities," "mutual appreciation of merits," and "voluntary association of individuals" were not Workman's. They were the words of Henry Billings Brown, words the Supreme Court justice in 1896 used to deny Homer Plessy—and all who shared his skin color—full equality as American citizens. They were the words with which the white South constructed and sustained a Jim Crow society whose recent end Workman, and so many other white Christians, lamented. And they were words that helped generations of white southerners interpret segregation as divinely ordered. At first blush, Workman's letter seemed to gesture at a new era of white Christians' acceptance of racial integration. But by appropriating word for word a line from the Supreme Court case that gave Jim Crow legal sanction in the South for nearly seven decades, Workman's letter also reveals ways in which the new language of colorblindness had its roots in the desire for segregation. Understanding the historical links between colorblindness and segregationist theology reveals a continuity of segregationist Christianity from the 1950s to the 1970s and a perpetuation of racial separatism by white Christians—even unwittingly so—into the decades beyond. This chapter tells that story.

Church polity dictated that denominationally mandated integration would never occur among the Baptists. Leaders of the Southern Baptist Convention may have urged their fellow Baptists to make their churches more inclusive and adopted endless reports to that effect, but congregational autonomy in Baptist churches meant individual churches themselves would ultimately hold that decision. At the state convention in November 1968, for example, the South Carolina Baptist Student Union presented a statement in support of integrated churches. "We do not see how a stand of racial prejudice or segregation can be derived from Christianity," the statement began. "Can we afford the vice of mental isolation that permits us to send missionaries to Kenya and Nigeria to establish Baptist churches among the black men there while we will not open membership in our churches to black men here?"[10] Defiant messengers responded to the students by receiving their statement as "information only."[11] Such pleadings in Southern Baptist statements and reports urging their convention churches toward racial inclusiveness could be taken or left, and more often than not, Baptist churches chose the latter. This was not so with the Methodists, who were beholden to an episcopal structure that meant denominational bodies and agencies could be made to go along with racial inclusivity whether they wanted to or not. Examining how such actions unfolded among Methodists in the late 1960s reveals how white Christians continued to find integration contradictory to the tenets of their faith and honed new language to resist racial mixing by the 1970s.

Understanding these Methodist actions begins seventeen years before the first shots of the American Civil War, when the Methodist Episcopal Church (MEC) split over the issue of a church bishop in the South holding slaves. In 1844, this situation was anathema to many northern members in the MEC, mirroring the deepening divide over slavery that existed in the country at that time. Because of this issue of slavery, the MEC ultimately divided along sectional lines, with southern Methodists establishing the Methodist Episcopal Church, South (MECS) in 1844 as an independent denomination comfortable with the existence of slavery.[12] In the years immediately following the Civil War, the vast majority of African American Methodists left the MECS, where they had been required to worship as slaves, and joined new black denominations or retained their affiliation with Methodism by establishing new churches in the South chartered and recognized as part of the northern MEC.[13] As memories of the Civil War faded and relations between the sections thawed in the early twentieth century, talk of reunifying the MEC and the MECS began in Methodist circles.[14] But the existence of black MEC churches in the South proved to be a sticking point in reunification discussions. If the MEC was to unite with the MECS, it was possible that black and white Methodist churches throughout the South could find themselves forced to integrate because of the church structure.

A *church* is the most elemental unit of the Methodist Church hierarchy. Methodism groups the churches in a region into *annual conferences*, so named because once a year each church in the region sends delegates to a meeting to conduct business ranging from ministerial appointments to budgeting on behalf of all the churches in the annual conference. The borders of annual conferences vary, but often they correspond with state boundaries, as is the case in South Carolina. All the MECS churches in South Carolina, therefore, composed the South Carolina annual conference.[15]

Every four years each annual conference elects delegates to attend the *General Conference* meeting of the global Methodist Church to conduct business on behalf of the entire denomination. The annual conference/General Conference system was the way Methodism had historically functioned in the United States from its inception in 1784.[16] Even when the denomination split in 1844, both the MEC and MECS maintained the annual conference/ General Conference arrangement in their respective region. But for white southern Methodists, reunification with the northern church necessitated rethinking this church structure. If the church reunited, black and white Methodist churches throughout the South would suddenly find themselves in the same annual conference, raising the specter of interracial conference meetings, cross-racial ministerial appointments, or even pressure to inte-grate black and white Methodist churches in the shared annual conference. From the white southern perspective, reunification of the Methodist Church required safeguards against such possible race mixing in their churches.

Such safeguards were first addressed in a 1910 proposal known as the "Chattanooga Plan," which would add a new layer to the traditional Methodist structure. Importantly for white southerners concerned about integration, this new layer would allow a reunified Methodist church to maintain racial segre-gation. Under the Chattanooga Plan, the denomination would insert an inter-mediary conference between the annual conference and General Conference called a *jurisdictional conference*.[17] The proposed jurisdictional conferences would allow for the continuation of racially segregated annual conferences by creating six jurisdictional conferences—five based on geography and the sixth based on race. Whereas white churches that composed various annual confer-ences would be assigned to a corresponding geographical jurisdictional confer-ence, all the black Methodist annual conferences, regardless of location, would be grouped into the race-based sixth jurisdictional conference called the Central Jurisdiction. The important part of this new jurisdictional structure for white southerners was that with creation of the Central Jurisdiction, black Methodist churches, irrespective of their geographic proximity to white Methodist churches, would belong to separate jurisdictional conferences and annual con-ferences than their white counterparts.[18] With the Central Jurisdiction, there was no danger of an African American pastor being assigned to a white church, and racially integrated churches and conference bodies could be avoided. Although this racially segregated jurisdictional plan was first proposed in 1910, it was not formally adopted for nearly thirty more years, when, in 1939, northern and southern Methodists finally repaired their antebellum breech and created a new nationwide denomination called the Methodist Church. In adopting the jurisdiction system with the all-black Central Jurisdiction, the new denomi-nation wrote racial segregation into its DNA, formally bringing Jim Crow into the church.[19] In South Carolina, two annual conferences were created after re-unification in 1939: one for all the white churches in the state, and the other for all the black churches. The same pattern followed throughout the country. A white Methodist church and a black Methodist church could stand only a city block apart and belong to the same denomination. Because of the jurisdictional structure, however, each church belonged to different annual conferences. The black and white churches of the state therefore held their own meetings, had their own agencies, and assigned their own ministers. In other words, black and white Methodist churches after 1939 were equal but separate.

The reunited denomination became the largest Protestant body in the country with over seven million members. The white South Carolina annual conference belonged in the Southeastern Jurisdiction, numerically the largest jurisdictional conference in the new denomination with over 27 percent of the nation's Methodist churches. As with all black annual conferences, the black South Carolina annual conference was assigned to the Central Jurisdiction. The Central Jurisdiction accounted for only 4 percent of the denomination's churches, but the South Carolina annual conference of the Central Jurisdiction was the jurisdiction's largest annual conference with over forty thousand members, making up 13 percent of the Central Jurisdiction's total.[20]

Not all white southern Methodists were willing to reunite with their northern counterparts, fearing that control of the new denomination would fall into "the hands of the . . . Northern and Negro element." Meeting in Florence, South Carolina, a year before reunification became official, these white Methodists made their concerns clear. In the reunified Methodist denomination, "Negroes will be on all General Boards and committees of the church." For these Methodists the creation of the Central Jurisdiction did little to alleviate their concerns about racial mixing, complaining that the jurisdiction would be overseen by "Negro Bishops [who] will largely live in the South, and will be entitled to the full recognition accorded to our white Bishops." Most troubling to these white Methodists was the reality that in a unified church, "any member, white or black, may transfer to any congregation he sees fit, and he must be received. Failure to receive a Negro in a white church will render the pastor of the latter liable to expulsion, and, if received, will disrupt the Southern congregation."[21] In the eyes of these Methodists, the Central Jurisdiction was only "a scheme to catch southern suckers and get them to vote for unification," and these wary Methodists predicted that once unification was achieved, the church would abolish the Central Jurisdiction and force integration upon the new denomination.[22] Rather than going along with reunification and the specter of integration they saw accompanying it, these white Christians instead created their own denomination, calling it the Southern Methodist Church. Among the distinctives of this new denomination, its founders declared, "The Southern Methodist Church is a segregated church. We do not believe that full integration, for which so many are clamoring, is the answer to current social problems. In fact, it is our opinion that integration would produce more problems than it would solve."[23] From the comfortable confines of their own denomination, the Southern Methodists consistently critiqued the unified Methodist Church. Three years into reunification, Southern Methodists reported in their denominational newsletter that "there can be no doubt in the mind of any person who keeps up—even in a small way—with what is going on in the Methodist Church, that it is determined to break down—if it can—all racial lines, not only in 'Methodist Institutions,' but in every way, everywhere, but particularly in the South."[24] As the years went by, more and more southern white Methodists would come to agree with this assessment.

Despite protests by the Southern Methodist Church, the segregation provided through the Central Jurisdiction was satisfactory for the majority of white Methodists throughout the South, though fear of one day losing the segregated structure loomed large in their imaginations. By 1950, church bishops had to assure white Methodists about their concerns. "I am in agreement with you that the abolishing of segregation in no way offers a solution to the race question," Bishop Costen J. Harrell assured a South Carolina parishioner anxious about possible integration in the denomination. "I cannot foresee the time when segregation will be abolished in the Methodist church," the bishop continued. "To do so would require a constitutional procedure, and we of the South could prevent it."[25]

As predicted by the founders of the Southern Methodist Church, many Methodists outside the South began clamoring to abolish the Central Jurisdiction, especially after World War II. When the Supreme Court ruled school segregation unconstitutional in 1954, the outcry over the Central Jurisdiction grew louder as northern Methodists viewed the all-black jurisdiction as hypocrisy for a denomination that had parroted the Supreme Court in denouncing racial segregation after the *Brown* decision.

Talk of abandoning the Central Jurisdiction and incorporating black Methodist churches into the geographical jurisdictions began in earnest at the 1956 General Conference. In a policy decision that mirrored the Supreme Court's mandate the year before that school desegregation should proceed "with all deliberate speed," a majority of Methodists in 1956 voted to abolish the Central Jurisdiction but set no timetable for doing so. Instead, General Conference delegates adopted an amendment to the denomination's constitution allowing for the *voluntary* transfer of black annual conferences out of the Central Jurisdiction and into their corresponding geographical jurisdictions. After the transfer, overlapping annual conferences in the same regional jurisdiction would *voluntarily* merge into a single racially inclusive annual conference. Voluntarism was at the heart of the 1956 change in the Methodist Church constitution, and as such, the amendment was largely accepted in the South because it did not *require* an end to segregation. Instead, voluntarism ensured the Central Jurisdiction would continue as the Jim Crow jurisdiction in Methodism as long as white southerners thought it necessary.[26]

Voluntarism was not viewed as favorably by Methodists outside the South. Even as delegates in 1956 adopted voluntarism, others spoke out against continuing the Central Jurisdiction because of the racial divisiveness it fostered in the church.[27] Acknowledging this growing chorus of voices, the 1956 General Conference created a commission to spend four years studying the jurisdictional system the church had adopted in 1939 and make recommendations to the 1960 General Conference if the system should be retained, reformed, or abolished. While the commission's work was framed to investigate all components of the jurisdictional system, the commission was tasked to pay particular attention to race and segregation during its years of study. Specifically, the General Conference dictated that the commission should "carry on studies and conduct hearings in all the jurisdictions on racial segregation in The Methodist Church and all other problems related to the jurisdictional system."[28] As the commission began its work and held hearings in the jurisdictions of the South, it became clear that the most significant matter to the majority of white southerners was the continuation of the Central Jurisdiction.

At a meeting the commission held in Louisiana in 1957, white Methodists wasted little time getting to heart of the matter: "We are disturbed by the recent action of the General Conference relative to the proposed ending of segregation in the Methodist Churches, and the action taken to change our jurisdictional system," one group of Methodist laymen expressed in a written statement presented at the meeting. "We view this move with misgiving and consider it as designed ultimately to eliminate the Central Jurisdiction. We are against integration. We are opposed to those in our church who— mistakenly, we believe—promote the idea that segregation is un-Christian and that integration, per se, is the will of God," the men wrote. "We remember that it was God Who [*sic*] divided the earth (Gen. 10:25) and scattered the

people abroad (Gen. 11:8)," the men declared, espousing traditional segregationist texts. "We cannot accept the inference that the General Conference
alone reflects the will of God in racial matters and that other Methodists and
other Methodist assemblies who took an opposite stand on the question of
race were outside the will of God."[29] But the men weren't finished: "We would
point out here that the acceptance of the pattern of segregation and the establishment of the Central Jurisdiction as the means thereto was the com-
promise by which unity was achieved in 1939, and we sincerely believe that
a reversal of this arrangement will provide a disruption of that unity."[30] The
men concluded that the Central Jurisdiction "should be maintained for one
of the specific purposes for which it was created, that is, to afford a workable
system within which racial harmony may prevail."[31]

Given that South Carolina had the largest number of black Methodist
churches in the country, the possibility of ending the Central Jurisdiction
was of significant consequence in that state, especially for white Methodists
who desired the segregated church. Unsurprisingly, in 1957 the Board of
Lay Activities for South Carolina's white annual conference prepared a
resolution for the commission studying the jurisdiction system: "The present Jurisdictional System of the Methodist Church has been and is func-
tioning satisfactorily and efficiently, and there is neither need nor sufficient
reason for any change to be made in such system," the resolution began.
"In no event should there be any further change in the present status of the
Central Jurisdiction." Repeating claims other white Methodists were making
throughout the South, the resolution recalled the debates between northern
and southern Methodists leading up to the 1939 reunification and defended
the continuation of separate jurisdictions for black and white Methodists.
"It has long been the understanding of this body and of the overwhelming
majority of our local church members that assurance was given to the
members of the Methodist Episcopal Church, South, and formally stipulated
at the time unification was agreed upon, that the Jurisdictional system, including the Central Jurisdiction, would be maintained and that no effort to
change that status would later be made."[32] The resolution ended with white
board members stating that if certain groups were upset about the racial arrangement of the Methodist Church, they should leave the denomination
rather than force their dissatisfaction "upon those loyal members who do
not themselves raise the issue."[33] If the separate jurisdictional conferences
were to be "sacrificed upon the alter of integration," the South Carolina lay
group told the denominational leaders, many white churches and white

church members would withdraw their support and membership from the denomination.[34]

Ultimately, the commission concluded that jurisdictional conferences remained useful for the Methodist Church and recommended to the General Conference in 1960 that the denomination maintain all jurisdictions and continue the policy of voluntary transfer and merger of the Central Jurisdiction conferences into the geographic jurisdictions as established in 1956.[35] The effect of this voluntarism had the same negligible impact in the South during its first decade as the Supreme Court's timeframe of "all deliberate speed" produced for school desegregation in its first ten years. In the South Central and Southeastern Jurisdictions, the two jurisdictional conferences consisting of all the states of the former Confederacy, not a single black annual conference from the Central Jurisdiction had transferred into the geographical jurisdictions, let alone had any overlapping conferences merged by 1964.[36] Unsurprisingly, eight years after the possibility first arose, the white annual conference of South Carolina had taken no steps toward transferring the black annual conference in the state into the Southeastern Jurisdiction.[37]

In November 1966, a special session of the Methodist General Conference met in Chicago to consider two pressing issues before the denomination. First was a vote on possible union of the Methodist Church with the Evangelical Brethren Church to create a new denomination to be called the United Methodist Church. For southern Methodists uneasy about the trend toward racial inclusiveness in their church, the second order of business at this special session was more important: a vote to abolish at last the Central Jurisdiction through a proposal known as the Omnibus Resolution. This resolution recommended that the Methodist Church pledge its "determination to do everything possible to bring about the elimination of any structural organization in The Methodist Church based on race at the earliest possible date and not later than the close of the Jurisdictional Conferences of 1972."[38] The Omnibus Resolution called for the immediate transfer of the Central Jurisdiction's black annual conferences into the five geographic jurisdictions as the first step in ending structural racism in the denomination. This plan would proceed only if each of the six jurisdictions approved the resolution by a two-thirds vote.

Once transferred into the same jurisdictions, the Omnibus Resolution additionally set a target date of 1972 for all overlapping black and white annual conferences to adopt plans of merger to form racially inclusive annual conferences throughout the country.[39] The target date was contentious because it abandoned the voluntarism that had thus far marked Methodist desegregation. For some delegates to the special session, imposing such a short timeline for conference mergers was seen as an unreasonable request for white southerners.

Leading the charge against the Omnibus Resolution at the 1966 General Conference was a lay delegate from Mississippi named John C. Satterfield. Satterfield and his fellow lay delegate, Edwin L. Jones of North Carolina, were both members of the denomination's Commission on Interjurisdictional Relations, the committee responsible for drafting the Omnibus Resolution. Neither Satterfield nor Jones agreed with their committee's decision to put forth the Omnibus Resolution. In fact, the two southerners felt strongly enough in their dissent that they wrote an alternative resolution to the one the other twenty-two members of their committee proposed. In their resolution, Satterfield and Jones noted that the Commission on Interjurisdictional Relations was unfairly disproportional in its representation. Each jurisdiction had four members on the commission. But Satterfield and Jones noted that their Southeastern Jurisdiction was composed of almost three million members, whereas the Central Jurisdiction had fewer than a quarter-million. Each jurisdiction having equal representation on the commission that drafted the Omnibus Resolution diluted the voice of white southerners while elevating the power of black Methodists by unfairly overrepresenting the Central Jurisdiction in the commission's deliberations.[40]

Taking the floor to defend his alternative resolution and its recommendation to maintain voluntarism, Satterfield explained to his fellow delegates that ramifications for conference mergers would be far different for his Southeastern Jurisdiction than for other jurisdictions in the church. "I hope that you from the Western Jurisdiction and the North Central and Northeast and probably the South Central realize . . . the tremendous difference in your area and in ours," Satterfield warned.[41] In South Carolina alone, Satterfield noted, there existed 340 African American Methodist churches. In Mississippi and Louisiana, the number of black Methodist churches was 216 and 153, respectively. In Satterfield's view, merging such a large number of black churches into a white annual conference required a more delicate approach than would be necessary in a region with only a small number of black Methodists. Satterfield quickly pointed out that his and Jones's alternative proposal was not a case of the southern white churches "dragging our feet or not acting in good faith."[42] In fact, Satterfield conceded, the white Southeastern Jurisdiction had already voted to approve the transfer of black annual conferences into their jurisdiction but had not devised plans to integrate black and white churches into single racially inclusive conferences.

Without a plan for merging the black and white conferences, the Central Jurisdiction had actually refused to approve the transfer of churches out of its purview, fearing that the annual conferences would remain indefinitely segregated. Such a concern was not new. Black bishops in the Central Jurisdiction had long been wary of their churches leaving the Central Jurisdiction to join the geographical jurisdictions. As early as 1957 the Central Jurisdiction bishops cautioned churches about being "too hasty . . . in breaking away from the Central Jurisdiction, and, except in cases of churches isolated from others in the jurisdiction, churches and conferences of the jurisdiction be encouraged to remain in the Central Jurisdiction until it is clear that the majority of our churches will be welcomed into the other jurisdiction on the basis of equality and mutual respect."[43] This perspective held nine years later. As a result, the Central Jurisdiction granted transfers from its jurisdiction only if a plan of merger for the black and white annual conferences was in place, an understandable position for black conferences that did not want to forgo their relative power in a segregated jurisdiction to become subservient members of an integrated jurisdiction. Seizing on this point, Satterfield noted that it was indeed the black jurisdiction rather than the white that had until now balked at transfer.[44]

While white Methodists in the Southeastern Jurisdiction displayed noble intentions by voting to accept transferred annual conferences from the Central Jurisdiction, Satterfield was certain they would not be as amenable to a plan forcing them to merge with black conferences by the 1972 deadline—a mere six years away. White Methodists in the South required time to digest the radical changes occurring in their society regarding race. In Satterfield's opinion, a heavy-handed mandate requiring a swift merger of black and white conferences would yield disastrous results in his home region. "After living and working in the Southeastern Jurisdiction for many, many years, it is my judgment that if this Conference by one means or another forces action to be taken which we know would be destructive of our Church . . . this Methodist church will lose a minimum of one million members and perhaps more," Satterfield predicted.[45] Speaking for the thousands of likeminded Methodists he represented, Satterfield declared he "could not, in good faith and in honor as a Christian and as a member of The Methodist Church vote for this [Omnibus] resolution which, in my opinion, amounts to a statement of coercion on any named date, to-wit, this one in 1972."[46]

When Satterfield yielded the floor, a dramatic back and forth ensued between supporters and detractors of the Omnibus Resolution. First, a delegate from India named Eric Mitchell rose to address the Mississippian's remarks. "The retention of the Central Jurisdiction is a stigma to the World Methodist Fellowship and to all Christians," Mitchell began. "I would like you to think, my friend, of the problem not only in the light of the domestic situation and of your present situation, but in the light of the world's needs."[47] Racial segregation in the Methodist Church in the United States undermined efforts of Methodists working around the world to combat secular movements whose rhetoric of anti-colonialism and social egalitarianism purportedly masked darker ambitions. "As I see it, there are two claims before us. The claim of Jesus Christ and the claim of Karl Marx," Mitchell concluded. "Communism has succeeded where the Christian witness has failed. We cannot win the world to Jesus Christ if we discriminate against people because of their race or color. We will drive them to Karl Marx. We will drive them into the fold of Communism."[48]

Satterfield's collaborator on the alternative resolution, Edwin Jones, agreed with Mitchell that attention to evangelism was needed in the denomination. But he disagreed with his brother from India about the importance of church structure for that evangelism to occur. "God will hold us responsible some day for not spending some time and some energy and some thought and some consideration on how to reach the unsaved and how to carry out Christ's last commission to his disciples," Jones told his fellow delegates. "There isn't a word in there [the Bible] about bothering yourself with the structure of the Church. I ask you to reread it." Jones reiterated the necessity of voluntarism for transfer and mergers to succeed and stated firmly, "I am unalterably opposed to trying to whiplash people into doing something which their conscience will not allow them to do at a certain time."[49]

K. Morgan Edwards, a delegate from California, followed Jones in the debate over the Satterfield and Jones alternative resolution and offered two points for consideration. First, Edwards noted that the racial issue was not merely a southern issue. "Those of us who are in the Far West will one day have to stand before the judgment bar of God and accept heavy responsibility for the real estate conspiracies, the lack of economic opportunity and all of the things which we did which produced the Watts riots," Edwards began. "I think none of us can think clearly unless we recognize that prejudice belongs just as much to those of us in the West and the North as it belongs to anybody in the South." Second, Edwards complicated the notion set forth by Jones in the latter's comments about white Methodists being forced to do something against their will. As Edwards explained, "There is compulsion, to be sure; but the compulsion which embarrasses me is the compulsion we are forcing upon our Negro brothers by depriving them of rights which are guaranteed by our Lord and underscored by the Constitution." Signaling his vote against Satterfield and Jones's alternative resolution, Edwards declared he was embarrassed that African Americans had been forced to wait so long to realize the equality granted to them by the Christian faith or the Constitution, declaring, "I'm unwilling to ask them to wait longer."[50]

Vincent Mouser, a delegate from Louisiana, spoke next and threw his support behind Satterfield and Jones. Mouser noted that the Methodist Church had historically established separate churches for ethnic groups such as Swedes or Germans and that the necessity of such churches naturally passed away as ethnic divisions faded. "I recognize that the Central Jurisdiction will pass away. I recognize that separate Negro Conferences will pass away. I recognize that eventually there will be no separate congregations," Mouser conceded. But he believed such a time could not be hastened by abolishing segregation in the church. The eradication of structural separation would only be effective when it "conform[ed] to the inward changes within hearts of Methodists, white and black, throughout the entire Southland where these changes actually will have the impact." Accordingly, Mouser pleaded with his fellow delegates to "give us time, give us the means by adopting [Satterfield and Jones's resolution], to have a little more time to attain and to have a little more voluntarism so that we can hope to bring the hearts and minds and thinking of our people into harmony with what we are now trying to require from a structural standpoint."[51]

Finally, Satterfield retook the floor to close the pro–alternative resolution arguments. Acknowledging that his thinking probably differed from the majority of the present delegates who would reject his alternative in favor of the Omnibus Resolution, Satterfield lamented, "I believe it will be the saddest day we have had in The Methodist Church since I became a member of the General Conference beginning the year 1952." Satterfield noted that adopting the Omnibus Resolution went against the wishes of the lay representatives for three million Methodists and would most likely push the denomination to "a point of no return."[52] After one last speech in favor of the Omnibus Resolution, the General Conference put the two proposals to a vote. By a show of hands the delegates defeated Satterfield and Jones's resolution and adopted the Omnibus Resolution.[53] The days of the Central Jurisdiction were now numbered.

The floor debate at the 1966 special session of the General Conference reveals the continuity of ideas about segregation that had held sway among southern white Christians. Allowing that the debate took place at the highest level of the Methodist denomination, it may initially seem significant that there was no questioning whether the abolition of the Central Jurisdiction should occur. Those who spoke against the Omnibus Resolution—publicly, at least—took issue with the timing, not the intent. At the same time, a careful read of the floor debate shows that the most noteworthy concern regarding the transfer and merger of the African American conferences rested on the presumed racial attitudes of white Methodists rather than other nonracialized apprehensions such as the bureaucratic or financial logistics of the transfer and merger process. Satterfield, Jones, and others who spoke against the Omnibus Resolution did not name it explicitly, but their hesitation toward the bill remained grounded in anxiety over racial mixing. In significant ways, the debate over Satterfield and Jones's alternative resolution was a continuation of segregationist arguments that southern moderates and conservatives had been making for a dozen years since the *Brown* decision. From 1954 on, southerners acknowledged their region was unique in its racial practices but reasoned that such a large southern black population necessitated that uniqueness. The disproportionate burden the South bore in desegregation was a mainstay of the segregationist response to critics outside the region. In fact, the high percentage of African Americans was precisely the rationale given by white South Carolina Methodists in 1954 for passing a resolution at the annual conference in Spartanburg denouncing the *Brown* decision. These Methodists noted that of the "approximately 15,000,000 Negro American citizens, [a]pproximately 9,000,000 of these live in the South," which meant that the impact of the Supreme Court's ruling would be felt much deeper in the former Confederacy. Expressing a sentiment that Satterfield and Jones resurrected twelve years later, the 1954 South Carolina annual conference cautioned that "these problems [of school desegregation] will not be resolved by hasty words or irresponsible sentiments but rather by a calm and patient consideration of all the factors involved and by a sincere desire to do what is best for all persons concerned." These 1954 delegates defined what was "best" in terms Satterfield and Jones could have written in 1966: "It is the judgment of this Conference that in situations where the minority race is present in large numbers, where the general sentiment of both races favors separate schools, and where the good of all is best served by separation, such voluntary separation is not contrary to the spirit and teaching of the Christian faith" and should therefore be supported.[54] While Satterfield and Jones made no explicit argument for the spiritual correctness of racial segregation, their call for an open-ended timeline for conference mergers due to the higher ratio of African American churches in the South was a continuation of segregationist thought and instincts from the prior decade.

At the same time, arguments against the Omnibus Resolution indicated that white racial attitudes had grown more conciliatory after the major successes of the civil rights movement. The resolution's opponents were primarily concerned that mandating the merger of black and white annual conferences by a set date risked destroying the tentative steps white Methodists in the South had taken toward racial equality. From Satterfield and Jones's perspective, white southerners would continue to accept racial changes in the Methodist Church, but the process could not be rushed. But with this argument too, Satterfield and Jones revisited a common trope racial moderates deployed to slow down civil rights demonstrations in the 1960s. Indeed, it was a Satterfield and Jones–like argument that Martin Luther King had railed against in his "Letter from Birmingham Jail." Writing to a group of white clergymen in 1963, King had "almost reached the regrettable conclusion that the Negro's great stumbling block in his stride toward freedom is not the White Citizen's Councilor or the Ku Klux Klanner, but the white moderate . . . who paternalistically believes he can set the timetable for another man's freedom. . . . Lukewarm acceptance is much more bewildering than outright rejection."[55] Satterfield and Jones's suggestion that the racial dilemma would solve itself if given more time was a long-standing argument of civil rights opponents and a position King and other civil rights leaders thoroughly rejected.

Interestingly, even the rationale given for adopting the Omnibus Resolution echoed logic used in the push for desegregation of American schools leading up to the *Brown* decision. Delegate Eric Mitchell's argument that the Central Jurisdiction was a blight on the Methodist Church that drove people away from Christianity into the arms of Karl Marx was almost identical to the Justice Department's amicus brief for the *Brown* case. In that brief, the Justice Department reasoned that "the existence of discrimination against minority groups in the United States has an adverse effect upon our relations with other countries. Racial discrimination furnishes grist for the Communist propaganda mills, and raises doubts . . . as to the intensity of our devotion to the democratic faith."[56] In many respects, then, the Methodist Church in 1966 was fighting the same battles that had raged in southern society for over a dozen years as southern white Methodists defended the segregated church structure using the same rationalizations that had defined the segregationist position for decades.

And yet, 1966 was not 1954; the tides of history had changed during those twelve years. The theological arguments of segregationists, while still motivating for Christian segregationists, had grown threadbare in broader society, proving ineffective against the moral force of the civil rights movement. If white Christians were going to avoid integration, they would need new arguments. Hints of a new tactic that would soon spread among conservative white Christians appeared in the 1966 floor debate concerning the Central Jurisdiction and foreshadowed the shift to a new position embraced by segregationists by the end of the decade. This shift revealed itself in the remarks made by delegate Vincent Mouser. Mouser's argument about the need to transform individual attitudes before addressing structural inequalities hinged on delaying the latter for the sake of the former. The need for separate black and white organizations would subside, Mouser suggested, "when we would have attained within our hearts that spirit of brotherhood, that communion of interest, that complete freedom from prejudice which we must achieve if all of these things we are talking about here are to do any good in God's service."[57] Mouser was thus positing that the inequality of the Methodist denomination segregating its black churches into a Jim Crow jurisdiction was best addressed not by undoing the *structure* that maintained the segregation but by *individuals* abandoning prejudicial feelings. Only when individual Christians had a change of heart would they be prepared to take on the inequality that existed around them. This emphasis on personal feelings reflected an attack on racism waged at the individual level, where the ultimate goal was to eradicate personal animus. According to this emerging argument, addressing structural inequalities before white individuals were willing to accept black men and women as equal remained a fruitless endeavor that would only lead to conflict. As subsequent debates about merging black and white annual conferences made clear, the evidence of a white Christian's transformed heart—that hoped-for moment when individual prejudice had been eradicated from the Christian's life—would be that race no longer mattered as old prejudices gave way to newfound colorblindness. In the years ahead, the call for individualistic colorblindness became the calling card of white Christians trying to hold onto a segregated world they saw slipping away. The conflict over merging black and white annual conferences in South Carolina well captures this change in segregationist Christianity.

John Satterfield had predicted that even if the General Conference adopted the Omnibus Resolution, it had no chance of passing in the Southeastern Jurisdiction with the necessary two-thirds majority needed for its implementation. White Methodists in South Carolina did their part to prove Satterfield prophetic. In fact, several Methodist groups in the Palmetto State had already made known their disapproval of abolishing the Central Jurisdiction prior to 1966 when the issue was formally put to a vote. At the annual conference meeting in 1964, for instance, the men's Bible class of Wesley Memorial Methodist in Yonges Island, South Carolina, expressed its belief that the 1939 Methodist reunification never would have occurred "had the people of the South known . . . the church would one day reverse its pledge to keep the Jurisdiction separate and seek to do away with the Central Jurisdiction," and the group pledged that they would "exercise all the powers at our command" to resist dissolving the Central Jurisdiction.[58] Similarly, the official board of the Pinewood Charge Methodist Church in Pinewood, South Carolina, requested that the annual conference "refrain from legislating any act which will integrate the Central Jurisdiction with the Southeastern Jurisdiction."[59] So disillusioned were two other South Carolina churches with the General Conference's approach to racial issues that they proposed that the South Carolina annual conference "withdraw completely from the General Church and set up the Methodist Church of South Carolina."[60]

The following year, disgruntlement with the denomination's treatment of race continued. Following the lead of the churches the previous year, St. Paul's Methodist Church proposed that the South Carolina annual conference withdraw from the denomination and form its own church in part due to a 1964 General Conference vote to financially support civil rights groups.[61] Meanwhile, anticipating the unthinkable, the official board of St. Mark Methodist in Charleston, South Carolina, proposed a measure stipulating that "in the area of race, the local church shall be integrated only by a 2/3 majority vote of the congregation."[62] The South Carolina annual conference did not adopt any of these resolutions in 1964 or 1965, but that such resolutions were even debated signaled that support of the Omnibus Resolution was far from solid. Indeed, when the delegates considered the Omnibus Resolution at the 1966 South Carolina annual conference, it was defeated, as it was at the annual conference of South Georgia, and the four annual conferences of Mississippi and Alabama.[63]

When all the Southeastern Jurisdiction's annual conferences' votes were tallied, the resolution received 67 percent of the vote, earning it the narrowest of passage in the jurisdiction. In adopting the Omnibus Resolution, the Southeastern Jurisdictional Conference tried to hold onto the spirit of voluntarism by amending 1972 as the target date for annual conference mergers with the timeline of "as soon as possible."[64] Despite the attempt to cling to voluntarism, the denomination overruled the amended timetable and mandated that black and white annual conferences throughout the Southeastern Jurisdiction merge by 1972. As a lay delegate from South Carolina reported after the Southeastern Jurisdictional meeting, "Make no mistake, the Methodist Church including the Southeastern Jurisdiction has committed itself to complete elimination of all racial lines and organization from the General Conference to the local church."[65] For religious conservatives resistant to integrated annual conferences, these were dark days. But in 1969, conservatives in the state learned that a group of concerned Methodists were organizing to help defeat forced racial inclusiveness in Methodism in South Carolina. Devising a defense against merging the black and white annual conferences, a new tool arose among these segregationist Christians: colorblindness.

As delegates across the state prepared for the 1969 South Carolina annual conference meeting, information arrived in their mailboxes about a new organization called the MCF. Sent by Don Herd, a Methodist layman and president of Lander College in Greenwood, South Carolina, the group's officers described the MCF as "a fellowship of Methodist Christians in South Carolina who love the Church, who love Methodism, and want it to continue to reach the people."[66] Herd touted the MCF as 160 ministers and 500 laymen concerned with the liberal direction of their denomination and who were now taking a stand against it. In his initial letter to the delegates, Herd offered few specifics about the group but made clear that the MCF was a conservative-leaning fellowship that wished to hear less about social issues from their pulpits and more about personal piety. "Some of our ministers seem to get marbles in their mouths when they try to say something about God or Christ or life after death but are flaming evangelists about the economic disorders of our times," Herd's letter stated.[67] The MCF letter ended with a pledge to hold a statewide meeting after the annual conference to further explain the group's purposes for anyone interested.

The creation of the MCF prior to the 1969 South Carolina annual conference was not coincidental. Following the passage of the Omnibus Resolution, the black annual conferences of the Central Jurisdiction were transferred into the geographical jurisdictions. Nineteen sixty-nine marked the first year black and white annual conferences in South Carolina belonged to the same jurisdiction and under the authority of the same bishop. The only thing keeping the two conferences separated was that neither had yet adopted a plan of merger. For white conservatives, this was a pivotal moment with a final bureaucratic step the only thing between them and an integrated church. And at the 1969 annual conference, delegates learned that this last step had already been initiated as the Conference Committee on Merger had begun meeting and would propose a plan of merger by the next annual conference.[68]

For white Methodists in the state concerned about the impending changes in the racial structure of their denomination, the MCF offered some hope. Although the MCF was supposedly organized as a brake against general liberalism in the denomination, some questioned the organization's true intent. In later years supporters of the merger called the MCF "racist," believing its sole purpose was to stop the black and white conferences from merging, and they described experiencing hostility when meeting with MCF members.[69] That the MCF disappeared shortly after the white and black annual conferences merged lends credence to this assertion that the MCF's chief concern was racial change. For their part, conservative Methodists were buoyed by the MCF's appearance. Dan Albergotti, a Methodist from Florence, South Carolina, for example, wrote, "Until the formation of the Methodist Christian Fellowship, I felt that I was fighting this battle alone and therefore was prepared to take individual action when and if the time arose." First among Albergotti's concerns was the integration of the Central Jurisdiction with the geographical jurisdictions. "As usual the conservative viewpoint is being expressed at the eleventh hour," Albergotti complained to a fellow MCF member, "but I hope and pray that we have not again come forward with 'too little-too late.'"[70] Like Albergotti, a Methodist layman from Williston, South Carolina, named Keith Whittle was grateful to hear about the MCF and was eager to help by covering mailing costs and spreading information about the fellowship in his native Barnwell County.[71] With the advent of the MCF,

Albergotti, Whittle, and thousands of other conservative Methodists at last had a vehicle to voice their concerns.

Whatever the initial reasons given for the MCF's founding, the issue that eclipsed all others in the fellowship's statements and correspondence dealt with race and the impending merger. Many who counted themselves part of the MCF retained the belief that segregation was compatible with Christian doctrine. But explicit sentiments of such ideas could no longer be comfortably expressed in a culture that was growing less tolerant of open expressions of racism. Still, some members of the MCF were less astute in grasping this new reality as evidenced by a letter to the editor of the *South Carolina Methodist Advocate* by one of the fellowship's members:

> Let me make this crystal clear. I do not believe that racial segregation is un-Christian. I believe that Christian relationships existed between individual white men and individual black men during slavery and during legal racial segregation and during voluntary racial segregation and can exist under any social order. The Methodist Episcopal Church, South, did not believe that segregation was un-Christian. The Methodist Church, as brought about by the Unification in 1939, did not believe that segregation was un-Christian because they created the racially segregated Central Jurisdiction. The [liberals] of our Church must have received a new revelation from God. I for one find it hard to believe that God would choose Earl Warren and the United States Supreme Court as His vessel to reveal this so-called truth to mankind.[72]

In rehashing the basic theological underpinnings of segregation that had been powerful in southern white Christianity, this letter demonstrates that for some white Christians, the thought of integration produced similar sentiments and emotions in 1970 as it had in 1955. But this letter notwithstanding, open expressions of such racial fears were considered impolitic by the 1970s. Throughout South Carolina in 1970, Methodist leaders heard comments such as "I don't want a black boy dating my daughter" and "I don't want a Negro man sitting by my wife in church" from church members, but such sentiments were now expressed in private conversations rather than in editorials or public letters as was the practice a decade before.[73] If white Christians were to stop a merger between the black and white conferences, they could not appeal to now-offensive segregationist theology as the public rationale, even as it continued to influence their private feelings. What they needed was new language to defend segregation. The MCF proved up to this challenge.

Not until early 1970 did the MCF officially codify its beliefs in a position paper sent to media outlets across the state. In the section covering the impending conference merger, the MCF professed, "Believing in the brotherhood of man under the Fatherhood of God, we stand for political, economic and religious freedom for all racial, cultural, and religious groups. We rededicate ourselves to resolving tensions between the races both within the Church and without, seeking to foster natural affinities, mutual appreciation of each other's merits and the voluntary association of individuals."[74] Utilizing polite appeals to voluntary association and natural affinities rather than railing against forced integration and mandated brotherhood served the MCF cause well; it could resist the merger without earning the fellowship a reputation for racism. But at the same time, the euphemistic phrases of "natural affinities" and "voluntary association" were drawn directly from the *Plessy* decision, revealing that the acceptable rhetoric in southern white churches in 1970 was rooted in a Jim Crow past. As the fight over the merger unfolded, the new language's ties to a segregated past grew sharper.

When white South Carolina Methodists gathered in Spartanburg in June 1970 for their annual conference, merger talk hung heavy in the air. A primary item on the agenda for the conference that year was presenting the plan to merge the black and white annual conferences in the state. "We, by some miracle, still have a chance to witness to the people of South Carolina that we do indeed believe that all baptized Christians are brothers," the Board of Christian Social Concerns informed the delegates.[75] The district superintendents were similarly hopeful for the promise of merger, stating in their report, "The merger of the two South Carolina Conferences in the immediate future calls black and white United Methodists to a new way of life based on forgiveness, reconciliation and human sensitivity."[76] When the proposed plan of merger was finally distributed, delegates read an idealistic preamble stating that the black and white annual conferences of South Carolina, "serving one Lord whose Gospel declares that in Christ there is neither Greek nor barbarian, bond nor free, male nor female, but that all of us are without distinction the children of God whose love is all inclusive, do now declare our earnest hope that The United Methodist Church in our area shall truly become an inclusive church."[77] The delegates were instructed to take the plan back to their churches, spend twelve months studying it, and then return to vote on its adoption the following year.

The year between the plan's introduction and vote was used for holding informational sessions, answering questions, and suggesting amendments. Congregations throughout the state held meetings to inform parishioners about the plan of merger and to hear feedback from the pews. Trenholm Road United Methodist in Columbia was one such congregation, and this church provided a unique window on various attitudes white Methodists held toward the proposed merger. Trenholm Road was the church home of two of the most significant leaders on both sides of the merger question: William Workman and Rhett Jackson. Workman was one of the most recognized and respected journalists in South Carolina, known for his uncompromising defense of segregation. Over a career that spanned decades, Workman wrote countless editorials in service to Jim Crow in the state's largest newspapers and in 1960 even published a book, *The Case for the South*, defending the region's resistance to integration. Two years later in 1962, Workman ran as a Republican candidate for Senate, one of the first among a generation of disaffected former Democrats unhappy with the national party's stance on civil rights. Workman lost to the incumbent Democrat, Olin Johnston, but received an impressive 42 percent of the vote, an almost unthinkable percentage for a Republican running in a Deep South state in 1962. After his foray into politics, Workman returned to journalism and in the late 1960s was a frequent guest on radio and television programs where he toed the line for the conservative politics of small government and states' rights. Not surprisingly, Workman was a prominent member of the MCF and played an instrumental role in both defining and defending the fellowship's position against the merger of the black and white annual conferences.[78]

Rhett Jackson was a member of the same congregation as Workman but was the reporter's ideological opposite. Unlike the segregationist Workman, Jackson was a theological and social liberal who eagerly anticipated the merger of the black and white annual conferences in the state. In 1966, South Carolina bishop Paul Hardin Jr. had appointed Jackson to chair a forty-member committee to investigate the feasibility of merging the black and white conferences in the state. Chairing the merger committee was an unenviable task as it guaranteed unpopularity in a state where the majority of white Methodists had little to no desire to merge with the black conference. Recognizing that leading the merger committee could lead to a tense situation between a white minister and his congregation, the nominating committee had the foresight to look for a well-positioned member of the laity to chair the merger committee. As a layman already heading the Board of Christian Social Concerns in South Carolina, Jackson fit the bill.[79]

Unusual though it was for a single congregation to have two such prominent members of the pro- and anti-merger factions—one as the mouthpiece of the MCF, the other as the chair of the merger committee—Workman's and Jackson's membership at Trenholm Road Methodist allowed their fellow churchgoers ample opportunities to weigh the proposed plan of merger. As did most of the Methodist churches in the state, Trenholm Road sponsored discussions over several months in the fall and winter of 1970 to ensure all church members thoroughly understood the plan. In one session, Workman and Jackson even appeared on the same panel to answer questions.[80] The fear of many white South Carolina Methodists was reflected in a list of questions and answers provided by Trenholm Road United Methodist Church to its members. First on the list was the question, "Will merger of the two conferences result in black ministers being assigned to white churches and vice versa?" The handout reassured church members that "for the immediate future it is not probable that ministers will be assigned across racial lines."[81]

In addition to participating in his home church's discussions on the merger, Jackson, along with Matthew McCollum, a black Methodist minister and former head of the South Carolina NAACP, traveled extensively throughout the state in 1970–1971 to inform church members of the plan. Jackson later recalled that he and McCollum often met resistance, occasional hostility, and only a few places where the two Christians could share a meal together.[82] Nonetheless, Jackson remained hopeful for the merger's prospects.

For its part, the MCF approached the merger with careful planning. Though it likely did not need the reminder, the MCF advisory committee was petitioned that the "South Carolina Conference is faced with the most serious decision it has had to deal with since the Civil War. The question of Merger should be prayerfully, seriously, and thoroughly dealt with by every Methodist in our Conference. It is too important and is fraught with far too great peril to let it go by default."[83] Although the MCF found many aspects of the proposed plan troubling, one particular component of the merger plan seemed like a weakness MCF members could exploit. Written into the plan of merger was a mandated quota of a 75 percent white and 25 percent black ratio for all conference boards, agencies, and leadership positions. To be in effect for twelve years following the merger, this ratio ensured a racial balance proportionate to the two annual conferences.[84] Also significant was the ratification process. The merger would take effect only if both the black and white conferences approved it with a simple majority. If merger opponents could find a cause to rally votes against the merger, integration could be, if not defeated, at least delayed. At Workman's suggestion, the MCF honed in on the racial quotas as the cause merger opponents needed.

The white annual conference convened in June 1971, a little more than two weeks after the black annual conference had met and approved the plan of merger by a huge margin, 241 to 9. If the white conference adopted the plan, the two conferences would go forward with the merger. Were the plan to fail, no merger would take place and a committee would have to devise an acceptable alternative plan. On the third day of the conference, the time to vote on the plan of merger came at last. The morning began with the hymn "Come Thou Almighty King" before Bishop Hardin declared the proposed plan of merger the order of the day.[85]

A member of the MCF instantly seized the initiative in trying to influence the vote's outcome. Roy C. Moore, an MCF member from Cheraw, South Carolina, asked if it was possible to vote on the planned merger by orders and if both orders would have to vote positively on the plan for it to pass. Voting by orders meant that rather than voting together as a single body of delegates, the laity and the clergy would vote separately. When Bishop Hardin answered both Moore's questions in the affirmative, the latter immediately moved that the vote on the merger be by orders.[86] Although Moore's motion was defeated, its intent was transparent. Thinking the laity more conservative than the clergy, restricting pastors to a separate voting pool could defeat the plan. The strategy of capitalizing on the conservative strength of the laity by creating a separate voting bloc had been foreshadowed by an MCF member in a letter to the *South Carolina Methodist Advocate* earlier in the year. Appalled that the vote on the merger was procedurally identical to any other mundane article of business, MCF member Dan Albergotti believed requiring a simple majority to adopt the plan was an outrage, especially when almost half the delegates to the conference were clergy members appointed by pro-merger bishops. It seemed appropriate to Albergotti that the merger vote be opened to *all* Methodists in the conference, not just those delegates serving at the annual conference meeting.[87] Had Moore's motion to vote by orders passed, it would have given more weight to the laity's opinion of the plan, as Albergotti had hoped. Rejecting Moore's motion signaled that the merger would not be defeated through procedural maneuvering by members of the MCF. But as Workman had suggested, there still existed another way to defeat the merger: defining it as racist.

In early 1971, Workman sent a letter to Jackson's merger committee expressing his concerns about the proposed plan. In Workman's interpretation, the plan violated the Constitution of the United Methodist Church. Citing the article in the church constitution that prevented discrimination in the denomination based on race, color, national origin, or economic condition, Workman declared that the mandated racial quotas for proportionate representation in the plan of merger were "clearly unconstitutional through any reasonable interpretation of the Constitution of the United Methodist Church" in that the quotas would exclude individuals for consideration because of their race.[88] Furthermore, Workman continued, the plan's scheme to "proportionately reflect" the racial makeup of South Carolina Methodists in church governing boards and agencies "makes for forced brotherhood 'by the numbers' and is inconsistent with the ethical spirit of inclusivity promulgated several years ago for and by the United Methodist Church."[89] Workman believed adopting the plan of merger as it was originally proposed "is likely to produce continuing friction and would perpetuate and emphasize race consciousness, since race would become a critical factor in determining church assignments and associations."[90] What was needed, Workman concluded, was to "eliminate racial distinctions or discriminations in the conduct of Methodist affairs." Quoting directly from the MCF's position paper as well as the *Plessy* decision, Workman wrote that creating an "atmosphere in which 'natural affinities, a mutual appreciation of each others' merits, and a voluntary consent of individuals' may contribute to the ultimate elimination of emotional as well as structural barriers between the races."[91]

Workman's letter represents something of a smoking gun in the transformation of segregationist Christianity. The problem conservative white Christians were battling by the early 1970s—the problem so clearly articulated in Workman's letter—was the continuing issue of race. It was not the existence of racial inequality that concerned these white Christians but the perpetual attention to race that, in their minds, did not allow racial scars to heal. How could these Christians get beyond race, Workman's letter asked, if they kept talking about race? What was needed in the battle over race was a new standard called colorblindness. Understood in this context, the shift to colorblindness for these Christians was more a defensive repositioning than a confession of past sins. With colorblindness, segregationist Christians were able to curtail the conversation. *They* were the ones who supposedly wanted to move on from race, the ones who wished to put the past behind them and march into a future where race no longer mattered. But recognizing the genesis of this colorblind position is crucial for understanding its true intent. Workman's channeling of *Plessy* in his appeal to colorblindness was intentional. Colorblindness had its roots in the segregationist movement, with this connection growing clearer as events in South Carolina's white annual conference unfolded.

Workman's strategy of questioning the constitutionality of the plan because of its racial language was also popular for opponents of the merger plan who parroted the same ideas in letters to the editor of the *South Carolina Methodist Advocate* leading up to the annual conference. Workman's strategy gave opponents of the conference merger a legitimate way to vote against the plan for reasons that avoided painting them as unreconstructed racists.

Rhett Jackson later recalled that he began to lose hope that the plan would be adopted as the debate continued and anger toward the merger became apparent.[92] Following almost three hours of debate, the time came to vote on the plan of merger. A period of silent prayer was called for, followed by the distribution of the ballots. After casting their ballots, the delegates broke for lunch with a few staying behind to tally the vote.[93] When Jackson returned from lunch, he found Bishop Hardin sitting in the almost empty conference hall with tears in his eyes. The tally was in; the plan was defeated by almost a hundred votes, 528 to 432.[94] The segregated church would continue.

Immediately following the vote, delegates shared the reasons that they voted against the plan. Many of these reasons dealt with either questioning the constitutionality of having racial quotas or opposing the mandated racial ratios, with some delegates calling the quotas "racist in nature." Other opponents of the merger said the entire plan "contained too many favorable leanings" toward the black conference. Delegates also expressed concerns about cross-racial ministerial appointments, and some opposed not the specific plan of merger itself but the idea of merging with the black annual conference in general.[95] Two months after the plan's defeat, with time to collect and catalog opposition to the merger, the white annual conference published a list of the reasons the 528 delegates cited for voting down the plan. First on this list was resistance to racial inclusiveness. Second was opposition over the mandated quotas.[96]

The appearance of these two items atop the list of reasons white Christians chose not to integrate with their black fellow Christians captures the way in which old notions of segregation and new arguments of colorblindness were related. It is not surprising that white Methodists' first reason for resisting the merger was that they opposed the idea of racial inclusiveness. After all, these were Christians raised with the teachings of segregationist theology. They did not oppose the merger out of spite or vindictiveness but because they believed that the Bible told them so. At the same time, the fact that opposition to racial quotas was second on the list only to rejecting racial inclusiveness shows the new direction of segregationist Christianity. Workman had shown the logical path from rejecting integration because it violated God's will to eschewing it because doing so only exacerbated racial tensions and damaged the brotherhood and goodwill God wants for all people. The way to achieve such harmonious relationships, a growing number of white Christians believed, was to replace segregationist theology with colorblindness, with the latter finding its purpose in the former. Colorblindness now became a way to ignore racial inequalities, and by not addressing such inequalities, they persisted. Yet "colorblind" individuals did not recognize ongoing structural or systemic inequities because they gave racism no credence beyond personalized feelings of animus or goodwill. So it was with the Methodist merger.

The Methodist Church required that all black and white annual conferences must merge by 1972; hence, the vote of white Methodists in South Carolina at first blush seemed only to delay the inevitable. But rejecting the merger did more than extend white Methodists one additional year of a segregated church; it also allowed them to change the terms of the merger. Immediately after the original plan of merger went down to defeat, Bishop Hardin appointed a committee of six individuals from both annual conferences to draft an alternative plan. Prior to crafting a new plan, white committee members published a letter reminding—or reassuring—Methodists that merging the two conferences did not require churches themselves to merge and would likely have little effect on individual congregations in the state.[97] The committee nonetheless recognized that white Methodists needed more than words of assurance to support a new plan of merger, thereby authoring an alternative plan that accounted for white apprehensions. Unsurprisingly, the new plan came at the expense of black Methodists.

Written with a mind toward the white conference, the committee proposed an alternative plan that mollified the concerns white delegates expressed toward the original plan of merger. Reducing the guaranteed time of racial quotas from twelve years to eight, the newly proposed plan also increased the racial percentage for white Methodists on boards and agencies to 80 percent while decreasing the percentage reserved for black Methodists to 20. Fearing that white Methodists would reject even these adjusted ratios, the new plan declared that these ratios were not mandated, but suggested. Indeed, the new plan stated that voting for membership on denominational boards and agencies should be done by "conscience rather than fixed quotas," essentially making the stated ratio meaningless. Three weeks after the white conference approved this new plan, the black conference rejected it.[98]

With the mandated deadline for merger quickly approaching, the black and white conferences ultimately agreed on a plan of merger. But, in keeping with the long history of American race relations, the adopted plan made concessions to the white conference at the expense of the black. The plan included provisions for racially diverse conference boards and agencies at a ratio approximately reflecting the racial composition of the newly merged conference, but again set no quotas for this ratio. Instead, delegates were to "follow their consciences on secret ballots to maintain the balance" when assembling denominational boards and agencies. And being intentionally inclusive in this manner was required only for eight years rather than twelve. Furthermore, the chairperson of the elected boards would be chosen "on the basis of merit, not racial quotas."[99] When the two conferences met in January 1972 to vote on the new plan of merger, the white conference approved the plan with 70 percent of the delegates voting yes. Only 68 percent of the African American delegates, however, voted for the plan, a significantly lower number than the 96 percent who had voted to accept the original plan the year before.[100] These black Christians recognized that they were making larger sacrifices for the merger to pass. With mandated ratios no longer required, white Methodists could enter this integrated annual conference with their colorblindness intact.

The mass exodus of white Methodists from the denomination as predicted by John Satterfield in 1966 did not materialize after the merger in South Carolina. In fact, South Carolina Methodism actually gained members in the five years after the merger.[101] Yet the absence of widespread white flight from the denomination was arguably because the merger changed little for the majority of white church members. Five years after the merger took place, not a single black minister had been assigned to a white church. Additionally, of the more than a thousand United Methodist churches in South Carolina in 1976, less than a dozen of these had both black and white members.[102] With the merger, just as with the *Brown* decision, everything changed and nothing changed.

In the final analysis, the story of the Methodist merger in South Carolina illuminates the transformation of segregationist Christianity in the late 1960s. Because segregationist theology grew quiet in public discourse during the latter half of the 1960s, it is possible to believe that southern white churches had rejected such teaching. And, if not fully receptive to the idea of racial inclusiveness, white conservative Christians could be seen as no longer convinced that racial segregation was something requiring a robust defense. The story of the Methodist merger complicates these assumptions by demonstrating how new expressions of segregationist Christians were related to older segregationist theology. To be sure, white Christians still adhered to traditional iterations of segregationist theology, but by the 1970s such beliefs were increasingly reserved for private correspondence. Eight months after the black and white annual conferences merged, for instance, William Workman received a letter from a friend and former Sunday School classmate, Mitzi Matthews, encouraging Workman and his family to leave Trenholm Road United Methodist Church and to join Matthews in a new church plant. With this letter, Matthews also sent Workman "the information I said I would send you" to help explain the reason for the new church plant: a seven-page exegesis of biblical passages that purportedly supported racial segregation.[103] As this example shows, early proponents of the colorblind rhetoric in the 1970s like Workman retained conversancy with the classical segregationist theology of an earlier generation.

Yet, something new developed in segregationist Christianity that the South Carolina merger helps reveal. The suggestions touted by Workman and the MCF to promote "natural affinities" between the races based not on forced interaction but on voluntary appreciation of merit presented themselves as new arguments for white religious conservatives in the late 1960s. What was needed, these conservatives argued, was not more attention to skin color, but less. Instead of creating intentional frameworks to ensure racial inclusiveness or working to identify and abolish structural inequalities between the races, white Christians argued that they should focus their efforts on interpersonal relations—"natural affinities"—based not on race but on "each others' merits." But it cannot be overlooked that in the same way these ideas were first espoused in the *Plessy* ruling to establish Jim Crow, these decades-old arguments were still marshalled in service to segregation. Shifting the focus from structural inequality to personal relationships would pay significant dividends for segregationist Christians in the decades to come. With this new rhetoric came a new paradigm of adjudicating racism, wherein individualized *feelings* of hostility or benevolence would serve as the barometer of racism rather than institutional *policies* or *actions* that produced or perpetuated racial inequities. The ultimate goal for white Christians espousing these colorblind arguments was ostensibly a heart that held no prejudice toward someone with a different skin color in order to arrive at a point where race held no meaning. Freed from the shopworn segregationist theology of the 1950s, the new rhetoric of individual colorblindness allowed conservative white Christians to argue against programs and policies that promoted racial inclusiveness and equity in the 1970s precisely because such initiatives violated colorblindness with their intentional attentiveness to race. And with individualized metrics of racism in place, white Christians could in good conscience built new "colorblind" structures of inequality to replace the outdated Jim Crow versions. Such was the case for white Christians in South Carolina in the 1970s who employed individualized colorblind rhetoric as they established private schools for their children after the state's public schools desegregated. This biblically inspired focus on their families trafficked in the new language of colorblind individualism even as it too was tied to the segregationist theology of old.

5

Focusing on the Family

Private Schools and the New Shape of Segregationist Christianity

In the fall of 1876, Wade Hampton, a cotton planter and former Confederate general whose wealth and military exploits won him widespread fame in South Carolina, was elected governor of the state. His election being by no means a pure expression of popular will, Hampton was swept into power as part of a deliberate campaign to intimidate, threaten, and ultimately disenfranchise black voters in South Carolina to re-establish "home rule" in the state. After more than a decade of black political gains following the Civil War, white conservatives took it upon themselves to reinstate white supremacy in 1876, declaring that it was their duty to "control the vote of at least one negro by intimidation, purchase, keeping him away [from the polls], or as each individual may determine."[1] One of these white leaders reminded his fellow comrades of the benefits of violence in the campaign to suppress black voters because "argument has no effect on them: They can only be influenced by their fears."[2] His listeners responded accordingly. The weeks preceding the 1876 election saw Hampton triumphantly tour the state on horseback, a reminder of his success in the Civil War as a Confederate cavalry officer. Hampton was accompanied on his tour by hundreds of red-shirted and armed supporters, a Praetorian Guard of his own in the making. Hampton's "Red Shirts" were not window dressings. As one historian recounts, Hampton's campaign corresponded with "[a] reign of terror reminiscent of Ku Klux Klan days . . . with freedmen driven from their homes and brutally whipped, and 'leading men' murdered."[3] The intended impact of the terrorism accomplished its aim: Hampton won the governorship. With his ascension to the executive mansion the following spring, South Carolina entered a new period, a "redemption" of the state from the hands of federal troops whose presence helped protect black political equality. Hampton's governorship marked the end of such equality and the start to relegating

The Bible Told Them So. J. Russell Hawkins, Oxford University Press. © Oxford University Press 2021.
DOI: 10.1093/oso/9780197571064.003.0006

> black Carolinians to second-class status, a position they held until the gains
> of the civil rights movement in the following century.

Ninety years after his supporters terrorized black citizens to ensure Hampton's election, a school in Orangeburg, South Carolina, named in the Confederate general's honor, graduated its first class of seniors. The commencement exercises at the Wade Hampton Academy in 1965 followed the same three-act ritual common to all such events. First, the cap-and-gown-clad seniors paraded in as their proud parents beamed. Next, the graduates fought to maintain focus during a local dignitary's invited remarks. Finally, the students made a short walk across the dais and received their diploma from the school's headmaster. But then the ceremony diverged from standard procedure, indicating that neither was the event a typical commencement nor was Wade Hampton a typical school. After receiving their diplomas, the school's headmaster, T. Elliott Wannamaker, called each of the seniors forward for an additional commendation, presenting each graduate with a lapel pin displaying the Confederate battle flag, a South Carolina Palmetto tree, and the word "survivor." Having distributed the pins, Wannamaker explained their meaning to both the seniors and their guests in attendance. Just as Confederate veterans in the 1860s had returned from the Civil War to rebuild and redeem South Carolina, Wannamaker intoned, "so we today, despite many evil signs we see about us . . . shall survive the fight, God willing; and with us will survive our Country, redeemed from those who would destroy it,—to be passed on to our children as a very precious heritage."[4] The nineteenth-century soldiers in Wannamaker's allusion fought to preserve slavery. One hundred years later, Wannamaker fancied himself a commander in the fight to preserve segregation.

Along with other white parents in Orangeburg, Wannamaker had founded Wade Hampton Academy to protect their children from the supposed danger posed by desegregated schools. The year before the school opened, a group of concerned citizens in Orangeburg County professed "that the separation of the races in education, in recreation, in living quarters, and in churches is in the best interest of both races and is essential to the preservation of racial integrity." Worried about a number of lawsuits pending in federal courts in 1963 that signaled the likely end of segregated schools in their community, the group concluded that "separate private school facilities must be provided . . . [to] avoid the pernicious 'experiment' being foisted upon the people of this state and nation."[5]

These South Carolinians resolved to create a private school for white students that would be operational by the start of the 1964 school year, Wade Hampton Academy being the fruit of their efforts. With the completion of the first school year in the spring of 1965, school leaders now sought to build on their success. More than simply a celebration of the graduates' achievement, the first Wade Hampton commencement was also a call to arms. When Wannamaker himself pinned the Wade Hampton graduates in 1965, he was commissioning new soldiers for the South's last stand against racial integration. The battlefields were public schools; the tactics were strategic retreats.

Wade Hampton the politician and Wade Hampton the private school both found their genesis in white fear over black equality. Hampton's white supporters in 1876 hoped his election would redeem the whole of their South Carolina society from the danger of black political sovereignty. The founders of the twentieth-century academy named in Hampton's honor had more modest aspirations than Hampton's Red Shirts, to be sure. But the same motive that drove white supremacists to disenfranchise black voters in the 1800s similarly inspired white parents a century later to establish Wade Hampton Academy: the redemption of their children from the imagined threat of their fellow black citizens. As the 1970s approached, white Christian parents increasingly viewed school desegregation as a lurking danger. As this chapter details, by embracing and espousing the colorblind individualism that was becoming vogue in conservative Christian circles, these parents played a significant role in the effort to maintain public school segregation. When these efforts failed, white Christians began an exodus out of integrated public schools and into white, segregated private schools, justifying their actions as defending their family as the Bible instructed.

Preserving segregated education was a fitting denouement to the story of segregationist Christianity in the civil rights era. Sustained deployment of segregationist theology as a reason to protect Jim Crow, after all, began after the Supreme Court declared segregated schools unconstitutional in 1954. But in the decade following the court's ruling, boycotts, sit-ins, and protest marches shifted attention to other areas of southern racial injustice such as segregated public accommodations and disenfranchised black voters. During this time, the school desegregation controversy simmered out of the spotlight, shining now on other fronts in the black freedom struggle. With civil rights victories mounting throughout the 1960s—and *because* of those victories—the issue of segregated schools eventually regained prominence in the civil rights movement. Coming full circle, the story of segregationist Christianity in the late 1960s returned to where it began fifteen years earlier: in the schools.

But much had changed in the decade and a half since 1954. Any designs white Christians formulated for retaining segregated public schools in the waning years of the 1960s were now countered by the executive and judicial branches of the federal government that were determined to see the *Brown* ruling at long last implemented. No longer could white southerners simply refuse to accommodate federal calls to desegregate their public schools. A government bent on seeing integrated classrooms necessarily required a change of strategy. And thus in the mid-1960s segregationist Christians began establishing a host of private schools like the Wade Hampton Academy, whose purpose was to avoid the federal government's perceived machinations and ensure that their children's education would continue in all-white classrooms.

As in other instances when white southerners fought against racial integration, segregationist theology played a pivotal role in the private school movement by justifying white families' retreats from public schools. But unlike previous theological arguments that explicitly declared segregation as God's will, the theology that buttressed these new private schools focused on the family. The parents of the Wade Hampton Academy class of 1965 would have no doubt agreed with the declaration made by other white proponents of private schools in that era: "Parents are accountable to God for the training of their children."[6] For many white Christian parents in the late 1960s, this accountability to the divine for their offspring's well-being entailed pulling their children out of public schools and enrolling them in newly created private academies. By justifying their actions with the language of familial obligations and values, these segregationist Christians simultaneously avoided naming black children as the entity in their minds that endangered their own children. Unquestioningly, however, the growth of white support for private schools in the mid-twentieth century was directly tied to public school desegregation.

Support for Private Schools in South Carolina: A Brief History

White desire for private schools ran cyclically throughout the 1950s and 1960s, with urgent calls for alternatives to public education corresponding with times when integration seemed imminent. In South Carolina, the idea of utilizing private schools to avoid public school desegregation actually predated the 1954 *Brown* decision when state leaders, perhaps acting as prognosticators regarding school integration, proposed measures to accommodate private education should the integration mandate come to pass. In a 1951 speech urging state lawmakers to allocate money for the construction of new schools for African American children, Governor James Byrnes suggested that if the courts forced public schools to desegregate, the newly built schools could be handed over to citizens to form their own private segregated schools.[7] In the post-*Brown* era, talk of encouraging private schools as a substitute for desegregated public schools did not surface among state officials until April 1957 when the Ways and Means Committee of the state's House of Representatives considered a bill to grant tax exemptions to parents whose children attended private schools.[8] The bill in question stalled when state senator Marion Gressette—whose eponymously named education committee was formed in 1951 at the direction of the governor specifically to maintain school segregation—reported that the state was sufficiently prepared "to meet any situation that may develop in the present [school desegregation] crisis" and announced that no need existed in 1957 to pass additional legislation.[9] In fact, the Gressette Committee had been instrumental in passing several legislative bills two years earlier in the wake of the *Brown* ruling, putting white South Carolinians on firmer legal ground to avoid school desegregation if and when that battle came. Such acts included repealing the compulsory school attendance law, thereby allowing parents to hold their children out of desegregated public schools without legal consequence, and granting more authority to local school boards, thus empowering communities to construct their own bureaucratic roadblocks to integration.[10] With Gressette's assurances of segregation's sustainability in the summer of 1957, state leaders envisioned no need to enact legislation promoting private schools and subsequently tabled the tax exemption proposal.

In the fall of 1957, Gressette's assurances crumbled. President Eisenhower's deployment of the United States Army to desegregate Central High School in Little Rock, Arkansas, shook white southern confidence about the future of segregated schools and resuscitated discussions of private education. In Washington, DC, Strom Thurmond fielded letters from concerned citizens asking if private schools might be exempt from desegregation orders even as Thurmond himself took to the floor of the Senate to warn presciently that if the federal government "persist[ed] in insisting on the racial integration of the public schools of the South, one inevitable result of this policy will be the closing of the public schools in many areas."[11]

Rather than passively allowing schools to close as a result of desegrega-tion, some South Carolinians actually urged state leaders to proactively abolish public education. In one such petition, concerned white citizen Sam C. Augustine wrote to Marion Gressette suggesting that all the state's public schools should be sold off to individuals who could then operate segregated private schools not bound by federal desegregation orders. In his response, Gressette acknowledged that he had occasionally received similar requests since the 1954 *Brown* decision, "but have felt that we should do everything possible to retain our public school system as long as we can." Gressette as-sured Augustine that "our program in South Carolina has been geared since the inception of this trouble and the formation of our Committee in 1951, to keep and preserve our public school system on a segregated basis." The state senator reminded Augustine that "to change over to a private school system would not prevent our enemies from trying to force our children to attend integrated schools. May I add that we anticipate such action on their part and that we have a good legal staff in South Carolina to defend and prosecute any such actions as may arise."[12]

Gressette and other state leaders may have viewed plans to eliminate public education as a bridge too far, but by the spring of 1958 fear that South Carolina was following the path of Central High in Little Rock became so widespread that white citizens began clamoring for some type of preven-tative action to counter the integrationist threat. One option to safeguard segregated education came that spring from the former president of the University of South Carolina and current gubernatorial candidate, Donald S. Russell. Standing before a meeting of the Olanta, South Carolina, Citizens' Council, candidate Russell assured the crowd that he thought "school inte-gration in this state is impossible" and that he and his fellow citizens were "united in their inflexible resolve that separate schools shall be maintained" in their state. The question at hand for Russell was not *if* the schools would stay segregated—of course they would; rather, the question was how to best maintain segregation. Russell came prepared with a plan. Contrary to those who wished to abolish public education altogether, Russell thought a hybrid between public and private education was preferable. His proposal that eve-ning to the segregationists of Florence County was to take the money the state allocated per pupil to each district and award it directly to the families to have them do with it as they saw best. In Russell's plan, "the state and the school district involved would provide the student with his tuition to attend a school, private or otherwise, of his choice in reasonable radius of his home;

but the student himself would select voluntarily the school he would attend and that school would not be under control of the State." Naturally, the private schools that Russell envisioned would conform to "local customs and patterns" as they pertained to segregation. Born from "an inflexible determination to have only segregated schools in this State," Russell's proposal and his school voucher program provided a means to that end.[13] Russell, however, did not win the governor's office in 1958; he would have to wait four more years to realize that prize. But the plan that he articulated on that spring evening would be revisited in the years to come.

In October 1958, a South Carolina legislator representing a county with a large black population once again sounded the call for private schools. Irritated by what he perceived as inaction by the Gressette Committee, Representative Sam Harrell of Florence County stated that the segregation committee "should do something to set up private schools before the courts act."[14] Harrell's perspective was no doubt colored by Eisenhower's intervention in Little Rock the previous autumn, as were those of many white South Carolinia Christians who responded to the situation in Arkansas with a pledge of support for their segregationist neighbors to the west. The men's club of St. Matthew's Methodist Church in Bishopsville, for instance, passed a resolution backing Arkansas governor Orval Faubus and his fight "against the unChristian and evil forces of the Supreme Court and federal government caused by the pressure of politicians, sociologists, psychologists and do-gooders, ignorant of the issues at hand."[15] Meanwhile, one Baptist minister urged members of the South Carolina Citizens' Council to send money to Arkansas to buttress the fledgling private school movement there. Reverend Marion A. Woodson believed the issue was important enough that South Carolinians needed to make personal sacrifices to build and maintain private schools. "We have reached the point," Woodson declared, "where we must be willing to give up the second car, cancel a vacation trip and buy less clothing in order to provide private schools for our children."[16]

The effort to provide private schools for South Carolina's white children was soon championed by the state's Farm Bureau and Citizens' Councils. In petitioning the state legislature in November 1958, the former group resurrected the radical plan to abolish public education in South Carolina altogether. Meanwhile, seven Citizens' Council groups in the Charleston area conducted a survey of the city's public buildings and churches to investigate the logistical feasibility for private schools should the need arise.[17]

Little Rock turned out to be an anomaly. In 1958, fears of soldiers integrating South Carolina schools at bayonet point went unrealized. Despite the concerns of white citizens, school desegregation in South Carolina was not imminent in 1958 or anytime soon thereafter. In fact, integration of public educational facilities did occur at any level in the Palmetto State for another half decade. Preserving segregated public education longer than any other state in the Union, South Carolina strictly enforced the color line until January 1963. Although South Carolina holds the ignominious distinction of having the longest run of segregated public education of any state in the nation, in point of fact, the decade following the *Brown* decision saw little integration in any southern public schools, particularly in the Deep South. The Supreme Court's 1955 vague ruling in *Brown II* that school integration should proceed "with all deliberate speed" all but guaranteed that school desegregation moved throughout the South at a glacial pace.[18] The year after the *Brown* ruling, for instance, less than one-fifth of 1 percent of black students in the South attended schools with white children. In 1962—eight years after the court had declared school segregation unconstitutional—the number of black students in the South who were enrolled in a school with white peers was still less than one-half of 1 percent.[19] As long as desegregation was merely talked about rather than enacted, the need for public school alternatives remained at bay. Despite occasional calls for private schools throughout the late 1950s and early 1960s, it was not until 1963 that the South Carolina legislature revisited the question of how best to support private schools as substitutes for the desegregated public versions.

In January 1963, weeks after Harvey Gantt integrated Clemson College, the South Carolina House of Representatives considered a bill to provide tuition grants to students who desired to withdraw from public schools and enroll in private institutions. This bill proposed that the state give parents the same amount of money that South Carolina spent per pupil—$225 a year for elementary school students, $250 for high school students in 1963—for use toward tuition at a private school of their choosing. To bypass First Amendment difficulties, the bill stipulated that the money could not be used at religiously affiliated schools, and to sidestep charges of discrimination, the grants were available to families regardless of race. In fact, so cautious were state lawmakers to avoid tainting the tuition grant proposal with accusations of racism that school desegregation was "not mentioned or in any way alluded to" when legislators presented the bill, despite that the legislation was proposed at a time when South Carolina was still abuzz about the desegregation of the state's first public educational facility.

Governor Donald S. Russell followed the legislature's lead in sidestepping the issue of race when casting his support for the proposed school vouchers by endorsing the tuition grant bill on the grounds that its passage would help keep public schools accountable to high standards through competition while simultaneously affording students and their parents greater freedom in choosing which schools they attended.[20] The language of school accountability and freedom of choice that the governor employed in 1963 had not been part of Russell's pitch for tuition grants five years earlier to the Olanta Citizens' Councils as a gubernatorial candidate. In that speech, Russell rooted the need for private school vouchers plainly in "the inflexible opposition of the white Southerner to school integration."[21] Five years later, Russell still supported tuition grants to be used at private schools, but his publicly stated rationale for doing so morphed. By emphasizing accountability and freedom rather than desegregation, Russell and other supporters of the tuition grants could plausibly—if not persuasively—maintain that the impetus behind the plan had nothing to do with race. Not coincidentally, however, at the same time that Russell and state legislators were endorsing the tuition grant bill, three desegregation suits filed against South Carolina schools were pending in federal courts.[22]

As careful as legislators and the governor had been in not mentioning race or school desegregation when debating the merits of tuition grants, the plan's progenitor was less discreet in discussing the need for the legislation. In fact, the 1963 tuition grant idea was the brainchild of Marion Gressette's segregation committee, which envisioned the tuition grants as a safeguard for segregation in the event that the courts ruled that South Carolina's public schools must integrate. Whereas Governor Russell was careful not to connect the line between race and private school vouchers, Senator Gressette did so willingly. In proposing the tuition grants, the committee declared, "South Carolina at all costs must prevent the development of its grammar and high schools into the lawless 'blackboard jungles' that integration has made" in other parts of the country.[23] Such words resonated with South Carolinians anxious about school desegregation. The idea that racial integration led directly to disorder and lawlessness was a theme white South Carolinians sounded time and again in the following decade, and in part explained why desire for private education in South Carolina always spiked when black children threatened to walk through the schoolhouse door.

Despite support from the governor, the majority of legislators, and a significant number of white parents who desired alternatives to racially integrated
schools, passage of the 1963 tuition grant bill was by no means a foregone
conclusion. Probably recognizing the true impetus for the grants, some
legislators foresaw problems with the bill's passing constitutional muster.
The state NAACP threatened immediate court action if the bill passed.
Additionally, state education officials, already financially pressed, were particularly critical of the tuition grant plan because state school funding was
directly tied to student enrollment. Some legislators believed the amount
of money the bill allocated for children to attend private schools was inade-
quate to cover the cost of tuition for most families and would therefore serve
only as a subsidy for wealthy South Carolinians who already had their children enrolled in private schools.[24]

One group, the Foundation for Independent Schools, supported the bill's
intent but worried that its exclusion of religious schools was too restrictive
and requested that the General Assembly amend the bill to allow tuition
grants to be used at church-related schools. George Cornish, the attorney
for the Foundation for Independent Schools, argued that barring the tuition
grants at religious schools discriminated against parents who wanted their
children educated in such institutions. More importantly, Cornish percep-
tively reasoned that even if a private school was not sponsored by a particular
church or explicitly religious in its intent, newly established private schools
would likely need to make use of church buildings to help defer overhead
costs until the time the schools could become financially stable enough to
move into their own facilities.[25]

Despite pressure from those who wanted the bill voted down and those
who desired an expanded version of the legislation, the General Assembly
ultimately passed the tuition grants bill in May 1963 with the attached clause
prohibiting their use at religious schools. The bill encountered no serious opposition from lawmakers in either chamber, passing seventy-eight to twenty-
eight in the House and thirty-five to four in the Senate. In its final version,
the legislature allocated $155 per pupil who opted out of public schools to
attend accredited nonreligious private institutions. It also provided that local
districts could decide for themselves if they wanted to participate and could
subsidize the grant with additional local money if thought prudent. One state
senator in the minority who opposed the bill took to the floor shortly before
the vote in an attempt to lay bare the bill's true intent. Although lawmakers
had consciously made no mention of school desegregation in debating the

bill, state senator Roger Scott declared bluntly, "We might as well say it, it's about white people and Negroes."[26] Whereas in 1958 an open connection between race and support for private education could be leveraged as a campaign issue, by 1963 such correlations had to be hidden. But Scott was not wrong. Private education in the 1960s was about race. And the history of the private education movement in South Carolina in subsequent years would bear out that truth.

For South Carolinians concerned about school desegregation, the tuition grants bill passed at a particularly fortuitous moment. Just months after the tuition grants bill became law, Judge Robert Martin, a United States district court judge in Columbia, South Carolina, heard arguments on whether twelve African American students could enroll in white high schools in Charleston for the 1963 school year. Nine years earlier, of course, the Supreme Court had already established that prohibiting a student's enrollment in a school solely because of his or her race was unconstitutional. The lawyers for the Charleston district therefore devised an alternative argument. To defend its segregation policy, the Charleston school district called an emeritus professor of anatomy from the University of North Carolina medical school to testify that black students were inherently inferior to white students. According to this expert witness, "Negroes have 'an innate lack of capacity' for matching the performance capabilities of whites," which justified the city of Charleston's decision to educate them separately from whites.[27] The emeritus anatomy professor based his analysis of the intellectual abilities of the races on the weight and perceived characteristics of the brains of whites and African Americans. According to this line of argument, black students in Charleston were not being discriminated against because of their race but because of their abilities. Segregation had to be retained because blacks had been marked by nature itself as intellectually lower than whites. In his decision, Judge Martin rejected the school district's defense and ruled that the black plaintiffs could attend one of the four white high schools in Charleston. Judge Martin also ruled that all the heretofore exclusively white Charleston schools would have to implement some amount of desegregation by the start of the 1964–1965 school year.[28] With Martin's ruling, the era of complete segregation in South Carolina's primary and secondary schools ended. In closing one sordid chapter of the state's racial history, Martin's 1963 ruling also marked the beginning of another in South Carolina: the rise of private schools to avoid desegregation.

School Desegregation and the Rise
of Private Schools

As the 1963 academic year began with four of Charleston's schools experiencing desegregation for the first time, white groups in the coastal city immediately began meeting to discuss opening private schools to take advantage of the newly enacted tuition grant program. Five separate groups in Charleston alone made plans for private schools, including the First Presbyterian Church of Charleston, which carefully wrote the school charter so it was unassociated with the church itself and thereby qualified for the grants.[29] This scene in Charleston was replicated across the state in the mid-1960s as court decisions and federal funding programs brought about desegregated schools in communities throughout South Carolina. Complying with court rulings and the Department of Housing Education and Welfare (HEW) guidelines that required desegregation in exchange for federal money, South Carolina school districts between 1964 and 1967 produced freedom-of-choice plans that gave parents the opportunity to enroll their children in the school of their choice. Critics of these freedom-of-choice plans noted that, at best, the plans produced "token" desegregation, as only a handful of black students actually matriculated in the previously all-white schools and not a single white student ever chose to attend a black school. Desegregation advocates argued that in many areas of the state, a "hostile community atmosphere" kept black parents from exercising their own freedom of choice to send their children to the white schools. Some black parents reported that they "do not send their children to the white schools because they fear their children will be subjected to physical abuse by other students and will be treated unfairly by an all-white teaching staff." Meanwhile, those families who did choose to pursue integration became vulnerable to other forms of retribution. As late as 1967, for example, after a black "parent chose a white school for his daughter, the white owner of the land on which he lived ordered him to move."[30]

For all intents and purposes, freedom-of-choice plans merely continued segregated education in the state. During the 1965–1966 school year, for instance, despite 80 percent of the state's school districts being in compliance with HEW guidelines for acceptable desegregation plans, only 1.5 percent of African American pupils in South Carolina attended school with white students.[31] The HEW guidelines changed segregation rates, but only at an incremental pace. And two years later at the beginning of the 1968 school year, 80 percent of black students still attended a school that enrolled not a single white pupil.[32]

Despite the minimal scale of desegregation from 1964 to 1968, a corresponding uptick in the creation of private schools nevertheless occurred in South Carolina during that same period. Token desegregation from the freedom-of-choice plans during these four years resulted in thirty-two new private schools opening their doors across the state, all being racially segregated. These schools were but a prelude of things to come as the federal government forced school districts to move beyond token integration.

In the spring of 1968, the United States Supreme Court issued a ruling in *Green v. County School Board of New Kent County* that substantially affected school integration in South Carolina and the rest of the South. In this case, the NAACP asked the court to rule on the constitutionality of the freedom-of-choice plans that heretofore had produced little integration in historically segregated school districts. New Kent County, Virginia, where the case originated, was such a district. The county's population was almost evenly split between whites and African Americans, and the county operated only two schools: the George W. Watkins School and the New Kent School. Watkins, on the county's west side, was a combined elementary and high school for the county's black students. New Kent, meanwhile, also being a combined elementary and high school, stood on the eastern side of the county and was reserved for the county's white students. In 1965, the county adopted a freedom-of-choice plan to remain eligible for federal education dollars, but during the next three years freedom of choice failed to produce substantial integration in New Kent County. In fact, by 1968 only 115 of the county's 740 black students were attending New Kent School, while not a single white student had enrolled at Watkins.[33]

In the *Green v. County School Board of New Kent County* case, NAACP lawyers argued before the court that freedom of choice in New Kent County had failed to produce substantial integration and therefore should be declared unconstitutional. The court agreed, but only to an extent. Writing for a unanimous court, Justice William J. Brennan declared that "in desegregating a dual system a plan utilizing 'freedom of choice' is not an end in itself." Citing a lower court judge, Brennan concurred that if a freedom-of-choice plan effectively produced substantial integration, "it is acceptable, but if it fails to undo segregation, other means must be used to achieve this end."[34] In other words, the court was interested only in seeing substantial integration in school districts. If that integration came as the result of freedom-of-choice plans, such results were acceptable. But if these plans produced only token integration, school districts needed to devise alternative strategies for making substantial integration a reality. "Freedom of choice is not a sacred talisman," Brennan wrote. "It is only a means to a constitutionally required end—the abolition of the system of segregation and its effects."[35] But for many white parents in South Carolina, freedom of choice *had* become sacred during the years it was enforced in their state. And losing the freedom to send their children to the schools they saw fit was tantamount to losing their religious freedom. In an appeal to Senator Strom Thurmond to intervene on behalf of South Carolina parents and protect freedom-of-choice plans, one father stated succinctly that "without freedom to choose for our children, there is no freedom of religion."[36] This father spoke for many other white parents in South Carolina who shared his sentiments regarding the venerability of choice. As school districts abandoned freedom of choice and adopted pupil placement plans to achieve the substantial integration required by the *Green* ruling, white parents showed themselves willing to leave public schools altogether rather than comply with the new plans.

Although freedom of choice became a dead letter by 1969, white families in South Carolina were not without alternatives to the integrated schools because the number of private schools in the state exploded that same year. Keeping with historical precedent, the rate at which these private schools were established was directly proportional to the amount of integration occurring in the state. In late 1969, the Supreme Court ruled in *Alexander v. Holmes County Board of Education* that the substantial desegregation called for in the *Green* decision could not be delayed and had to be in place throughout the South by the following spring.[37] As a result of the *Alexander* decision, 93 percent of South Carolina's African American students attended desegregated schools by the spring of 1970. The previous year, only 29 percent had done so. Not coincidentally, 1970 also marked the advent of thirty-six newly segregated private schools in South Carolina, the most in a single year.[38] Between 1964 and 1972, when the majority of school desegregation in South Carolina occurred, white South Carolinians formed 111 new private schools. Seventy-nine of these schools sprang up after the *Green* decision in 1968. By 1973, these schools that had been established less than a decade before enrolled twenty-five thousand white students.[39]

As the number of private schools in South Carolina mounted, so did the concern of white parents who found themselves unable to afford the new schools and were left coping with the worst fears their minds could conjure about the now integrated schools. "Must the parents of any whites who are unable financially to send their children to a private school, have to subject them to a lower level of education, expose them to the degradation of morals and, perhaps, physical and sexual dangers?" a concerned mother named Naomi Floyd asked Strom Thurmond in 1969. "The establishment of private schools is going to create a more definite segregation in the [S]outh than has ever been experienced since the days of slavery.... The less fortunate whites who have to attend public schools will become absorbed by the negro population," warned Floyd.[40] Another mother wrote to Senator Ernest Hollings to ask him to intervene on behalf of the white children who faced the prospect of attending school with black children. Government officials, wrote Mrs. Eugene Hill, "can not [sic] possibly know what they are forcing upon our children. My daughter, Karen, is in Jr. High and she is completely terrified of the Negro students." Hill continued that with school integration came integrated buses, which held other dangers. "How can the white people who live in rural areas allow their little girls to get on the bus with Negro drivers before the sun has even come up. Would you?" she asked Hollings.[41]

Other white parents pleaded for assistance in delaying the required integration until they had the time to get a private school up and running. One mother wrote to Hollings that her children would likely forego school after the forced integration "because there isn't room in all the private schools and we don't have time to get them organized."[42] "The people [of South Carolina] has [sic] nothing against negroes," another parent assured Thurmond. "They're just a race of people that belong together. God made them just as they are and wanted them to stay that way. If he had wanted us half and half, don't they know he would have made them that way? They're trying to change God's will."[43] Other white parents in South Carolina clearly shared this sentiment and acted accordingly to avoid the integrated schools. By the mid-1970s, South Carolina—the last state in the Union to desegregate their public schools—had enrolled a higher percentage of students in private schools than any other southern state.[44]

South Carolina's post-1964 private school boom mirrored a broader phenomenon that occurred across the southern United States. The meteoric growth in southern private schools that began in the mid-1960s reached its peak in the wake of the 1971 Supreme Court decision in *Swann v. Charlotte-Mecklenburg Board of Education*, a court decision that sanctioned busing as an acceptable instrument to achieve school desegregation.[45] In October 1969, an estimated three hundred thousand white students throughout the South were enrolled in private schools where racial segregation was upheld. Following the *Alexander* decision the next month, a ruling that ordered school districts to integrate "at once," the enrollment in private schools jumped 33 percent. By 1971, the number of pupils attending segregated private schools in the South topped a half-million and continued to rise.[46] By 1974, twenty years after the Supreme Court handed down its *Brown* decision, education experts estimated that between three and four thousand private schools had been established in southern states whose roots could be found in the desegregation of public schools. Attendance at these "segregationist academies," as their critics called them, accounted for an estimated three-quarters of a million white schoolchildren whose parents pulled their children from publicly funded schools and paid to enroll them in these newly established private institutions.[47]

Despite the intentions of state lawmakers, families were indeed the ones footing the bill for tuition at the new schools since court challenges had frozen money that several states, including South Carolina, had earmarked to help parents pay for private education.[48] South Carolina's tuition grant program, for example, was halted almost as soon as the first payments were dispersed in 1963. Opponents of the payments won an injunction against the state-sponsored tuition grants, and in 1968 the courts ultimately ruled them unconstitutional. Despite this obstacle, the growth of private schools in South Carolina remained unabated after school desegregation began in 1963.[49] The same scenario held for white families across the South: as the 1960s progressed and schools integrated, hundreds of thousands of southern white parents proved willing to bear the financial burden of private school tuition to keep their children out of racially integrated public schools. Faced with the requirement to send their children to desegregated public schools, parents chose to create their own schools, some parents believing they had no other option. The local board of education and HEW "have left us no choice but [to create] a private school for our white school children," complained a resident of Dale, South Carolina.[50] Such openly racialized admissions proved difficult to navigate for the new private schools. Although there was an undeniable racial element to the schools' rise, leaders of the private school movement took pains to explain the schools' popularity in other terms. This elision of race as a causal factor for private schools can be clearly seen in the history of the South Carolina Independent School Association.

The South Carolina Independent
School Association

In the minds of some, the new wave of private schools in South Carolina in the mid-1960s necessitated an organization to further private education in the state. Accordingly, in 1965 T. Elliot Wannamaker, the Wade Hampton Academy headmaster who presented his graduates with lapel pins of the Confederate battle flag, invited representatives from seven of the other newly formed private schools to his hometown of Orangeburg to discuss the creation of an independent school association. As a result of that meeting, the South Carolina Independent School Association (SCISA) requested and received a corporate charter from the state.[51] The newly formed association recruited a young lawyer, Tom Turnipseed, from Barnwell County, South Carolina, to serve as the SCISA executive secretary and public relations liaison. As one of the founders of the Jefferson Davis Academy in Blackville, South Carolina, Turnipseed was personally committed to utilizing private education to avoid racial integration, and being one of the association's few public faces, it fell to Turnipseed to obfuscate the connection between the new SCISA schools and race. During his two-year tenure with the SCISA, Turnipseed was instrumental in establishing private schools throughout the state and using his legal training to ensure the new schools were tax exempt. The majority of these schools were located in the South Carolina low country where the African American population density was highest. Turnipseed spent much time in this part of the state to help promote and rally support for private education. In his public relations duties for the SCISA, Turnipseed developed a race-neutral message to explain the appeal of the new schools: quality of education. In speeches and public writings on behalf of the SCISA, Turnipseed emphasized that the new association was not a segregationist outfit but a group of prominent citizens concerned about quality education in their state.[52]

While the SCISA never publicly mentioned race, Turnipseed later admitted that the private school movement of the mid-1960s in South Carolina "had everything to do with race,"[53] a truth made plain in a letter Turnipseed authored to Senator Strom Thurmond in 1965. Turnipseed wrote to ask the senator if he might pledge money to "help the financially handcapped [sic] send their children" to the Jefferson Davis Academy in Barnwell County, South Carolina, and to help underwrite the school's operational costs. In his missive, Turnipseed confessed that Jefferson Davis Academy was being formed because "we are in a rather dire situation in Barnwell County as far as our public schools are concerned with a 50 percent Negro population equally interspersed throughout the County and no convenient ghettos for them or any sort of 'across the Potomac' sanctuary to run to ourselves."[54] Out of options to avoid the impending school integration, white parents in Barnwell County established a private school as a last resort to maintain segregated education.

In subsequent years, Jefferson Davis Academy would highlight its legacy of academic excellence while downplaying the racialized impetus for its establishment. This strategy was consistent with other member schools of the SCISA and followed the example laid out by the SCISA itself. While the SCISA was consistent with claims that the association was concerned chiefly with academic performance, it left unspoken the source of those concerns. But in the mid-1960s the SCISA hired a scientific expert to explain at a retreat of association board members and school headmasters that the frontal lobes of African Americans' brains lacked the deep folds found in those of whites, supposedly inhibiting the former's capacity for critical thinking.[55] Ideas such as these were the basis on which the Charleston school district had petitioned the US district court to uphold segregation in the city's public schools. When the district court rejected these supposedly scientific findings and ruled that Charleston schools must integrate, the school district appealed the decision all the way to the Supreme Court in 1964. While the Supreme Court rejected without comment the notion of the innate intellectual inferiority of black students, such ideas still had purchase among the supporters of the private schools in South Carolina.[56] And these private school proponents trafficked in the colorblind rhetoric of "quality education" to mask assumptions about black inferiority.

That the two most prominent leaders of the SCISA, Wannamaker and Turnipseed, supported private education in part because of concerns about racial mixing belied the mantra that the association was founded for quality education alone. Wannamaker, for instance, had written two years before founding the private school association that the "separation of the races in education, in recreation, in living quarters, and in churches is in the best interest of both races and is essential to the preservation of racial integrity."[57] As executive secretary of the SCISA, Turnipseed shared Wannamaker's racial views and even withdrew from the Methodist denomination to join the Southern Methodists, who remained firmly committed to segregation of the races.[58] Beneath the veneer of "quality education" that the SCISA espoused to justify its schools, the racialized underpinnings of the private school association were not too difficult to ascertain. Even a headmaster of one of the schools in the SCISA conceded that "there can be no doubt that one of the major factors affecting the growth of those (independent) schools and the establishment of a great number of private schools in 1964 and the following years in South Carolina was the beginning of mass integration of black students into the public schools."[59] Just as race was a significant part of the private school movement, so too was religion. While the long-standing segregationist strain in their theology helped justify the schools' creation, emerging sensibilities of conservative Christians about protecting the family kept the schools' rosters full.

Religion and the Private Schools

With white migration to private schools well underway by the early 1970s, the headmaster of one of these southern private academies disclosed that "religion is an integral part of the [private] school movement because it's an integral part of the South. Our people—supporters of the Independent Schools—are convinced that God is behind us. That I am sure of, we are doing God's work. . . . If you don't include that [the religious] aspect you're missing a good part of the motivation behind this movement. People believe full heartedly that God doesn't want us to mix."[60] This candid assessment of the private school movement captured the new shape of white Christian resistance to integration in the early 1970s and exemplified the significant change in how conservative Christians discussed segregation. While this headmaster affirmed the centrality of religion for the private school movement, his evaluation skirted explicit mention of race. "God doesn't want us to mix" did indeed hold enough ambiguity to sustain a segregationist movement into the 1970s when public pronouncements of God as the author of racial segregation had fallen out of favor. But white Christians' appeal to the divine in justifying segregation had not ended; it had merely taken a new form. The theology of segregation that evangelicals once employed to thwart racial mixing was recalibrated to endorse a biblically inspired defense of the family. The God who had demanded racial integrity now became the God who required familial protection, with the result being the same. White Christians avoided contact with black people, and segregation remained in practice if not in pronouncements. In the private school movement that began in the late 1960s, the shift from a theology of segregation to a focus on the family was made plain.

In South Carolina, white churches were essential in forming many of the member schools in the SCISA. In fact, as president of the SCISA, Elliott Wannamaker encouraged groups interested in starting private schools to work with local churches that could house the schools during the week in the buildings' ample Sunday School space. Wannamaker's own school, Wade Hampton Academy, spent the first year of its existence housed in the Northside Baptist Church in Orangeburg. In time the school was able to raise enough capital to move out of the church building and construct its own facilities, but for Wade Hampton Academy, Northside Baptist was instrumental in getting the school off the ground.[61]

Many churches in South Carolina did more than house newly formed private schools. While some churches granted private schools use of their facilities without a formal association with the schools, a number of churches established racially segregated schools that operated under church authority. Of the 111 racially segregated private schools in South Carolina by 1973, more than one-third were church sponsored and operated. These schools meeting in church basements, Sunday School classrooms, and fellowship halls in the wake of desegregation did so with God's implied sanction.[62] The statement that these church-affiliated schools tacitly made was that God supported the practice of racial segregation. The very argument conservative white Christians had preached explicitly in previous decades was now perpetuated through covert appeals to racial orthodoxy couched in new language. The message sent by a racially segregated school created under the aegis of a church was clear: divine favor for such a school and the principles for which it was founded. This truth was not lost on religious leaders responsible for the segregated schools. When asked about using church property for a private school, one Baptist minister told his parishioners that to do so "would be to sanction segregation in the name of God."[63] For many white Christians, that was precisely the point.

The importance of religion to private schools was not limited to those institutions directly associated with local churches. Even secular private academies had religious underpinnings that buttressed the righteousness of the segregationist cause, for such schools with no church affiliation relied heavily on Christian reputations to justify their existence. Many of these purportedly secular private schools emphasized Christian principles in their classrooms that appealed to white Christian families. According to one survey of southern private schools, even the nonsectarian schools "open classes with prayer . . . [which is] expanded into a considerable devotional exercise, with readings from the Bible."[64] In throwing his political weight behind the SCISA, Senator Strom Thurmond reiterated the idea that independent schools, although often unassociated with any church, maintained a palpable religious identity. As Thurmond told his constituents in South Carolina, the newly created independent schools "are unabashedly Christian in outlook and daily practice," despite not being officially church related.[65]

The Southern Council Academy provides a useful example of how schools not affiliated with local churches still imbued their students with Christian teachings. Established in September 1971 at the height of the desegregation movement, the Southern Council Academy was one of 396 institutions in a network of schools overseen that year by the national organization of the Citizens' Councils of America.[66] "Although Southern Council Academy is not affiliated with any church group," the school's handbook informed potential applicants, "it is a 'Christian' school. A basic premise for our school is 'The fear of God is the beginning of knowledge.' " In addition to the quote from the book of Proverbs, the handbook assured parents that "every home room teacher daily conducts devotions during the home room period." The headmaster of the school "is also a Christian minister, [and] teaches a Bible class daily." Furthermore, the school required chapel once a week for both the elementary and high school students who attended.[67]

Although the Southern Council Academy was established the year after the Supreme Court mandated the immediate desegregation of southern schools, any mention of race was conspicuously missing from the school's informational handbook. This omission was likely due in part to changes in IRS tax codes that required private schools to strike any mention of racial discrimination from their institutional charter to maintain tax-exempt status.[68] But other issues were also at play. At the time Southern Council Academy leaders wrote the school handbook in the early 1970s, open admission that segregation was a driving purpose for these private schools went unmentioned. By the 1970s, overt conveyances of this type were outside the bounds of social acceptability even in the Deep South. As one observer of the private school movement noted, "As middle class whites in the South have become more conscious of their image in racial matters, they have begun to say (and to believe) that they have many reasons for patronizing the schools that have little to do with race."[69] This statement was certainly true for South Carolinian Christian parents in the early 1970s who, in their letters to state leaders, avoided casting their concerns about schools in racial terms and instead articulated their frustration with the dangers the desegregated schools posed to their children's education and physical well-being. For these parents, protecting their children became the rallying cry in justifying their retreat from the public schools. "Why don't you tell the Courts and the HEW that the children do not belong to the State. They belong to God and to the parents as stewards of their well-being, education, and safety," one mother wrote a state official at the highpoint of South Carolina's desegregation movement.[70] C. C. Duncan spoke for many parents in identifying what was at the heart of the emerging focus on the family: "We believe that a child is a gift of God, and that God will call each parent to a strict accounting for training and teaching of their children, for there are many passages of Scripture, which are too numerous to mention in this letter that clearly makes the parent responsible. Will you please inform us how we may fulfill our obligation to God unless we have a choice, as to where our children go, with whom they associate, what they are taught and by whom they are taught?"[71]

What often went unmentioned in these jeremiads to elected officials were explicit references to race. Parents cited hearsay anecdotes of behavioral problems and railed against the diminished academic standards they saw as being inevitable in desegregated public schools, without directly naming the perceived source of the poor behavior and lower academics. At a 1973 public forum to discuss the possibility of busing children to achieve integration in Columbia, South Carolina, schools, white parents presented their arguments against the integration plan in race-neutral terms. A school board member present at the forum later recalled, "One after another, white [parents] laid out the charges—fights on the playground, terrorism in the restrooms, vulgar language, attempted sexual acts, chaos in the classrooms. Still no mention of race. Finally a black man said it: "You people oughta cut out the code language. What you're saying is, 'It ain't the busin', it's the niggers.'"[72]

But by the 1970s, few white parents made open appeals to race, now grounding their support of private schools in the language of behavior standards and academic achievement instead. For some Christian parents, these justifications dovetailed nicely with an emerging theological emphasis on familial responsibility and values. "Parents' rights come from God by way of the natural law," wrote one parent referring to private schools.[73] Whereas segregationist Christians viewed public schools as attempting to strip away parental rights, the private schools existed to reinforce them. And whereas segregationist Christians saw public schools as a threat to their children's safety and quality education, private schools enhanced both. What was at stake for these Christian parents who sent their children to all-white private schools was nothing less than parental rights and obligations. In their assessment, race was not a factor.

Denying that race was the cause for enrolling children in private schools did not make it so. But it did begin the process of allowing southern white Christians—intentionally or otherwise—to elide the connection between their school choices and race. A researcher who attended a convention in the early 1970s for private school students noted this lack of awareness in the students themselves. Every student at the convention "said they were attending the private school because their parents did not want them in integrated schools." But none of the students described this decision as race based. One of the students' comments captured it perfectly: "Niggers are dumb, can't learn; and when you have a majority of low standard in a school, they will pull all the rest down. It's not really a race issue, just a matter of lowering standards."[74] With the mantra that they were acting on the divine mandate to protect their children, white Christian parents ceased talking about race. Further, as demonstrated in the words of the young man at the private school convention, white Christians failed to recognize *when* they were talking about race. Physical safety and academic standards became the metrics by which parents could gauge success in protecting their family. How race influenced either of those categories remained unmentioned. In time, unmentioned assumptions became unexamined beliefs.[75]

The Lamar Incident

The new matrix of school desegregation, private education, religion, and familial responsibility was clearly displayed in an incident that occurred in Lamar, South Carolina, in 1970. The previous year the public schools in Lamar had undergone token desegregation. Being historically white, the Lamar elementary and high school had nine and ten black students, respectively, while the historically black Spaulding high school and elementary school on the other side of town had no white students. In January 1970, following the Supreme Court's directives in the *Alexander* ruling, the US Fourth District Court of Appeals declared that the schools in Lamar must move immediately beyond token desegregation. To accomplish this court-ordered desegregation, city officials drew zoning plans that sent 520 African

American students to the white Lamar schools and transferred 120 white students into the all-black Spaulding schools.

On March 3, 1970, the second day of the implementation of the new desegregation plan, a group of nearly two hundred white parents waited outside the Lamar school with axe handles, bricks, and bottles. When a bus of black students tried to pull up to the school building, the mob blocked the road while some members tore open the engine hood and ripped out cables, rendering the bus immobile. The sixteen black students aboard (including the driver, a senior at Lamar High) got out of the bus and ran into the school as the mob showered the vehicle with rocks and broke out the windows with their axe handles. When a second bus of black students arrived, it was blocked by the first disabled bus. This time the white parents did not bother to wait until the children were off the bus before smashing the windows. Covered in broken glass, the children exited the bus to shouts of "Run, nigger, run!" as South Carolina highway patrolmen tried to repel the mob with tear gas. Before the rioters had been dispersed, they managed to overturn both school buses on the side of the road.[76]

In the fallout of the Lamar school incident, thirty-seven men were charged with rioting. Freed on bail, these men departed the county courthouse to the cheers of an appreciative crowd. A journalist covering the scene reported that "the mention of God and 'the good Lord' was made often. A man said, 'God made men white and God made men black and he sure didn't mean for them to mix together.'"[77] This sentiment was shared by Mrs. M. V. Thomas, who wrote to South Carolina governor Robert McNair to explain the reaction at Lamar. "You claim you want the best or as you say a quality education for the younger generation. We believe there is no way to give them the best except to separate them. It is better for the blacks as same as the whites," Thomas wrote the governor. She continued, "We know the blacks are God's children as same as we are. We believe if God had intended for us to mix he would have made us all the same color or put us together in the first place. Birds and animals don't mix."[78] Rufus Phillips and his wife also wrote McNair to express their displeasure with the desegregation at Lamar. "We are a Christian family of 5, with children ranging in age from an infant to 8 years old. We are indeed concerned for their welfare and we depend on our state leaders to show some concern for our children and for the problems we are now facing," the Phillipses wrote. The solution the Phillipses desired was the same as many other Christian parents: "We are in favor of freedom of choice in our school system and want this freedom returned to us."[79]

For white community members in Lamar who shared Thomas's perspective that God did not desire the races to mix, and others who, like the Phillipses, desired the option of sending their children to a nonintegrated school, Lake Swamp Baptist Church in nearby Timmonsville was an answer to prayer. Anxious about the impeding desegregation order, deacons at Lake Swamp Baptist had called a former Lamar elementary school principal on a Friday evening to gauge his interest in overseeing a proposed private school. Securing his agreement, the church hastily held registration, and within ten days the Lake Swamp Baptist School was operational. The school immediately enrolled four hundred students and turned two hundred others away for lack of space. All were white.

The Lake Swamp Baptist School proved so popular that the sponsoring church could not hold all the students, and school officials were forced to locate other venues for classroom space. Pine Grove United Methodist Church made its space available for the Lake Swamp Baptist School's seventh grade, even though the church had received a memo from state denominational leaders advising against such action. In February 1970, only weeks before massive integration was set to take place across the state, Methodist leaders on the church's statewide Board of Christian Social Concerns disseminated a letter to ministers in South Carolina regarding the use of Methodist church buildings for private schools: "In some sections of our state private schools are being organized in response to court-ordered desegregation of public schools," the memo read. "Methodist churches may be asked for the use of their buildings and facilities by these privately operated schools. As 'pastor in charge,' the minister of the local congregation has the final authority regarding the use of church facilities."[80]

Although not expressly forbidden to use their church buildings for private schools, the South Carolina Board of Christian Social Concerns included four pages of material for ministers' consideration that suggested doing so would not be in the church's best financial or spiritual interests. "As you arrive at your decision and exercise your responsibility in the light of your conscience, please know that we share the heavy weight of your responsibility," the letter concluded.[81] Weighing his options, the pastor of Pine Grove United Methodist Church apparently thought it best to reflect the desires of white families in the community in supporting the private school, demonstrating that even in the 1970s local pastors continued to understand the importance of adhering to the racial sensitivities of their congregations rather than following the racial inclusiveness of denominational leaders. Baptist leaders responded similarly as their Methodist counterparts. Editors of Baptist state newspapers also adopted a resolution in February 1970 to "respectfully remind churches and individuals of the serious financial, racial, political, social, and religious dangers involved in conducting private schools in church buildings to avoid integration in public schools."[82] Nevertheless, Lake Swamp Baptist went forward with the school.

For his part, the pastor of Lake Swamp Baptist Church hoped that the creation of his school did not give the wrong impression. Pastor Ed Duncan told a reporter that his church's establishment of a private school had nothing to do with desegregation in and of itself. At issue was the timing of the desegregation. "Now, some got the idea it [setting up the private school] was done through racial prejudice. If the government had waited until summer and done this the following fall, there wouldn't have been anything like as much trouble," Duncan surmised. "The public would permit token integration," the Baptist minister continued, "but it's when a school isn't a white school anymore that you have a problem."[83] One of the community members who had participated in attacking the school buses carrying black students echoed the pastor's sentiments that race was not the primary issue at stake in the controversy. "It definitely was never a race issue," Jeryl Best told a reporter. "It's simply the matter of education, quality of education. I'm not going to get my daughter drug down in her education."[84]

Under its founders' original plan, the Lake Swamp Baptist School was to be opened only for the remainder of the 1970 school year, homage to the idea that it was the timing rather than integration that was the real impetus behind the school. But the private school proved to be more popular than perhaps anticipated, and many white families in the community clamored for it to remain open. By 1973, it had moved out of the Baptist church and was housed in a former furniture renovation factory that had previously been owned by the Darlington Country School District; it also had joined the SCISA.[85]

As overtly racist pronouncements became publicly rare in the state by the mid-1970s, many South Carolinians sounded seemingly sincere appeals for private education. Some parents saw private education as good and necessary regardless of its ties to segregation, past or present. "Parents are prohibited from giving their children the school environment they would like," one South Carolina father noted. "When pupils are bused away from their communities to achieve the kind of integration our courts seem to desire, it not only hurts the child, but it hurts the community socially. . . . It is not so much the integration but rather the environment in the public schools to which

I object."[86] One South Carolina mother spoke for many who were growing tired of the constant association between private schools and racism: "It is a little exasperating that 'private school' has become a dirty word, synonymous with racism and sin."[87] By 1975, for many South Carolina parents private schools were not likely regarded as intentionally segregationist havens, despite the institutions' history. They were instead viewed as something necessary to make sure the white sons and daughters of South Carolina received the best education available, thereby fulfilling their God-given duty to their children.

But in the end, the southern private academies of the late 1960s and early 1970s cannot be understood apart from their segregationist origins. In a 1972 interview, the founder of Clarendon Hall, a private school in Summerton, South Carolina, claimed that the school—which operated in the county in which *Briggs v. Elliot* originated—"was started not so much because of integration as [it was] the Supreme Court decisions on prayer and teaching the Bible in school."[88] Although this kind of justification for private schools was becoming popular in the 1970s, it is notable that such rhetoric came from the staunch Christian segregationist S. Emory Rogers, a lawyer who had argued for segregated schools before the Supreme Court in 1954 and later served as the president of the South Carolina Association of Citizens' Councils. In addition, Rogers published an influential pamphlet on the compatibility of Christian love and segregation that circulated across the South in the 1960s.

Clarendon Hall's enrollment history suggests a different reason for the school's success than those offered by Rogers. When Clarendon Hall opened in conjunction with a Baptist church in 1968, 127 students attended; the following year enrollment stood at 124. In 1970, however, the first year Clarendon County saw significant school integration, Clarendon Hall's student body swelled to 434 pupils. By 1972, enrollment topped 500, and the school was no longer associated with the Baptist church.[89] That enrollment at Clarendon Hall exploded after desegregation and continued to grow even when the school was no longer operated by the Baptist church casts doubts on the idea that concerns about school prayer and Bible readings were the primary motivation behind the county's largest private academy. Another factor remained unmentioned in Rogers's analysis whose import to Clarendon Hall's success was likely more pivotal: black students.

By the early 1970s the South teemed with schools like Clarendon Hall that were created in the years between 1954 and 1973 as first the threat and then the realization of school desegregation spread throughout the region. As southern author Walker Percy noted in his novel *Love in the Ruins*, written during the heyday of the private school movement, these institutions were founded "on religious and patriotic principles and to keep Negroes out."[90] In this description, Percy perhaps used one conjunction too many. Schools "founded on religious and patriotic principles *to* keep Negroes out" would have been a more accurate description of the segregationist academy movement that took hold in the South by the mid-1960s.

The private schools that sprang up across the South during this period are the most significant artifacts from the Jim Crow era. Unlike poll taxes and "whites only" signs that have vanished after federal intervention, many of the private schools specifically created to avoid desegregation still exist today, a lasting testament—albeit one rarely acknowledged—to white Christians' historic discomfort with racial mixing and their enduring ability to avoid it.

Epilogue

The Heirs of Segregationist Christianity

On a spring day in 1968, President Lyndon Johnson welcomed members of the Southern Baptist Convention's (SBC's) Christian Life Commission (CLC) to the White House Rose Garden. The CLC members were in Washington, DC, as part of the commission's Christian citizenship seminar, whose purpose that year was to explore factors contributing to racism and urban unrest.[1] Five years earlier, John F. Kennedy had invited religious leaders to the East Room of the White House, hoping to gain their assistance in passing a strong civil rights act. Following his predecessor's lead, Johnson was hosting Christian leaders in hopes of mobilizing them for the common good: "We believe—in fact we think we know—that the past few years have been a time of considerable progress that history will take due note of," Johnson told the Southern Baptists that cloudy afternoon in 1968.[2] Johnson was not wrong; the efforts of black Americans had forced the federal government into action over the previous half decade and, as a result, had changed the country. Fire hoses, police dogs, bombings, and beatings had been the cost for legislation that ensured for the first time that all Americans, regardless of race, would have equal access to public facilities. Black Americans had similarly wrested the power of the ballot away from the white supremacists who for generations had kept their right to vote from them. That right had also come at a high price for the protestors who suffered tear gas, nightsticks, and even death in their quest for voting rights. Yet those atrocities had swayed the nation's conscience and helped secure at last the vote for black southerners. With legislative accomplishments like the 1964 Civil Rights Act and the 1965 Voting Rights Act, Johnson could rightly claim racial progress since Kennedy's meeting with religious leaders in 1963.

Johnson, however, was not content with his "considerable progress" but resolved to press on, announcing in the Rose Garden that despite the achievements, "we know that there must be even more work and even more rapid progress in the days ahead."[3] Although his administration was actively

The Bible Told Them So. J. Russell Hawkins, Oxford University Press. © Oxford University Press 2021.
DOI: 10.1093/oso/9780197571064.003.0007

considering next steps, solving completely the lingering problem of racism that still plagued the country was a task, Johnson told his guests that day, that "lies far beyond these government programs. The only lasting solution won't cost a cent," the president continued, "but it is going to be, really, the hardest to achieve. It will require, actually, a great change—a change in men's hearts—in the way that men treat their neighbors. It will require a change in men's eyes—in the way they see their neighbors. There, my dear friends, is where each of you can come in," Johnson told the Southern Baptists. "You are teachers. You are preachers. You are religious leaders of a great congregation in a great section of this country, the American South."[4] Reiterating talking points from previous speeches, Johnson highlighted that racism was not a southern problem or a northern problem, but simply an American problem. Even still, the Texan confessed, "Because much of that American problem began in the region which you and I call home, I would like the solutions to begin there, too. So I am glad that each of you has shown your concern about it. I am looking to you for action and for leadership and for inspiration."[5]

President Kennedy had summoned religious leaders to the White House to ask for their help in changing the book of law. Now, Johnson was content to seek Southern Baptist aid in changing people's hearts. This change in requests was significant and fitting. By the late 1960s, southern white Christians were leaning ever more into individualistic "heart changes" that trafficked in appeals to colorblindness to address—or ignore—racism. Such appeals were rooted in desires to avoid further structural reforms of their churches, their schools, and their society. A few weeks after Johnson's meeting with the Southern Baptists in the Rose Garden, the latter reassembled in Houston, Texas, for their annual convention and elected W. A. Criswell president of the SBC, a fitting choice for the new era of colorblindness toward race.

Wallie Amos Criswell was well suited for the work of individual heart change for which Johnson was hoping from southern white Christians in 1968, for Criswell was a living embodiment of the transformation that segregationist Christianity had undergone in the civil rights period. By the late 1960s, Criswell had enjoyed a long and distinguished career, having first risen to national prominence in the early 1950s as the pastor of the First Baptist Church of Dallas, the largest SBC congregation in the country. Because of his influential position, Criswell was often invited to guest preach in pulpits around the country. One such particularly important address occurred in February 1956, when the South Carolina Baptist Convention's annual evangelism conference featured Criswell as a speaker.[6] Criswell's appearance in

South Carolina corresponded with the growing backlash to the *Brown* decision among white Christians in the state. Perhaps that was the reason that Criswell used his sermon before a packed sanctuary in the First Baptist Church of Columbia—the same space where South Carolina Baptists eight years later would vote to keep their colleges segregated—to attack racial integration, "as a denial of all that we believe in."[7] Criswell believed that the book of Genesis had made clear that blacks were intended to be a servant race and therefore should not mix with whites.[8] Accordingly, in his sermon at the evangelism conference, Criswell blasted the NAACP as "two-by scathing, good-for-nothing fellows who are trying to upset all of the things that we love as good old Southern people and as good old Southern Baptists," and declared that people who were pushing for integration "are just as blasphemous and unbiblical as they can be."[9]

George Bell Timmerman Jr. was among those listening to Criswell's sermon in the Columbia First Baptist sanctuary. Timmerman, the staunch segregationist governor of South Carolina whose father had been instrumental in having Jackson Stafford dismissed from his pulpit the year before, was so impressed with Criswell that he invited the pastor to give an address before the state legislature the following day. Criswell accepted. Strom Thurmond, riding a wave of popularity due to his recently announced Southern Manifesto that had committed southern senators and congressmen to resisting integration, was coincidentally back in his home state at the time of Criswell's visit. Thurmond lent additional importance to the Texan's address to the joint session of the legislature when the well-regarded South Carolina senator introduced Criswell.[10]

Criswell's address to the South Carolina lawmakers was essentially a repeat of the previous day's denunciation of integrationists and those trying to change southerners' way of life, but this second address drew more attention. When Dallas newspapers published selections of Criswell's remarks in South Carolina, his hometown press praised the preacher for his forthright defense of segregation. Meanwhile, Criswell's best-known parishioner, Billy Graham, found it necessary to distance himself from his minister: "My Pastor and I have never seen eye to eye on the race question," Graham told reporters.[11] Given the evangelist's growing stature in American society, Graham likely hoped his personal pastor's remarks in South Carolina would fade quickly from public memory; such was not to be. Instead, Criswell's address took on a life of its own after copies of his speech to the South Carolina legislature were printed and would for years be distributed throughout the South by Citizens' Councils who were no doubt happy to have Billy Graham's pastor on record against race mixing.

By 1968, the times had changed, and on the eve of Criswell's election to the SBC presidency, the pastor belatedly changed with them. Anticipating that his rise to the pinnacle of the nation's largest Protestant body would prompt questions about his past racial views, Criswell held an emergency meeting with his church deacons a week before the convention to implement a new nonracially exclusive open-door policy at the First Baptist Church of Dallas. This decision was well timed because, as Criswell had suspected, in his meeting with reporters following his election as SBC president, questions indeed arose whether he still held the same segregationist beliefs that had garnered him so much attention in South Carolina twelve years earlier. "I've changed," Criswell responded to reporters, adding, "I have enlarged my sympathies and my heart during the past few years."[12] In other words, Criswell had purportedly done the hard work to which Lyndon Johnson had called Southern Baptists in the Rose Garden just weeks before: a change of racial perspective through a change of heart.

In his SBC presidential sermon in 1969, Criswell touted the same remedy for solving racism that he had supposedly employed himself: " 'Old Time Religion.' Makes me love everybody, it'll take us all to heaven, it's good enough for me," Criswell quoted from the gospel standard. "Makes me love everybody," Criswell again emphasized before turning to specifics using a different well-known melody: "Red and yellow black and white, they are precious in His sight, Jesus loved the many peoples of the world. The arms of the cross outstretched, wide, wide open; far as the east goes east and the west goes west, the arms of our Lord outstretched to the whole earth. And like our Savior," Criswell told the gathered Baptists, "our arms are outstretched: open arms, open hearts, open doors, open churches, open schools, open colleges, open seminaries. As wide as the world is wide, our arms are outstretched to the peoples of the earth."[13] Criswell's presidential sermon was the perfect distillation of colorblind individualism: by allowing that "old time religion" to transform one's heart, white Christians would be able to move past the now supposedly unimportant barriers of race and love everyone equally.[14] As this book has argued, however, the emergence of colorblindness among southern white Christians in the late 1960s must be understood within the historical context of segregation. Criswell's life proves instructive on this point as well. Three years after his presidential address, Criswell conceded in an unpublished oral memoir that the segregationist position he espoused before the South Carolina legislature in 1956 represented his views much longer than his public sentiments would indicate. "My soul and attitude may not have changed," Criswell confessed, "but my public statements did."[15] As historian Curtis Freeman points out, Criswell's statement was "a stunning admission that indicates his 'change' may have been more a matter of social decorum than personal conviction."[16] Evidence that Criswell's newfound colorblindness may not have been as radically transformative for his perspectives on race was further evident when desegregation came to Dallas schools. Speaking on the topic in 1984—twenty-eight years after he railed against it in South Carolina—Criswell confessed, "I've had to accommodate my spirit to it, but I still am against some of it, like busing. The associations you make, you and your family, it has to come out of your heart."[17]

The life of W. A. Criswell perfectly captures the transformation and persistence of segregationist Christianity in the civil rights era. Criswell's address before the South Carolina legislature in 1956 was emblematic of white southerners who interpreted the Bible to support segregation and held fast to those convictions, gripping such beliefs even stronger after the *Brown* decision as they fought the civil rights movement occurring around them. Despite these white Christians' efforts to save Jim Crow, legal segregation ended in the South and changed how polite society discussed the topic. Criswell's admission—"*My soul and attitude may not have changed, but my public statements did*"—could be said of a generation of white Christians who came of age with segregationist theology but by the mid-1960s found themselves in a world that no longer tolerated public espousals of such ideas. Instead of jettisoning this theology, these Christians repackaged it. In 1956, white Christians like Criswell could denounce integration as unbiblical. But once the force of law made integration unavoidable, the reasons for opposing it changed: it now undermined God-given parental authority. As it was for Criswell—"*I've had to accommodate my spirit to it, but I still am against some of it. . . . The associations you make, you and your family, it has to come out of your heart*"—so it was for countless other southern white Christians who embraced the new "colorblind" perspective that viewed imposed integration, whether in churches or schools, as damaging to race relations. Such integration ultimately threatened the sanctity of families by exposing them to something they were not prepared to accept. Only when individuals arrived at a sincere desire to associate with others of a different race—that is, only when racial difference lost all meaning through the embrace of colorblindness—could the problems caused by racism be addressed.

But constituted in this way, colorblindness was always a dead end because it reduced and reclassified the problem of race to metrics of personal feelings rather than structural realities. According to the logic of colorblindness, a person's ill will toward others was the central problem and could only be remedied through transformed feelings. But a change of feelings does not automatically lead to an elimination of racial discrimination in the systemic and structural realms where access to material resources and political power are unequally distributed along racial lines. It is entirely possible, for instance, for a society to exist in which no one has a "racist bone" in their body and yet racial disparities in wealth, privilege, opportunities, and prestige still abound. Furthermore, as this book has shown, such a society was precisely the original point of the colorblind perspective. For segregationist Christians like Criswell who promoted colorblindness in the late 1960s, the rhetoric was about plausible deniability, not racial justice.

Decades later, some of the heirs of those segregationist Christians began pursuing the racial justice their forebears had fought. Six decades after the *Brown* decision first ignited southern white Christians' long defense of segregation, a political scientist published a study of a growing movement among conservative evangelical Christians who hoped to bring about racial healing in the United States this side of heaven. According to Nancy Wadsworth, the study's author, participants in this racial justice movement sought to "foster a body of believers who know how to identify and dismantle racist attitudes, beliefs, and behaviors, and are able, wherever feasible, to thrive in racially and ethnically heterogeneous, culturally syncretic congregations in which no single worship or leadership style dominates."[18] The effort toward creating multiracial churches has borne significant fruit. Between 2000 and 2019, the number of multiracial evangelical congregations in the United States tripled.[19] In a reversal of the biblical interpretations that segregationist Christians promoted a half-century earlier, these latter-day conservative Christians embrace racial diversity as a biblical command.[20]

And yet, studies find that the majority of white Christians who attend multiracial churches are actually more likely than non-Christians to reentrench the racial divisions these evangelicals claim they are interested in overcoming.[21] Wadsworth, for instance, found that the evangelicals she studied were curiously unconcerned with pursuing racial justice at a structural or systemic level.[22] Rather than advocate for a change of laws, or push to implement new social policies, or adopt different institutional practices that would mitigate the racial inequities that persist in the United States, the vast majority of white Christians in the evangelical racial justice movement and in this new crop of multiracial churches choose to address racism by pursuing racial reconciliation *between individuals*. In this way, these white Christians have identified racial injustice as a continuing problem but believe the way to solve this problem is simply by building relationships across racial lines. These are not the Christians in the East Room during the Kennedy years, marshalling their social capital to help pass new legislation. Rather, these contemporary white evangelicals are the Southern Baptists of Lyndon Johnson's Rose Garden, hoping for social change one heart transformation at a time.

This ineffective strategy of racial justice is due in part to the persistence of the individualistic colorblind approach to racial issues championed by segregationist Christians of an earlier generation. As colorblind rhetoric metastasized among conservative white Christians in the early years of the twenty-first century, it reinforced the racial separatism its original proponents had intended the century before. Such separatism lingers today—albeit unintentionally—even with white Christians who desire to see racial unity in their society. As sociologists Michael Emerson and Christian Smith explain, "Many race issues that white evangelicals want to see solved are generated in part by the way they themselves do religion, interpret their world, and live their own lives."[23] Emerson and Smith identify three components of contemporary white evangelical theology and practice that are primary contributors to the difficulty in bridging racial divides in American churches and society: "Accountable free will individualism, relationalism (attaching central importance to interpersonal relationships), and antistructuralism (inability to perceive or unwillingness to accept social structural influences)."[24] According to Emerson and Smith, these basic rudiments of conservative white Christians' faith "direct them to see the world individualistically . . . and to desire a color-blind society."[25] This dual emphasis on individualism and colorblindness has ironically led modern-day white evangelicals to believe that *overcoming* racism requires something akin to the very strategy segregationist Christians called for when trying to *avoid* racial integration in the late 1960s: "natural affinities, mutual appreciation of each other's merits and the voluntary association of individuals."[26]

Most black Christians, however, view the world differently than white evangelicals and believe that ending racism necessitates addressing structural and systemic racism, the disparities that exist in opportunities,

privilege, and power along racial lines within American institutions and society. But because of the significant influence of individualism, relationalism,
and anti-structuralism, conservative white Christians often fail to even recognize the *existence* of structural and systemic racism, let alone conceive of
ways to address such inequality. As Emerson and Smith note, emphases on
individualism and attempts at colorblindness lead white evangelicals "to as-
sess the race problem in divergent and nonreconciliatory ways" from black
Christians. The sociologists conclude that "this large gulf in understanding
is perhaps part of the race problem's core, and most certainly contributes
to the entrenchment of the racialized society."[27] Ironically, then, although a
growing number of conservative white Christians profess a desire to solve
the problem of race, they are hindered in such efforts by the colorblind theology they inherited from their segregationist forebears.

To say contemporary white evangelicals are influenced by their past is to
say something unremarkable. We all are products of our history. Southern
white Christians of the twentieth century lived in a world shaped profoundly
by their nineteenth-century predecessors, as the opening vignettes in each
chapter of this book have demonstrated. The placement of the Confederate
statue in Orangeburg and the celebration of the Lost Cause it commemo-
rated helped shape the way the First Baptist congregation across the street
viewed the world and forced Fred Laughon from his pulpit. The exodus
of free blacks from Camden First Baptist Church after the Civil War gave
the white parishioners left behind the racial isolation necessary to develop
a robust theology of segregation they would adamantly defend after 1954.
South Carolinians' decision to leave the Union to protect slavery in the
1860s influenced Baptist efforts a century later to protect segregation at
Furman. The legacy of the *Plessy* decision was partially responsible for white
Methodists' fight to keep their South Carolina annual conferences separate but equal. And the veneration of a white supremacist Civil War general
helped explain why the parents of Wade Hampton Academy were willing to
establish a school named in his honor to avoid desegregated classrooms. All
individuals are influenced by the history that precedes them. As it was for
southern white Christians in the last century, so it is for their heirs today.
White evangelicals who champion racial justice through individual heart
changes, or reconciled relationships, or appeals to colorblindness are using
the tools fashioned and utilized by their segregationist forebears precisely to
avoid the racial justice their descendents now seek. It should not surprise us,

therefore, that studies find these latter-day racial reconciliation efforts fall spectacularly short of their goals.[28]

Achieving the racial justice so many conservative white Christians today purportedly desire will require them to forge new tools and adopt new approaches, starting perhaps with an acknowledgment of their history and attentiveness to that history's lasting residue. The evangelical world these Christians inhabit has been shaped in part by a segregationist Christianity whose influence lingers on unrecognized today. If segregationist theology justified fighting the desegregation of Christian colleges and universities, its historical residue is seen in the cultural and structural homogeneity of such institutions today.[29] If segregationist theology justified the adoption of colorblind individualistic rhetoric to mask its intent during a time of social change, its historical residue lives on in the ridicule of "identity politics" and dismissive response to systemic racism by conservative white Christians today.[30] If segregationist theology justified an abandonment of desegregating public schools for the sake of white children, its historical residue can be felt in the resegregation of American public schools to unprecedented levels while white evangelical children are taught at home or enrolled in private schools.[31] And if segregationist theology justified maintaining the color line in church sanctuaries, its historical residue explains recent surveys reporting that, while 11:00 Sunday morning continues to be the most segregated hour of the week, most white Christians are just fine with that.[32]

In the closing decades of the twentieth century, John Perkins, a self-identified black evangelical Christian, embarked on a ministry of racial reconciliation among Christians of his native South. As he traveled throughout his home region sharing his vision of reconciled lives and beloved community, Perkins discovered that many of the white conservative Christians who embraced his message did so without expressing repentance. "I find that they want my relationship, but they want more to quickly forget the brutality and the injustice that their people put upon many of us in the name of Christianity," Perkins wrote in his 1976 autobiography.[33] Perkins's words continue to resonate today. White evangelicals desiring a solution to the problem of race would do well to begin their search for answers by acknowledging and addressing the "brutality and the injustice" of the segregationist theology that has so deeply shaped their past even as it continues to influence their present.

Notes

Introduction

1. Martin Luther King Jr. quoted in Taylor Branch, *Parting the Waters: America in the King Years 1954–1963* (New York: Simon and Schuster), 822 (first quote); "Memorandum for the President June 14, 1963," Box 97, Folder "Meeting with Religious Leaders," President's Office Files: Civil Rights, John F. Kennedy Library (second quote).

2. "Meeting of the President with Religious Leaders, June 17, 1963," Box 97, Folder "Meeting with Religious Leaders," President's Office Files: Civil Rights, John F. Kennedy Library. The meeting is briefly mentioned in two books by senior Kennedy aides. See Theodore C. Sorenson, *Kennedy* (New York: Harper and Row, 1965), 501–2; and Arthur M. Schlesinger Jr., *A Thousand Days: John F. Kennedy in the White House* (Boston: Houghton Mifflin, 1965), 966–67.

3. "Meeting of the President with Religious Leaders, June 17, 1963," Box 97, Folder "Meeting with Religious Leaders," President's Office Files: Civil Rights, John F. Kennedy Library.

4. "Meeting of the President with Religious Leaders, June 17, 1963," Box 97, Folder "Meeting with Religious Leaders," President's Office Files: Civil Rights, John F. Kennedy Library. In the same folder with the transcript of the meeting between Kennedy and the religious leaders is a two-page memo that Albert Garner wrote to the president that further explained the position he vocalized during the meeting in the East Room. Garner's memo suggested three points for Kennedy to consider: "FIRST, It is our finding that segregation was the social pattern of life of the Old Testament Hebrew people, long followed with much glory to their history. This social pattern was given and administered by Divine Command. SECOND, It is our finding that PRIOR TO THIS CENTURY neither the Hebrew Religion, the Christian Religion, nor ANY DENOMINATION OF THE CHRISTIAN RELIGION ever held that integration of the races into a close social pattern was necessary to obey God or follow the teachings of Jesus Christ. THIRD, It is our finding that the philosophy of close social integration of the races, prior to this century, has been basically held and promoted by anti-Christian religions, atheists, and infidels." Garner ended his memorandum by telling Kennedy, "We shall pray that God may strengthen you and guide you as you face the racial crisis of the hour and that the decisions you make can be justified by the Word of God and experiences of Historical Christianity." Albert Garner, "Segregation Memento to the President of the USA," Box 97, Folder "Meeting with Religious Leaders," President's Office Files: Civil Rights, John F. Kennedy Library.

5. Sorenson, *Kennedy*, 502 (first quote); "Meeting of the President with Religious Leaders, June 17, 1963," Box 97, Folder "Meeting with Religious Leaders," President's Office Files: Civil Rights, John F. Kennedy Library (second quote).

6. "Meeting of the President with Religious Leaders, June 17, 1963," Box 97, Folder "Meeting with Religious Leaders," President's Office Files: Civil Rights, John F. Kennedy Library.

7. "Meeting of the President with Religious Leaders, June 17, 1963," Box 97, Folder "Meeting with Religious Leaders," President's Office Files: Civil Rights, John F. Kennedy Library.

8. Hobson A. Wolfe to Strom Thurmond, August 22, 1963, Box 4, Folder "Civil Rights Legislation 5," Subject Correspondence 1963, Mss 100, Strom Thurmond Collection, Special Collections, Clemson University Libraries.

9. C. W. Kemmerlin to Strom Thurmond, August 3, 1963, Box 4, Folder "Civil Rights Legislation 5," Subject Correspondence 1963, Mss 100, Strom Thurmond Collection, Special Collections, Clemson University Libraries.

10. Schlesinger, *A Thousand Days*, 924.

11. David L. Chappell, *A Stone of Hope: Prophetic Religion and the Death of Jim Crow* (Chapel Hill: University of North Carolina Press, 2004); Lewis V. Baldwin, *The Voice of Conscience: The Church in the Mind of Martin Luther King, Jr.* (New York: Oxford University Press, 2010).

12. Chappell, *Stone of Hope*, 44–66.

13. The terms "evangelical," "conservative white Christians," and "conservative white Protestants" I use interchangeably throughout this book.

14. John Shelton Reed, *The Enduring South: Subcultural Persistence in Mass Society* (Chapel Hill: University of North Carolina Press, 1972), 58–59. For further statistical evidence of evangelicalism's dominance in the South during the mid-twentieth century, see Edwin S. Gaustad, "Religious Demography of the South," in *Religion in the Solid South*, ed. Samuel S. Hill Jr. (Nashville: Abingdon Press, 1972), 143–78.

15. Samuel S. Hill, *Southern Churches in Crisis* (Tuscaloosa: University of Alabama Press, 1966), 39.

16. Mark Newman, *Getting Right with God: Southern Baptists and Desegregation, 1945–1995* (Tuscaloosa: University of Alabama Press, 2001), viii.

17. Ironically, a chief proponent of nullifying religion's importance to the anti–civil rights movement is historian David L. Chappell, who has persuasively argued for the importance of prophetic Christianity in the civil rights movement's success. Having published numerous chapters, articles, and a book on the subject, Chappell has contributed more pages of scholarship to the religious thought of southern segregationists than any other historian. By drawing on all that he has written about the subject, Chappell's thesis on white Christians' resistance to the civil rights movement is as follows: Integration proceeded relatively swiftly in the South because the southern white churches "failed in any meaningful way to join the anti-civil rights movement" and "gave no significant support to segregation." Because the clear biblical mandate that had existed for pro-slavery theologians in slavery debates of the antebellum period had no comparable validity for segregationists in the twentieth

century, segregationists were left on tenuous theological ground when seeking to prove the practice's divine sanction. The justifications for segregation that southern whites were able to extract from the Bible were therefore strained to the point that "segregationists do not seem to have had much confidence in these biblical or theological arguments and did not use them much." Ultimately, the inability of southern religious leaders to articulate any viable defense of segregation was a primary reason segregation in the South failed. See Chappell, *A Stone of Hope,* 107 (first and third quotes). David L. Chappell, "Religious Ideas of the Segregationists," *Journal of American Studies* 32, no. 2 (1998): 239 (second quote). Chappell also explores the religious beliefs of segregationists in David L. Chappell, "Disunity and Religious Institutions in the White South," in *Massive Resistance: Southern Opposition to the Second Reconstruction,* ed. Clive Webb (Oxford: Oxford University Press, 2005), 136–50. Chappell's claims loom large in publications exploring white evangelical resistance to black civil rights over the previous decade.

18. For instance, Carolyn Renee DuPont, *Mississippi Praying: Southern White Evangelical and the Civil Rights Movement, 1945–1975* (New York: New York University Press, 2013); Stephen R. Haynes, *The Last Segregated Hour: The Memphis Kneel-Ins and the Campaign for Southern Church Desegregation* (New York: Oxford University Press, 2012); Carter Dalton Lyon, *Sanctuaries of Segregation: The Story of the Jackson Church Visit Campaign* (Jackson: University Press of Mississippi, 2017); Joseph T. Reiff, *Born of Conviction: White Methodists and Mississippi's Closed Society* (New York: Oxford University Press, 2016); and Ansley L. Quiros, *God with Us: Lived Theology and the Freedom Struggle in Americus, Georgia 1942–1976* (Chapel Hill: University of North Carolina Press, 2018); Joseph Crespino, *In Search of Another Country: Mississippi and the Conservative Counterrevolution* (Princeton, NJ: Princeton University Press, 2007), 144–72; and Charles Marsh, *God's Long Summer: Stories of Faith and Civil Rights* (Princeton, NJ: Princeton University Press, 1997). In addition to these, other historians have conducted studies of the racial attitudes of various religious denominations. Though ancillary to their projects, some information about the specific role religion played in defending segregation can be culled from these historians' works. See, for instance, Peter Murray, *Methodists and the Crucible of Race 1930–1975* (Columbia: University of Missouri Press, 2004); Donald E. Collins, *When the Church Bell Rang Racist: The Methodist Church and the Civil Rights Movement in Alabama* (Macon, GA: Mercer University Press, 1998); Gardiner H. Shattuck, *Episcopalians and Race: Civil War to Civil Rights* (Lexington: University of Kentucky Press, 2000); Joel L. Alvis, *Race and Religion: Southern Presbyterians, 1946–1983* (Tuscaloosa: University of Alabama Press, 1994); and Newman, *Getting Right with God.* Two chronological histories of religion in Mississippi and Southern Baptists in Alabama also contain helpful chapters in discerning southern white religion's endorsement of Jim Crow. See Randy J. Sparks, *Religion in Mississippi* (Jackson: University Press of Mississippi, 2001), 221–47; and Wayne Flynt, *Alabama Baptists: Southern Baptists in the Heart of Dixie* (Tuscaloosa: University of Alabama Press, 1998), 455–516.

19. Historian Paul Harvey coined the term "segregationist folk theology" in *Freedom's Coming: Religious Culture and the Shaping of the South from the Civil War through the*

Civil Rights Era (Chapel Hill: University of North Carolina Press, 2005). Harvey also explicates the idea of segregationist theology in "Religion, Race, and the Right in the South, 1945–1990," in *Politics and Religion in the White South,* ed. Glenn Feldman (Lexington: University Press of Kentucky, 2005), 101–23; and in "God and Negroes and Jesus and Sin and Salvation: Racism, Racial Interchange, and Interracialism in Southern Religious History," in *Religion in the American South: Protestants and Others in History and Culture,* ed. Beth Barton Schweiger and Donald G. Mathews (Chapel Hill: University of North Carolina Press, 2004), 285–91. Although my scholarship is deeply informed by Harvey's, I chose to exclude the term "folk" from my description of this religious belief system, calling it simply "segregationist theology."

20. Nathan O. Hatch, "Evangelicalism as a Democratic Movement," in *Evangelicalism and Modern America,* ed. George Marsden (Grand Rapids, MI: Eerdmans Publishing Company, 1984), 79.

21. James Baldwin, "The White Man's Guilt," in *James Baldwin Collected Essays,* ed. Toni Morrison (New York: Library of America, 1998), 723.

Chapter 1

1. "Sherman's March into Orangeburg Marked at River," *Orangeburg Times and Democrat* (June 28, 2014), https://thetandd.com/100_objects/objects-day-sherman-s-march-into-orangeburg-marked-at-river/article_458f73ec-fe69-11e3-9a14-001a4bcf887a.html (accessed July 14, 2019).

2. A history of the First Baptist Church can be found at http://fbcorangeburg.org/who-we-are/history/ (accessed June 19, 2014).

3. Information about the Orangeburg Confederate memorial is available at http://www.waymarking.com/waymarks/WM9PC0_Orangeburg_Confederate_Monument_Orangeburg_SC (accessed June 19, 2014).

4. *The Laruens Advertiser* (October 24, 1893) online at https://chroniclingamerica.loc.gov/lccn/sn93067760/1893-10-24/ed-1/seq-1/# (accessed June 15, 2018).

5. *The Laruens Advertiser* (October 24, 1893) online at https://chroniclingamerica.loc.gov/lccn/sn93067760/1893-10-24/ed-1/seq-1/# (accessed June 15, 2018).

6. A history of the First Baptist can be found at http://fbcorangeburg.org/who-we-are/history/ (accessed June 19, 2014). Information about the Orangeburg Confederate memorial is available at http://www.waymarking.com/waymarks/WM9PC0_Orangeburg_Confederate_Monument_Orangeburg_SC (accessed June 19, 2014).

7. Fred Laughon to A. C. Miller, June 25, 1957, Box 21, Folder "Race Relations Letters Expressing Alarm or Opposition 1957," Christian Life Commission Papers, Southern Baptist Historical Library and Archives.

8. Fred Laughon to A. C. Miller, June 25, 1957, Box 21, Folder "Race Relations Letters Expressing Alarm or Opposition 1957," Christian Life Commission Papers, Southern Baptist Historical Library and Archives.

9. Fred Laughon to A. C. Miller, June 25, 1957, Box 21, Folder "Race Relations Letters Expressing Alarm or Opposition 1957," Christian Life Commission Papers, Southern Baptist Historical Library and Archives.

10. J. Nates Blanton to Brooks Hays, June 27, 1957, Box 21, Folder "Race Relations Letters Expressing Alarm or Opposition 1957," Christian Life Commission Papers, Southern Baptist Historical Library and Archives; "Resolution of First Baptist Church, Orangeburg, SC," Box 21, Folder "Race Relations Letters Expressing Alarm or Opposition 1957," Christian Life Commission Papers, Southern Baptist Historical Library and Archives; *Baptist Courier* (October 31, 1957), 14.

11. Fred Laughon to A. C. Miller, July 17, 1957, Box 21, Folder "Race Relations Letters Expressing Alarm or Opposition 1957," Christian Life Commission Papers, Southern Baptist Historical Library and Archives.

12. Fred Laughon to A. C. Miller, June 25, 1957, Box 21, Folder "Race Relations Letters Expressing Alarm or Opposition 1957," Christian Life Commission Papers, Southern Baptist Historical Library and Archives; Fred Laughon to A. C. Miller, July 15, 1957, Box 21, Folder "Race Relations Letters Expressing Alarm or Opposition 1957," Christian Life Commission Papers, Southern Baptist Historical Library and Archives.

13. Fred Laughon to A. C. Miller, July 17, 1957, Box 21, Folder "Race Relations Letters Expressing Alarm or Opposition 1957," Christian Life Commission Papers, Southern Baptist Historical Library and Archives.

14. Charles Reagan Wilson, *Baptized in Blood: The Religion of the Lost Cause 1865–1920* (Athens: University of Georgia Press, 2009), 16.

15. For a sampling of the historiography of antebellum proslavery theology see John Patrick Daly, *When Slavery Was Called Freedom: Evangelicalism, Proslavery, and the Causes of the Civil War* (Lexington: University Press of Kentucky, 2002); Eugene D. Genovese, *The Slaveholders' Dilemma: Freedom and Progress in Southern Conservative Thought, 1820–1860* (Columbia: University of South Carolina Press, 1992); Genovese, *A Consuming Fire: The Fall of the Confederacy in the Mind of the White Christian South* (Athens: University of Georgia Press, 1998); Elizabeth Fox-Genovese and Eugene D. Genovese, *The Mind of the Master Class: History and Faith in the Southern Slaveholders' Worldview* (New York: Cambridge University Press, 2005); Charles F. Irons, *The Origins of Proslavery Christianity: White and Black Evangelicals in Colonial and Antebellum Virginia* (Chapel Hill: University of North Carolina Press, 2008); Mark A. Noll, *The Civil War as a Theological Crisis* (Chapel Hill: University of North Carolina Press, 2006); and Mark A. Noll, *America's God, From Jonathan Edwards to Abraham Lincoln* (New York: Oxford University Press, 2002), 367–401.

16. Luke E. Harlow, "Slavery, Race, and Political Ideology in the White Christian South Before and After the Civil War," in *Religion and American Politics: From the Colonial Period to the Present*, 2nd ed., ed. Mark A. Noll and Luke E. Harlow (New York: Oxford University Press, 2007), 212–20.

17. Quoted in Kenneth K. Bailey, *Southern White Protestantism in the Twentieth Century* (New York: Harper and Row, 1964), 140.

18. Quoted in Bailey, *Southern White Protestantism in the Twentieth Century*, 138.

19. Bailey, *Southern White Protestantism in the Twentieth Century*, 136–37.

20. Michael J. Klarman, "How Brown Changed Race Relations: The Backlash Thesis," *Journal of American History* 81 (June 1994): 81–118.

21. Ernest Queener Campbell and Thomas F. Pettigrew, *Christians in Racial Crisis: A Study of Little Rock's Ministry* (Washington, DC: Public Affairs Press, 1959), 137–38.

22. Campbell and Pettigrew, *Christians in Racial Crisis*, 137–38.

23. Mark Newman, *Getting Right with God: Southern Baptists and Desegregation, 1945-1995* (Tuscaloosa: University of Alabama Press, 2001), 24.

24. Audiotape Collection, Historical Commission of the Southern Baptist Convention.

25. Audiotape Collection, Historical Commission of the Southern Baptist Convention, quoted in Charles Marsh, *God's Long Summer: Stories of Faith and Civil Rights* (Princeton, NJ: Princeton University Press, 1997), 99.

26. Audiotape Collection, Historical Commission of the Southern Baptist Convention.

27. *Southern School News* (December 1954), 13; *Baptist Courier* (November 18, 1954), 24.

28. Mark Newman, "The Baptist State Convention of South Carolina and Desegregation, 1954-1971," *Baptist History and Heritage*, Spring 1999, 56. For a general examination of the disparity between the SBC and local churches across the South, see Newman, *Getting Right with God*.

29. Newman, "The Baptist State Convention of South Carolina and Desegregation," 58.

30. Ralph E. Lattimore to A. C. Miller, September 24, 1956, Box 20, Folder "Race Relations—Letters Expressing Alarm or Opposition (1956)," Christian Life Commission Resource Files, Southern Baptist Historical Library and Archives.

31. Ralph E. Lattimore to A. C. Miller, September 24, 1956, Box 20, Folder "Race Relations—Letters Expressing Alarm or Opposition (1956)," Christian Life Commission Resource Files, Southern Baptist Historical Library and Archives.

32. Ralph E. Lattimore to A. C. Miller, September 24, 1956, Box 20, Folder "Race Relations—Letters Expressing Alarm or Opposition (1956)," Christian Life Commission Resource Files, Southern Baptist Historical Library and Archives.

33. C. Doyle Burgess to the Christian Life Commission, April 24, 1956, Box 20, Folder "Race Relations—Letters Expressing Alarm or Opposition (1956)," Christian Life Commission Resource Files, Southern Baptist Historical Library and Archives.

34. Harry E. Dawkins to Rev. G. Avery Lee, September 21, 1956, Box 20, Folder "Race Relations—Letters Expressing Alarm or Opposition (1956)," Christian Life Commission Resource Files, Southern Baptist Historical Library and Archives.

35. G. P. Lanier to the Christian Life Commission, September 24, 1956, Box 20, Folder "Race Relations—Letters Expressing Alarm or Opposition (1956)," Christian Life Commission Resource Files, Southern Baptist Historical Library and Archives.

36. G. P. Lanier to the Christian Life Commission, September 24, 1956, Box 20, Folder "Race Relations—Letters Expressing Alarm or Opposition (1956)," Christian Life Commission Resource Files, Southern Baptist Historical Library and Archives.

37. G. P. Lanier to the Christian Life Commission, September 24, 1956, Box 20, Folder "Race Relations—Letters Expressing Alarm or Opposition (1956)," Christian Life Commission Resource Files, Southern Baptist Historical Library and Archives.

38. W. W. Lancaster to A. C. Miller, November 18, 1957, Box 21, Folder "Race Relations—Letters Expressing Alarm or Opposition (1957)," Christian Life Commission Papers, Southern Baptist Historical Library and Archives.

39. A. C. Miller to Dr. C. C. Warren, November 19, 1957, Box 21, Folder "Race Relations—Letters Expressing Alarm or Opposition (1957)," Christian Life Commission Papers, Southern Baptist Historical Library and Archives.

40. A. C. Miller to Dr. C. C. Warren, November 19, 1957, Box 21, Folder "Race Relations—Letters Expressing Alarm or Opposition (1957)," Christian Life Commission Papers, Southern Baptist Historical Library and Archives.

41. George Lowell to Dr. C.C. Warren, November 7, 1957, Box 21, Folder "Race Relations—Letters Expressing Alarm or Opposition (1957)," Christian Life Commission Papers, Southern Baptist Historical Library and Archives.

42. "Resolution," Edisto Baptist Church, July 7, 1957, Box 21, Folder "Race Relations—Letters Expressing Alarm or Opposition (1957)," Christian Life Commission Papers, Southern Baptist Historical Library and Archives.

43. "Resolution," Ebenezer Baptist Church, July 7, 1957, Box 21, Folder "Race Relations—Letters Expressing Alarm or Opposition (1957)," Christian Life Commission Papers, Southern Baptist Historical Library and Archives.

44. *Baptist Courier* (October 31, 1957), 14.

45. Newman, "The Baptist State Convention of South Carolina and Desegregation," 62.

46. *Southern School News* (September 1957), 2.

47. *Baptist Courier* (September 12, 1957), 23.

48. *Southern School News* (October 1957), 13.

49. Quoted in *Southern School News* (November 1957), 15.

50. Quoted in *Southern School News* (December 1957), 7.

51. Marion A. Woodson to the Christian Life Commission, April 15, 1958, Box 21, Folder "Race Relations—Letters of Opposition (1958)," Christian Life Commission Papers, Southern Baptist Historical Library and Archives.

52. Charles Marsh, *The Last Days: A Son's Story of Sin and Segregation at the Dawn of a New South* (New York: Basic Books, 2001), 174.

53. James Byrnes, "Memo" undated, Box 44, Folder 13, Series 8, Post-Gubernatorial Papers, Mss 90, James F. Byrnes Papers, Special Collections, Clemson University Libraries.

54. "Batesburg Minister Resigns in Dispute Over Segregation," *News and Courier* (November 2, 1955).

55. G. Jackson Stafford to William Workman, January 11, 1956, Box 27, William D. Workman Jr. Papers, South Carolina Political Collections, The University of South Carolina.

56. "Batesburg Minister Resigns in Dispute"; Howard H. Quint, *Profile in Black and White: A Frank Portrait of South Carolina* (Washington DC, Public Affairs Press, 1958), 60.

57. G. Jackson Stafford to Judge George Bell Timmerman, June 29, 1955, Box 1, Folder "1955—Annual, SBC," Race Relations and Southern Baptists, Southern Baptist Historical Library and Archives.

58. G. Jackson Stafford to Judge George Bell Timmerman, July 25, 1955, Box 1, Folder "1955—Annual, SBC," Race Relations and Southern Baptists, Southern Baptist Historical Library and Archives.

59. Judge George Bell Timmerman to G. Jackson Stafford, July 29, 1955, Box 1, Folder "1955—Annual, SBC," Race Relations and Southern Baptists, Southern Baptist Historical Library and Archives.

60. Judge George Bell Timmerman to G. Jackson Stafford, July 29, 1955, Box 1, Folder "1955—Annual, SBC," Race Relations and Southern Baptists, Southern Baptist Historical Library and Archives.

61. Newman, *Getting Right with God*, 43.

62. Quoted in Newman, "South Carolina Baptist Convention and Desegregation," 60.

63. *Southern School News* (November 1954), 14.

64. Stephanie R. Rolph, *Resisting Equality: The Citizens' Council 1954–1989* (Baton Rouge: Louisiana State University Press, 2018), 29, 32.

65. For more on the Citizens' Councils see Neil McMillen, *The Citizens' Council: Organized Resistance to the Second Reconstruction, 1954–1964* (Urbana: University of Illinois Press, 1971).

66. McMillen, *The Citizens' Council*, 74–77.

67. For more on the spread of the Citizens' Council movement in South Carolina, see John W. White, "Managed Compliance: White Resistance and Desegregation in South Carolina, 1950–1970" (PhD diss., University of Florida, 2006), 181–89.

68. White, "Managed Compliance," 186.

69. Kingstree Citizens' Council to Strom Thurmond, December 23, 1955, Box 32, Folder "Segregation, States Rights IV," Thurmond Papers Subject Correspondence 1955, Mss 100, Strom Thurmond Collection, Special Collections, Clemson University Libraries.

70. Day Bondeson to Strom Thurmond, January 6, 1956, Box 12, Folder "Segregation I," Thurmond Papers Subject Correspondence Series 1956, Mss 100, Strom Thurmond Collection, Special Collections, Clemson University Libraries.

71. White, "Managed Compliance."

72. Strom Thurmond to G. L. Ivey, February 10, 1956, Box 12, Folder "Segregation I," Thurmond Papers Subject Correspondence Series 1956, Mss 100, Strom Thurmond Collection, Special Collections, Clemson University Libraries.

73. John D. Britton to Strom Thurmond, February 12, 1956, Box 12, Folder "Segregation II," Thurmond Papers Subject Correspondence Series 1956, Mss 100, Strom Thurmond Collection, Special Collections, Clemson University Libraries.

74. S. L. Gentry to Strom Thurmond, July 21, 1961, Box 3, Folder "Civil Rights 3," Thurmond Papers Correspondence Series 1961, Mss 100, Strom Thurmond Collection, Special Collections, Clemson University Libraries; Dr. D. M. Nelson, "Conflicting Views on Segregation," Box 36, Folder 475, Mss 91, Edgar Allan Brown Papers, Special Collections, Clemson University Libraries; Attorney General Eugene Cook, "The Ugly Truth about the NAACP," Box 36, Folder 475, Mss 91, Edgar Allan Brown Papers, Special Collections, Clemson University Libraries.

75. *Southern School News* (February 1957), 11.

76. Marion Woodson to Strom Thurmond, February 13, 1958, Box 24, Folder "Civil Rights," Thurmond Papers Subject Correspondence Series 1958, Mss 100, Strom Thurmond Collection, Special Collections, Clemson University Libraries.

77. "A Resolution," Kingstree Citizens' Council, July 2, 1957, Box 27, Folder "Segregation, States Rights," Thurmond Papers Subject Correspondence 1957, Mss 100, Strom Thurmond Collection, Special Collections, Clemson University Libraries.

78. B. A. Graham to Strom Thurmond, March 1, 1958, Box 6, Folder "Civil Rights Commission," Subject Correspondence Series 1958, Mss 100, Strom Thurmond Collection, Special Collections, Clemson University Libraries.

79. *Southern School News* (October 1956), 4.

80. Quoted in *Southern School News* (July 1957), 4.

81. "Statement by the Council of Bishops of the Methodist Church, Chicago, November 18–21, 1954," quoted in Campbell and Pettigrew, *Christians in Racial Crisis*, 154.

82. South Carolina Annual Conference Southeastern Jurisdiction, *Journal and Yearbook* (1954) 158–60.

83. South Carolina Annual Conference Southeastern Jurisdiction, *Journal and Yearbook* (1955) 159.

84. "Rev. McKay Brabham Explains Resolution," *Bamberg Herald* (September 8, 1955).

85. "Citizens Councils," *Charleston News and Courier* (September 12, 1955).

86. "What the Conference Said," *South Carolina Methodist Advocate* (September 15, 1955), 3.

87. "A Conference to Be Proud Of . . . ," *South Carolina Methodist Advocate* (September 8, 1955), 3.

88. "Dislikes Editorial 'We,'" *South Carolina Methodist Advocate* (September 22, 1955), 10. Emphasis not in original.

89. "Rise of the Citizens Councils," *Charleston News and Courier* (August 31, 1955).

90. "Church Protests," *Charleston News and Courier* (October 26, 1955).

91. "Methodist Laymen Endorse Forming Citizens' Councils," *Charleston News and Courier* (October 21, 1955).

92. "S.C. Methodist Groups Back Segregation," *Charleston News and Courier* (October 25, 1955).

93. "Norway Methodists Support Aims of Citizens' Councils," *Charleston News and Courier* (December 11, 1955).

94. "Official Board of Kingstree Methodist Church Passes Resolution Condemning Annual Conference Resolution," *South Carolina Methodist Advocate* (October 6, 1955), 7.

95. "Hemingway Groups Oppose Integration," *Charleston News and Courier* (December, 8, 1955); "Hemingway Church Opposes Further Integration Moves," *Charleston News and Courier* (December 28, 1955).

96. "Amen to Mr. Pok, Etc.," *South Carolina Methodist Advocate* (October 6, 1955), 10.

97. "Supports Economic Pressure," *South Carolina Methodist Advocate* (September 29, 1955), 10.

98. "Protest to Methodist," *Charleston News and Courier* (September 6, 1955).

99. "A Minister Writes His People," *South Carolina Methodist Advocate* (November 10, 1955), 10.
100. "Orangeburg Minister Outlines Views in Behalf of Segregation," *Charleston News and Courier* (September 6, 1955).
101. "The Minister as Prophet," *South Carolina Methodist Advocate* (October 20, 1955), 10.
102. "S.C. Methodist Condemn Forming of Citizen Councils," *Charleston News and Courier* (August 28, 1955).
103. "Conference Should Change Rules," *South Carolina Methodist Advocate* (November 24, 1955), 10.
104. "Orangeburg Minister Outlines Views in Behalf of Segregation," *Charleston News and Courier* (September 6, 1955).
105. "Methodist Laymen Endorse Forming Citizens' Councils," *Charleston News and Courier* (October 21, 1955).
106. "Supports Economic Pressure," 10. Emphasis in original.
107. "No Halfway Ground," *South Carolina Methodist Advocate* (September 8, 1955), 11.
108. "Co-Author of Resolution Condemning Citizens Councils Rejected by Area Methodists," *Orangeburg Times and Democrat* (September 12, 1955).
109. "Minister Makes No Comment on Change," *Charleston News and Courier* (September 16, 1955).
110. "Springfield Methodist Church Bulletin," September 11, 1955, in author's possession.
111. "Upset over Conference," *South Carolina Methodist Advocate* (December 15, 1955), 10.
112. "Concerned Over Post-Conference Move," *South Carolina Methodist Advocate* (October 20, 1955), 10. Emphasis in original.
113. "The World Knows About South Carolina," *South Carolina Methodist Advocate* (December 8, 1955), 11.
114. For additional studies of white ministers who faced consequences for speaking out in favor of civil rights, see Joseph, T. Reiff, *Born of Conviction: White Methodists and Mississippi's Closed Society* (New York: Oxford University Press, 2016); and Elaine Allen Lechtreck, *Southern White Ministers and the Civil Rights Movement* (Jackson: University Press of Mississippi, 2018).
115. Brabham to Workman, January 18, 1956, Box 27, William D. Workman, Jr., Papers, South Carolina Political Collections, The University of South Carolina.
116. For more on Brabham's career as the editor of the South Carolina *Methodist Advocate*, see Susan Pierce Johnston, *The* South Carolina United Methodist Advocate *and Civil Rights: One Editor's Stand* (Columbia: South Carolina United Methodist Advocate, 1992).
117. Murray to Workman, January 5, 1956, Box 27, William D. Workman, Jr., Papers, South Carolina Political Collections, The University of South Carolina.
118. Herman Melville, *Moby Dick* (1851; repr., New York: W. W. Norton and Company, 2002), 47.

Chapter 2

1. Joan A. Inabinet, *His People: A History of the Camden (First) Baptist Church of South Carolina 1810–1985* (Camden, SC: Pine Tree Publishing Company, 1985).

2. John B. Boles, *The Irony of Southern Religion* (New York: Peter Lang, 1994), 37–72.

3. Inabinet, *His People*, 47–50.

4. Inabinet, *His People*, 50. Emphasis not in original.

5. "Memo from First Baptist Church Camden, SC," November 4, 1957, Box 21, Folder "Race Relations—Letters Expressing Alarm or Opposition 1957," Christian Life Commission Papers, Southern Baptist Historical Library and Archives.

6. "Resolution by Clarendon Baptist Church, Alcolu, SC," October 24, 1957, Box 21, Folder "Race Relations—Letters Expressing Alarm or Opposition 1957," Christian Life Commission Papers, Southern Baptist Historical Library and Archives.

7. W. C. George, "Race, Heredity, and Civilization," Box 432, Folder 5, Thomas R. Waring Jr. Papers, South Carolina Historical Society.

8. Fetus F. Windham, *A Bible Treatise on Segregation: An Analysis of Biblical References to Determine the True Relationship of the Races* (New York: William-Frederick Press, 1957), 15.

9. Mack P. Stewart Jr., "Why I Am a Segregationist," June 18, 1961, sermon reprint found in Box 33, William D. Workman, Jr., Papers, South Carolina Political Collections, The University of South Carolina.

10. William Talley, *The Wayward Winds*, undated booklet found in University of Iowa, *The Right Wing Collection of the University of Iowa Libraries, 1918–1977*, microfilm edition, 177 rolls (Glen Rock, NJ: Microfilming Corporation of America, 1978), roll 26, frame C28, 14.

11. G. T. Gillespie, "A Christian View on Segregation," Address delivered before the Synod of Mississippi of the Presbyterian Church in the U.S., November 4, 1954, pamphlet found in *Right Wing Collection of the University of Iowa Libraries*, roll 26, frame C28, 5.

12. Carey Daniel, "God the Original Segregationist," pamphlet reprint found in *Right Wing Collection of the University of Iowa Libraries*, roll 26, frame C28, 4.

13. A. C. Lawton Sr., "Christianity vs. Integration," *The Councilor* (October 20, 1963).

14. H. C. McGowan, *God's Garden of Segregation* (New York: Vantage Press, 1961), 9–10.

15. Pointing to God's favor for the South in the 1950s as justification for segregation echoed the call southern divines issued a century earlier in defending the Confederacy as being part of the will of God. See Daniel Stowell, *Rebuilding Zion: The Religious Reconstruction of the South, 1863–1877* (New York: Oxford University Press, 1998), 33–38.

16. "Farmerville First Baptist Church Adopts Resolution Against Race Mixing," *The Councilor* (December 1957), 7.

17. Medford Evans, "A Methodist Declaration of Conscience on Racial Segregation," reprinted pamphlet found in *Right Wing Collection of the University of Iowa Libraries*, roll 26, frame C28.

18. Maylon D. Watkins, "Segregation of the Races Is Biblical and Therefore Christlike," article reprint found in Box 457, Folder 3, Thomas R. Waring, Jr. papers, South Carolina Historical Society.

19. C. W. Howell, "Segregation: It Is Scriptural, It Is Natural, It Is Sensible, It Is Imperative," Box 5, Folder "White Supremists [sic]," Christian Life Commission Resource Files, Southern Baptist Historical Library and Archive. Emphasis in the original.

20. Genesis 11:1–9.

21. Stuart O. Landry, "Rebuilding the Tower of Babel," pamphlet found in Box 457, Folder 3, Thomas R. Waring, Jr. papers, South Carolina Historical Society.

22. Montague Cook, "Racial Segregation Is Christian," pamphlet found in Box 59, Folder "Race," Clifton J. Allen Papers, Southern Baptist Historical Library and Archives. Emphasis in the original.

23. For one segregationist publication that cites nearly every instance of biblical intermarriage, see Humphrey K. Ezell, *The Christian Problem of Racial Segregation* (New York: Greenwich Book Publishers, 1959).

24. Montague Cook, "Racial Segregation Is Christian," pamphlet found in Box 59, Folder "Race," Clifton, J. Allen Papers, Southern Baptist Historical Library and Archives.

25. Lawton, "Christianity vs. Integration."

26. Parson Jack, "God Orders Segregation," Box 5, Folder "White Supremists [sic]," Christian Life Commission Resource Files, Southern Baptist Historical Library and Archives, 4.

27. Jane Dailey argues that "it was through sex that racial segregation in the South moved from being a local social practice to a part of the divine plan for the world. It was thus through sex that segregation assumed, for the believing Christian, cosmological significance." Dailey, "The Theology of Massive Resistance: Sex, Segregation, and the Sacred after *Brown*," in *Massive Resistance: Southern Opposition to the Second Reconstruction,* ed. Clive Webb (Oxford: Oxford University Press, 2005), 154. Dailey also advances this argument in "Sex, Segregation, and the Sacred after *Brown*," *Journal of American History* 91 (June 2004): 119–44. I agree with Dailey that there is certainly a significant connection between sex and the importance of segregation, but I would reverse her syllogism. It is because racial segregation had cosmological significance that policing interracial sexual practices became so important to white Christians.

28. C. H. Hardin, "What the Bible Says About Integration: Segregation Commanded of All of God's Creation," pamphlet found in Box 457, Folder 3, Thomas R. Waring, Jr. papers, South Carolina Historical Society.

29. This passage is found in Leviticus 19:19. For an example of a segregationist publication that appealed to this verse, see Stewart, "Why I Am a Segregationist," 2.

30. Matthew 5:17–18. The idea of Jesus defending Old Testament law as a defense of segregation was cited in C. R. Dickey, "The Bible and Segregation," pamphlet found in Box 457, Folder 3, Thomas R. Waring, Jr. papers, South Carolina Historical Society, 16.

31. Dickey, "The Bible and Segregation," 16.

32. Matthew 25:32, cited in Marvin Brooks Norfleet, "Forced Racial Integration: In Its Religious, Social and Political Aspects—Principally Applied to School Integration of

the White and Negro Races," pamphlet found in Box 34, William D. Workman, Jr., Papers, South Carolina Political Collections, The University of South Carolina, 6.

33. William F. Johnson, "Do You Fight the Creators Will?," document found in Box 24, Folder "Segregation," Subject Correspondence Series 1958, Mss 100, Strom Thurmond Collection, Special Collections, Clemson University Libraries.

34. J. U. Teague, *What the Bible Teaches on the Race Question: Segregation vs. Integration* (Henderson, NC: the author, 1957), 3.

35. I Corinthians 14:40; Watkins, "Segregation of the Races Is Biblical and Therefore Christlike," 2.

36. E. Earle Ellis, "Segregation and the Kingdom of God," pamphlet found in Box 457, Folder 3, Thomas R. Waring, Jr. Papers, South Carolina Historical Society.

37. Acts 17:26.

38. Henry W. Fancher Sr., "Segregation: God's Plan and God's Purpose," 1954, Box 61, Folder "Segregation," Clifton J. Allen Papers, Southern Baptist Historical Library and Archives.

39. For a further explanation of the importance of Acts 17:26, see Paul Harvey, *Bounds of Their Habitation: Race and Religion in American History* (Lanham, MD: Rowman and Littlefield, 2017), 3–10. For an explanation of how the Curse of Ham influenced proslavery theologians in the nineteenth century, see Stephen R. Haynes, *Noah's Curse: The Biblical Justification of American Slavery* (New York: Oxford University Press, 2002).

40. J. Elwood Welsh, "Is Racial Segregation Right and Christian?," sermon reprint found in Box 436, Folder 6, Thomas R. Waring, Jr. Papers, South Carolina Historical Society.

41. Galatians 3:28.

42. W. Clyde Odeneal, "Segregation: Sin or Sensible?," pamphlet found in Box 33, William D. Workman, Jr., Papers, South Carolina Political Collections, The University of South Carolina, 4.

43. Daniel, "God the Original Segregationist," 3.

44. *South Carolina Methodist Advocate* (November 11, 1954), 3.

45. Rev. J. Paul Barrett, "The Church and Segregation," Box 5, Folder "White Supremists [*sic*]," Christian Life Commission Resource Files, Southern Baptist Historical Library and Archives, 7.

46. Nathan O. Hatch, "Evangelicalism as a Democratic Movement," in *Evangelicalism and Modern America,* ed. George Marsden (Grand Rapids, MI: Eerdmans Publishing Company, 1984), 79.

47. *News and Courier* (April 19, 1959).

48. *Southern School News* (June 1959), 9.

49. James Copeland to Thomas Waring, June 10, 1959, Box 393, Folder 4, Thomas R. Waring, Jr. Papers, South Carolina Historical Society.

50. Thomas Waring to James Copeland, June 11, 1959, Box 393, Folder 4, Thomas R. Waring, Jr. Papers, South Carolina Historical Society.

51. William Stackhouse to Thomas Waring, June 13, 1959, Box 393, Folder 4, Thomas R. Waring, Jr. Papers, South Carolina Historical Society.

52. "Most Southern Pastors Favor Obeying Court," *The State* (October 20, 1958).

53. Carey Daniel to Dr. A. C. Miller, September 23, 1956, Box 20, Folder "Race Relations—Letters Expressing Alarm or Opposition 1956," Christian Life Commission Resource Files, Southern Baptist Historical Library and Archives. Emphasis in original.

54. *The Citizen's Council* (May 1956), 2, quoted in McMillen, *The Citizens' Council*, 174, note 43.

55. "The Citizen' Councils . . . Their Platform," pamphlet found in Box 393, Folder 7, Thomas R. Waring, Jr. Papers, South Carolina Historical Society.

56. McMillen, *The Citizens' Council*, 174–75.

57. "Pastor Talks to Hartsville Citizens Body," newspaper clipping found in Box 47, William D. Workman, Jr., Papers, South Carolina Political Collections, The University of South Carolina.

58. Ed Roberts to M. A. Woodson, March 7, 1959, Box 393, Folder 4, Thomas R. Waring, Jr. Papers, South Carolina Historical Society.

59. George Bell Timmerman to Rev. John B. Morris, October 29, 1957, Box 5, Folder "White Supremists [*sic*]," Christian Life Commission Resource Files, Southern Baptist Historical Library and Archives.

60. John B. Morris to George Bell Timmerman, January 17, 1959, Box 5, Folder "White Supremists [*sic*]," Christian Life Commission Resource Files, Southern Baptist Historical Library and Archives.

61. George Bell Timmerman to Rev. John B. Morris, January 21, 1958, Box 5, Folder "White Supremists [*sic*]," Christian Life Commission Resource Files, Southern Baptist Historical Library and Archives.

62. George Bell Timmerman to Rev. John B. Morris, January 21, 1958, Box 5, Folder "White Supremists [*sic*]," Christian Life Commission Resource Files, Southern Baptist Historical Library and Archives.

63. T. E. Wilburn to Strom Thurmond, December 21, 1955, Box 32, Folder "Segregation (Aiken Office) February–December 23, 1955," Subject Correspondence 1955, Mss 100, Strom Thurmond Collection, Special Collections, Clemson University Libraries. Emphasis in original.

64. L. W. Briggs to Olin D. Johnston, June 11, 1954, Box 40, Olin DeWitt Talmadge Johnston Papers, South Carolina Political Collections, The University of South Carolina.

65. I. D. and Marion Yonce to Olin D. Johnston, July 7, 1954, Box 40, Olin DeWitt Talmadge Johnston Papers, South Carolina Political Collections, The University of South Carolina.

66. Thomas Howe to Olin D. Johnston, May 26, 1954, Box 40, Olin DeWitt Talmadge Johnston Papers, South Carolina Political Collections, The University of South Carolina.

67. Jan Revill to Olin D. Johnston, May 24, 1954, Box 40, Johnston Papers; James B. Davis to Olin D. Johnston, May 25, 1954, Box 40, Olin DeWitt Talmadge Johnston Papers, South Carolina Political Collections, The University of South Carolina.

68. *Charleston News and Courier* (August 28, 1955).

69. "Court's Segregation Decision Called Invitation to Race War," Box 32, Folder "Segregation and States' Rights August 1–30, 1955 III," Subject Correspondence

1955, Mss 100, Strom Thurmond Collection, Special Collections, Clemson University Libraries.

70. *Southern School News* (July 1959), 10.

71. R. K. Wallace to Strom Thurmond, March 31, 1959, Box 3, Folder "Civil Rights (Race Relations) I," Subject Correspondence Series, Mss 100, Strom Thurmond Collection, Special Collections, Clemson University Libraries.

72. "Orderly Is Held on Rape Count," Box 32, Folder: "Segregation and States' Rights August 1–30, 1955 III," Subject Correspondence 1955, Mss 100, Strom Thurmond Collection, Special Collections, Clemson University Libraries.

73. Strom Thurmond to E. A. Wilder, July 27, 1955, Box 32, Folder "Segregation and States' Rights August 1–30, 1955 III," Subject Correspondence 1955, Mss 100, Strom Thurmond Collection, Special Collections, Clemson University Libraries.

74. Ann White to Herbert Brownell, February 28, 1956, Box 12, Folder "Segregation February 14–March 13, 1956 II," Subject Correspondence 1956, Mss 100, Strom Thurmond Collection, Special Collections, Clemson University Libraries. Emphasis in the original.

75. N. Y. Mathis to Senator Olin D. Johnston, March 8, 1956, Box 12, Folder "Segregation February 14–March 13, 1956 II," Subject Correspondence 1956, Mss 100, Strom Thurmond Collection, Special Collections, Clemson University Libraries.

76. W. H. B. Simpson to Senator Paul H. Douglas, July 8, 1958, Box 24, Folder "Segregation May 10–September 16, 1958 II," Subject Correspondence 1958, Mss 100, Strom Thurmond Collection, Special Collections, Clemson University Libraries. In Mark 9:42, Jesus states, "And whosoever shall offend one of these little ones that believe in me, it is better for him that a millstone were hanged about his neck, and he were cast into the sea."

77. Mabel Harvey to Strom Thurmond, November 28, 1958, Box 24, Folder "Segregation October 7–December 22, 1958 II," Subject Correspondence 1958, Mss 100, Strom Thurmond Collection, Special Collections, Clemson University Libraries.

78. R. T. Matthews to Strom Thurmond, April 18, 1959, Box 3, Folder "Civil Rights and Race Relations January 6–April 23, 1959 I," Subject Correspondence 1959, Mss 100, Strom Thurmond Collection, Special Collections, Clemson University Libraries.

79. A. B. Conolly to National Council of Churches, January 3, 1961, Box 3, Folder "Civil Rights 3 (Race Relations)," Subject Correspondence 1961, Mss 100, Strom Thurmond Collection, Special Collections, Clemson University Libraries.

80. Gary C. Posey, "God the Author of Segregation," Box 3, Folder "Civil Rights 3 (Race Relations)," Subject Correspondence 1961, Mss 100, Strom Thurmond Collection, Special Collections, Clemson University Libraries.

81. James T. Bowen to Strom Thurmond, June 13, 1963, Box 3, Folder "Civil Rights January 7–November 23, 1963," Subject Correspondence 1963, Mss 100, Strom Thurmond Collection, Special Collections, Clemson University Libraries.

82. "What Is God's Will?," Box 3, Folder "Civil Rights I (Civil Rights Legislation) II," Subject Correspondence 1963, Mss 100, Strom Thurmond Collection, Special Collections, Clemson University Libraries.

83. Strom Thurmond to Boyd Hull, June 26, 1963, Box 3, Folder "Civil Rights I (Civil Rights Legislation) II," Subject Correspondence 1963, Mss 100, Strom Thurmond Collection, Special Collections, Clemson University Libraries.

84. Percy A. & Margretta E. Nauglie to Strom Thurmond, July 23, 1963, Box 3, Folder "Civil Rights Legislation IV," Subject Correspondence 1963, Mss 100, Strom Thurmond Collection, Special Collections, Clemson University Libraries.

85. *Southern School News* (June 1964), 16.

Chapter 3

1. Quoted in Walter Edgar, *South Carolina: A History* (Columbia: University of South Carolina Press, 1998), 350.

2. Kenneth Townsend, *South Carolina: On the Road Histories* (Northampton, MA: Interlink Books, 2009), 167.

3. Of the 582 members of the First Baptist congregation in 1860, only 120 were white. The remaining 462 were black slaves. See "First Baptist Church, Columbia, South Carolina," pamphlet in author's possession.

4. William Cox Allen, *A History of the First Baptist Church Columbia, South Carolina* (Columbia, SC: First Baptist Church, 1959), 38–41. Although the initial vote to pursue secession occurred in Columbia, subsequent votes that actually severed South Carolina's ties with the Union occurred in Charleston. The convention moved to the coastal city upon widespread fears of smallpox outbreak in Columbia.

5. Allen, *A History of the First Baptist Church*, 45–46. Sherman's troops did burn the original First Baptist church building that stood a few blocks away from the new First Baptist. It could be, therefore, that Union troops simply burned the wrong First Baptist. Other versions have it that a black janitor at First Baptist misled Union troops about which church was First Baptist, causing the troops to burn the Methodist church across the street from First Baptist.

6. *Southern School News* (December 1964), 6; *South Carolina Baptist Convention Journal* (1964), 44.

7. George Gallup, "76 Pct. In South See End of Segregation," 1961, Box 145, Folder "Segregation Race Relations I," Mss 100, Strom Thurmond Collection, Special Collections, Clemson University Libraries.

8. Jason Sokol, *There Goes My Everything: White Southerners in the Age of Civil Rights, 1945–1975* (New York: Vintage Books, 2006), 182–237.

9. Sokol, *There Goes My Everything*, 182–237.

10. *Southern Schools News* (September 1961), 1.

11. Kenneth K. Bailey, *Southern White Protestantism in the Twentieth Century* (New York: Harper and Row Publishers, 1964), 147.

12. *Greenville News* (October 29, 1961).

13. *South Carolina Baptist Convention Journal* (1961), 44–45; *Greenville News* (November 16, 1961); *Southern School News* (December 1961), 16.

14. Statement by Bonner in Response to Student Poll, Folder 42 ("Integration"), John Plyer Papers, Special Collections and Archives, Furman University.

15. Statement by Bonner in Response to Student Poll, Folder 42 ("Integration"), John Plyer Papers, Special Collections and Archives, Furman University; *Southern School News* (January 1962), 15; Courtney Louise Tollison, "Moral Imperative and Financial Practicality: Desegregation of South Carolina's Denominationally-Affiliated Colleges and Universities" (PhD diss., University of South Carolina, 2003), 101–2.

16. L. R. Wells to Dr. John Plyer, December 21, 1961, Folder 42 ("Integration"), John Plyer Papers, Special Collections and Archives, Furman University.

17. E. G. Spencer to the Faculty and President of Furman University, December 14, 1961, Folder 42 ("Integration"), John Plyer Papers, Special Collections and Archives, Furman University.

18. E. G. Spencer to the Faculty and President of Furman University, December 14, 1961, Folder 42 ("Integration"), John Plyer Papers, Special Collections and Archives, Furman University.

19. W. W. Williams to Dr. John L. Plyer, December 14, 1961, Folder 42 ("Integration"), John Plyer Papers, Special Collections and Archives, Furman University. Emphasis in the original.

20. Mrs. T. Adden Player to Dr. John Plyer, December 15, 1961, Folder 42 ("Integration"), John Plyer Papers, Special Collections and Archives, Furman University.

21. Eric W. Hardy to Dr. John Plyer, January 16, 1962, Folder 42 ("Integration"), John Plyer Papers, Special Collections and Archives, Furman University.

22. Eric W. Hardy to Dr. John Plyer, January 16, 1962, Folder 42 ("Integration"), John Plyer Papers, Special Collections and Archives, Furman University.

23. Untitled Press Release found in Folder 42 ("Integration"), John Plyer Papers, Special Collections and Archives, Furman University.

24. Winfield Martins to Dr. John Plyer, letter undated, Folder 42 ("Integration"), John Plyer Papers, Special Collections and Archives, Furman University.

25. L. R. Wells to Dr. John Plyer, December 21, 1961, Folder 42 ("Integration"), John Plyer Papers, Special Collections and Archives, Furman University.

26. Eric W. Hardy to Dr. John Plyer, January 16, 1962, Folder 42 ("Integration"), John Plyer Papers, Special Collections and Archives, Furman University.

27. Sapp Funderburk to Eric W. Hardy, January 25, 1962, Folder 42 ("Integration"), John Plyer Papers, Special Collections and Archives, Furman University

28. Tollison, "Moral Imperative and Financial Practicality," 103. See also Melissa Kean, *Desegregating Private Higher Education in the South: Duke, Emory, Rice, Tulane, and Vanderbilt* (Baton Rouge: Louisiana State University Press, 2008).

29. *Southern School News* (April 1963), 14. For details on Harvey Gantt's desegregation of Clemson, see Maxie Myron Cox Jr., "1963—The Year of Decision: Desegregation in South Carolina" (PhD diss., University of South Carolina, 1996).

30. "Minister Says Gantt Contact Lost His Post," *Augusta Chronicle* (March 28, 1963).

31. "Preacher Says Contact with Gantt Cost His Job," *Charleston News and Courier* (March 28, 1963).

32. "Preacher Says Contact with Gantt Cost His Job," *Charleston News and Courier* (March 28, 1963). Elaine Allen Lechtreck, *Southern White Ministers and the Civil Rights Movement* (Jackson: University of Mississippi Press, 2018), 45–47.

33. *Baptist Courier* (October 17, 1963), 5; "Integration Approved by Furman Trustees," *Charleston News and Courier* (October 9, 1963).

34. Quoted in Tollison, "Moral Imperative and Financial Practicality," 106; "Integration Approved by Furman Trustees," *Charleston News and Courier* (October 9, 1963).

35. Resolution of Cameron Baptist Church, October 22, 1963, Box 53, Folder "Race Relations (1963–1964)," Sunday School Board Executive Office Records, Sothern Baptist Historical Library and Archives.

36. W. Ray Avant to Porter W. Routh, October 22, 1963, Box 53, Folder "Race Relations (1963–1964)," Sunday School Board Executive Office Records, Sothern Baptist Historical Library and Archives.

37. *Baptist Courier* (October 23, 1963), 2.

38. *Southern School News* (November 1963), 12.

39. *South Carolina Baptist Convention Journal* (1963), 40–41.

40. *Southern School News* (December 1963), 4. In fact, the persistence of segregation in American churches *was* a significant problem for overseas missions. See Melani McAlister, *The Kingdom of God Has No Borders: A Global History of American Evangelicals* (New York: Oxford University Press, 2018), 17–29.

41. *South Carolina Baptist Convention Journal* (1963), 41. As detailed in Chapter 3, Ezra Chapters 9 and 10 were common Old Testament passages cited by segregationist theologians. In these two chapters the Israelites, recently returned from their Babylonian exile, are convicted by Ezra for taking non-Jewish wives. In repenting of this violation of Jewish law, the Israelite men promised to purify themselves by separating from their non-Jewish wives. Segregationists used this story to suggest that God abhorred the idea of mixed-race marriages.

42. *South Carolina Baptist Convention Journal* (1963), 42. One woman who attended the state convention in 1963 reported later that were it not for the large amount of lay Baptists espousing the idea that segregation was in line with Christian belief, the state convention likely would have acquiesced to the Furman trustees' plan to immediately open school admissions to students of all races. See Zilla Hinton to Senator Strom Thurmond, July 30, 1964, Box 8, Folder "Private Schools," Thurmond Papers, Clemson University Library.

43. "H1164: Bill Providing for the Removal of Trustees and the Appointment of Successor Trustees of Certain Trusts Created for Educational, Charitable, or Religious Purposes," Folder 42 ("Integration"), John Plyer Papers, Special Collections and Archives, Furman University.

44. "Baptists Are Sharply Split on Question of Integration," *Greenville News* (May 1, 1964).

45. "Introductory Statement: South Carolina Baptist Conference on Race Relations," April 30, 1964, Folder "Baptist Convention 1964," John Plyer Papers, Special Collections and Archives, Furman University, "Baptists Are Sharply Split on Question of Integration," *Greenville News* (May 1, 1964).

46. "Baptists Are Sharply Split on Question of Integration," *Greenville News* (May 1, 1964).

47. "Baptists Are Sharply Split on Question of Integration," *Greenville News* (May 1, 1964).
48. "Baptists Are Sharply Split on Question of Integration," *Greenville News* (May 1, 1964).
49. "Baptists Are Sharply Split on Question of Integration," *Greenville News* (May 1, 1964).
50. "Baptists Are Sharply Split on Question of Integration," *Greenville News* (May 1, 1964).
51. "Baptists Are Sharply Split on Question of Integration," *Greenville News* (May 1, 1964).
52. Tollison, "Moral Imperative and Financial Practicality," 107–13. The loss of federal money for noncompliance with racially inclusive practices was a real issue after the 1964 Civil Rights Act. In 1966 Anderson College, a Baptist school in South Carolina, was denied federal loans for students after the institution refused to sign nondiscrimination compliance forms as required by the 1964 law. See "Government Refuses Funds for South Carolina College," December 15, 1966, Box 1, Folder "1966— Clippings, Notes, Press Releases," Race Relations and Southern Baptists, Sothern Baptist Historical Library and Archives.
53. *Baptist Courier* (October 22, 1964), 23.
54. "Baptist Battle Coming Up," *Greenville News* (November 11, 1964).
55. *Southern School News* (December 1964), 6; *South Carolina Baptist Convention Journal* (1964), 42.
56. *Southern School News* (December 1964), 6; *South Carolina Baptist Convention Journal* (1964), 44.
57. "Baptist Colleges," *Charleston News and Courier* (November 13, 1964).
58. Tollison, "Moral Imperative and Financial Practicality," 114–15; *Southern School News* (January 1965), 1.
59. *Southern School News* (January 1965), 8.
60. *Southern School News* (January 1965), 8.
61. *Southern School News* (February 1965), 7.
62. James M. Copeland, "Cheers for Furman" undated newspaper clipping, Box 4, Folder 54, Papers of President Charles F. Marsh, Archives, Sandor Teszler Library, Wofford College.
63. Edgar A. Brown to W. J. McLeod Jr., March 17, 1960, Box 153, Folder 1003, Mss 91, Edgar Allan Brown Papers, Special Collections, Clemson University Libraries.
64. Edgar A. Brown to W. J. McLeod Jr., March 17, 1960, Box 153, Folder 1003, Mss 91, Edgar Allan Brown Papers, Special Collections, Clemson University Libraries. See Frank J. Kendrick to Ernest F. Hollings, March 13, 1960, Box 153, Folder 1003, Mss 91, Edgar Allan Brown Papers, Special Collections, Clemson University Libraries.
65. South Carolina Annual Conference Southeastern Jurisdiction, *Journal and Yearbook* (1962), 80.
66. *Southern School News* (July 1962), 11.
67. *Southern School News* (July 1962), 11.
68. South Carolina Annual Conference Southeastern Jurisdiction, *Journal and Yearbook* (1962), 80; *Southern School News* (July 1962), 11.
69. South Carolina Annual Conference Southeastern Jurisdiction, *Journal and Yearbook* (1963), 91.
70. South Carolina Annual Conference Southeastern Jurisdiction, *Journal and Yearbook* (1963), 91.

71. South Carolina Annual Conference Southeastern Jurisdiction, *Journal and Yearbook* (1963), 91.

72. "Resolution," June 18, 1963, Box 4, Papers of President Charles F. Marsh, Archives, Sandor Teszler Library, Wofford College.

73. "Confidential Statement to the Members of the Board of Trustees of Wofford College," Box 4, Papers of President Charles F. Marsh, Archives, Sandor Teszler Library, Wofford College.

74. "Confidential Statement to the Members of the Board of Trustees of Wofford College," Box 4, Papers of President Charles F. Marsh, Archives, Sandor Teszler Library, Wofford College.

75. C. F. Nesbitt to C. F. Marsh, January 7, 1964, Box 4, Papers of President Charles F. Marsh, Archives, Sandor Teszler Library, Wofford College.

76. Conley T. Snidow to Dr. Charles F. Marsh, January 18, 1964, Box 4, Papers of President Charles F. Marsh, Archives, Sandor Teszler Library, Wofford College.

77. C. E. Cauthen to Dr. Charles F. Marsh, January 22, 1964, Box 4, Papers of President Charles F. Marsh, Archives, Sandor Teszler Library, Wofford College.

78. Howard M. Pegram to Dr. Charles F. Marsh, January 25, 1964, Box 4, Papers of President Charles F. Marsh, Archives, Sandor Teszler Library, Wofford College. Emphasis in the original.

79. "Minutes of Special Committee of the Board of Trustees on Wofford College Admission Policies," Box 4, Papers of President Charles F. Marsh, Archives, Sandor Teszler Library, Wofford College.

80. "Resolution," February 24, 1964, Box 4, Papers of President Charles F. Marsh, Archives, Sandor Teszler Library, Wofford College.

81. Charles F. Marsh to Members of the Wofford Faculty, Administrative Staff and Student Body, May 19, 1964, Box 4, Papers of President Charles F. Marsh, Archives, Sandor Teszler Library, Wofford College.

82. "Statement Made by Colonel Marcus S. Griffin, Professor of Military Science, Wofford College, for the Special Study Committee Established by the Board on October 7, 1963," December 17, 1963, Box 4, Papers of President Charles F. Marsh, Archives, Sandor Teszler Library, Wofford College.

83. "Opposed Wofford Action," *South Carolina Methodist Advocate* (June 11, 1964), 5. Emphasis in the original.

84. George C. James, Secretary of the Official Board, Trinity Methodist Church to Charles F. Marsh, May 25, 1964, Box 4, Folder 55, Papers of President Charles F. Marsh, Archives, Sandor Teszler Library, Wofford College.

85. South Carolina Annual Conference Southeastern Jurisdiction, *Journal and Yearbook* (1964), 243.

86. *Southern School News* (July 1964), 7.

87. South Carolina Annual Conference Southeastern Jurisdiction, *Journal and Yearbook* (1964), 101.

88. South Carolina Annual Conference Southeastern Jurisdiction, *Journal and Yearbook* (1964), 102.

89. E. B. Woodward to Charles F. Marsh, May 26, 1964, Box 4, Folder 55, Papers of President Charles F. Marsh, Archives, Sandor Teszler Library, Wofford College.

90. Paul W. Harless to Charles F. Marsh, June 20, 1964, Box 4, Folder 55, Papers of President Charles F. Marsh, Archives, Sandor Teszler Library, Wofford College.

91. "A Letter from Manning," *South Carolina Methodist Advocate* (July 2, 1964), 12–13.

92. Dan R. McDaniel to Charles F. Marsh, May 14, 1964, Box 4, Folder 55, Papers of President Charles F. Marsh, Archives, Sandor Teszler Library, Wofford College.

93. Tollison, "Moral Imperative and Financial Practicality," 139.

94. Tollison, "Moral Imperative and Financial Practicality," 140–41.

95. W. Kenneth Suggs to Charles F. Marsh, July 6, 1964, Box 4, Folder 55, Papers of President Charles F. Marsh, Archives, Sandor Teszler Library, Wofford College.

96. W. W. Alman to Charles F. Marsh, May 22, 1964, Box 4, Folder 55, Papers of President Charles F. Marsh, Archives, Sandor Teszler Library, Wofford College.

97. "Wofford's First Black Students Remember Struggle," *The State* (February 25, 2013).

98. Courtney Louise Tollison, "Principles over Prejudice: The Desegregation of Furman University, Wofford, Columbia, and Presbyterian Colleges" (Master's thesis, University of South Carolina, 2001), 55.

99. Brian Neumann, "Progress, Pragmatism, and Power: Furman's Struggle Over Desegregation," https://www.furman.edu/diversity-inclusion/commemorating-desegregation/wp-content/uploads/sites/169/2020/01/BrianNeumann.pdf (accessed June 1, 2020).

100. Joab M. Lesesne to Edward L Tullis, April 4, 1973, Folder: "Merger Review and Evaluation: Columbia, South Carolina," Drew University Archives. 1526-5-1:23

101. Integrated Postsecondary Education Data System, https://nces.ed.gov/ipeds/datacenter/Data.aspx (accessed May 10, 2018).

102. R. A. Patterson to Charles F. Marsh, January 29, 1964, Box 4, Papers of President Charles F. Marsh, Archives, Sandor Teszler Library, Wofford College.

103. For additional reading on the sociology of white institutional spaces, see Glenn E. Bracey II and Wendy Leo Moore, "'Race Tests': Racial Boundary Maintenance in White Evangelical Churches," *Sociological Inquiry* 87, no. 2 (May 2017): 282–302. According to Bracey and Moore, a white institutional space "is created through a process that begins with whites excluding people of color, either completely or from institutional positions of power, during a formative period in the history of an organization. During this period, whites populate all influential posts within the institution and create institutional logics—norms of operation, organizational structures, curricula, criteria for membership and leadership—which imbed white norms into the fabric of the institution's structure and culture," 285.

104. "Furman Reflects on Desegregation," *Greenville News* (September 4, 2014); "Wofford's First Black Students Remember Struggle," *The State* (February 25, 2013).

105. "Basis for Race, Attitudes Reported," February 27, 1964, Box 71, Folder "Race Relations- 1964/1965," Wilmer C. Fields Papers, Southern Baptist Historical Library and Archives.

106. See Sokol, *There Goes My Everything*, 182–237.

107. *Southern School News* (April 1960), 4; I. A. Newby, *Black Carolinians: A History of Blacks in South Carolina from 1895 to 1968* (Columbia: University of South Carolina Press, 1973), 314–60. See also James L. Felder, *Civil Rights in South Carolina: From Peaceful Protests to Groundbreaking Rulings* (Charleston, SC: History Press, 2012).

108. James Davison Hunter, *American Evangelicalism: Conservative Religion and the Quandary of Modernity* (New Brunswick, NJ: Rutgers University Press, 1983), 90.

109. J. C. Hubbard to Charles Marsh, June 24, 1964, Box 4, Folder 55, Papers of President Charles F. Marsh, Archives, Sandor Teszler Library, Wofford College.

110. "The Pulse of the Church," *South Carolina Methodist Advocate* (July 9, 1964), 2–3.

Chapter 4

1. Steve Luxenberg, *Separate: The Story of* Plessy v. Ferguson, *and America's Journey from Slavery to Segregation* (New York: W. W. Norton & Company, 2019), 431–33; Richard Kluger, *Simple Justice: The History of* Brown v. Board of Education *and Black America's Struggle for Equality* (New York: Random House, 2004), 72.

2. *Plessy v. Ferguson* 163 U.S. 537 (1896). For more on the *Plessy* decision, see Kluger, *Simple Justice*, 73–80; and Luxenberg, *Separate* 477–80.

3. Henry Louis Gates Jr., *Stony the Road: Reconstruction, White Supremacy, and the Rise of Jim Crow* (New York: Penguin Press, 2019), 1–39.

4. Harvard Sitkoff, *The Struggle for Black Equality* (New York: Hill and Wang, 2008), 5.

5. Frederick Douglass, "The Color Line," *North American Review*, June 1881.

6. Quoted in *Southern School News* (January 1965), 8.

7. For a fuller biography of William Workman, see J. Russell Hawkins, "Religion, Race, and Resistance: White Evangelicals and the Dilemma of Integration in South Carolina 1950–1975" (PhD diss., Rice University, 2009), 14–66.

8. Workman to the Joint Committee on the Merger, January 7, 1971, Box 23, William D. Workman, Jr. Papers, South Carolina Political Collections, The University of South Carolina.

9. Workman to the Joint Committee on the Merger, January 7, 1971, Box 23, William D. Workman, Jr. Papers, South Carolina Political Collections, The University of South Carolina.

10. Quoted in Mark Newman, "The Baptist State Convention of South Carolina and Desegregation, 1954–1971," *Baptist History and Heritage*, Spring 1999, 68–69.

11. Quoted in Newman, "The Baptist State Convention of South Carolina and Desegregation," 69.

12. See Mark Noll, *The Civil War as a Theological Crisis* (Chapel Hill: The University of North Carolina Press, 2006) for more information on how American Protestant denominations were caught up in the battle over slavery prior to 1861.

13. Charles H. Lippy, "Towards an Inclusive Church: South Carolina Methodism and Race, 1972–1982," in *Rethinking Methodist History: A Bicentennial Historical*

Consultation, ed. Russell E. Richey and Kenneth E. Rowe (Nashville: Kingswood Books, 1985), 221.

14. Edward J. Blum, *Reforging the White Republic: Race, Religion, and American Nationalism, 1865–1898* (Baton Rouge: Louisiana State University Press, 2005).

15. Depending on the number of churches, some states have multiple annual conferences.

16. Peter C. Murray, *Methodists and the Crucible of Race 1930–1975* (Columbia: University of Missouri Press, 2004), xv–xvi.

17. Morris L. Davis, *The Methodist Unification: Christianity and the Politics of Race in the Jim Crow Era* (New York: New York University Press, 2008), 5.

18. Murray, *Methodists and the Crucible of Race,* 31–52; Davis, *The Methodist Unification,* 86–88.

19. Davis, *The Methodist Unification,* 4–5. For more on the reconciliation of religious northerners and southerners throughout the late nineteenth century, see Edward J. Blum, *Reforging the White Republic: Race, Religion, and American Nationalism 1865–1898* (Baton Rouge: Louisiana State University Press, 2007). Blum's work supports the idea that the conciliatory stance of northern and southern Methodists after the Civil War was typical of most white Christians in the two regions in the post–Civil War decades.

20. Murray, *Methodists and the Crucible of Race,* 45–46.

21. John C. Smith Jr., "Organizational History of the Sou. Methodist Church," *Southern Methodist* 29, no. 1 (January 1971): 6.

22. "The Negro Jurisdiction of the Partly Merged Methodist Church," *Southern Methodist Layman* 10, no. 13 (December 15, 1947): 9.

23. "General Information of the Southern Methodist Church," *Southern Methodist* (October 1957), 2.

24. "Gradual Elimination of Segregation," *Southern Methodist Layman* 4, no. 26 (May 1, 1942): 12.

25. Costen J. Harrell to Frank W. Hollingsworth, May 1, 1950, Box 39, William D. Workman, Jr. Papers, South Carolina Political Collections, The University of South Carolina.

26. Murray, *Methodists and the Crucible of Race,* 86–90. Murray's book is the best source for explaining the very complicated process of abolishing racially defined governing structures from the whole of the Methodist denomination. South Carolina white Methodists reacted negatively to the idea of transferring and merging black and white conferences but were relieved that the process was completely voluntary. See *Southern School News* (June 1956), 14.

27. "Report to the 1960 General Conference of the Methodist Church," March 18, 1959, Folder "1336-2-8:01 Committee to Study the Jurisdictional System: Minutes and Reports to the 1960 General Conference (Drafts) 1956–1959 (1974-005)," Interjurisdictional Relations, Drew University Methodist Library.

28. "Report to the 1960 General Conference of the Methodist Church," March 18, 1959, Folder "1336-2-8:01 Committee to Study the Jurisdictional System: Minutes

and Reports to the 1960 General Conference (Drafts) 1956–1959 (1974-005)," Interjurisdictional Relations, Drew University Methodist Library.

29. "Statement Concerning the Jurisdictional System of the Methodist Church," October 16, 1957, Folder "1336-4-3:02 Personal Statements Made at Jurisdictional Hearings—Folder 1 1957 (2003-061)," Jurisdictional Study, Drew University Methodist Library.

30. "Statement Concerning the Jurisdictional System of the Methodist Church," October 16, 1957, Folder "1336-4-3:02 Personal Statements Made at Jurisdictional Hearings—Folder 1 1957 (2003-061)," Jurisdictional Study, Drew University Methodist Library.

31. "Statement Concerning the Jurisdictional System of the Methodist Church," October 16, 1957, Folder "1336-4-3:02 Personal Statements Made at Jurisdictional Hearings—Folder 1 1957 (2003-061)," Jurisdictional Study, Drew University Methodist Library.

32. "Jurisdictional Hearings October 30-31 in Charlotte," *South Carolina Methodist Advocate* (October 24, 1957).

33. "Jurisdictional Hearings October 30-31 in Charlotte," *South Carolina Methodist Advocate* (October 24, 1957).

34. Quoted in *Southern School News* (December 1957), 7.

35. "Report to the 1960 General Conference of The Methodist Church," March 18, 1959, Folder "1336-2-8:01 Committee to Study the Jurisdictional System: Minutes and Reports to the 1960 General Conference (Drafts) 1956–1959 (1974-005)," Interjurisdictional Relations, Drew University Methodist Library

36. Murray, *Methodists and the Crucible of Race*, 184.

37. Frederick A. Shippey, PhD, "Annual Conference Actions on Integration: United States, 1952-1958, The Methodist Church," Folder "1336-2-8:01 Committee to Study the Jurisdictional System: Minutes and Reports to the 1960 General Conference (Drafts) 1956-1959 (1974-005)," Interjurisdictional Relations, Drew University Methodist Library.

38. The Methodist Church General Conference, *Journal* (1966), 3078–79.

39. Murray, *Methodists and the Crucible of Race*, 185.

40. The Methodist Church General Conference, *Journal* (1966), 3096.

41. The Methodist Church General Conference, *Journal* (1966), 3096.

42. The Methodist Church General Conference, *Journal* (1966), 2613.

43. "Resolution," Folder "1336-2-8:01 Committee to Study the Jurisdictional System: Minutes and Reports to the 1960 General Conference (Drafts) 1956–1959 (1974-005)," Interjurisdictional Relations, Drew University Methodist Library.

44. The Methodist Church General Conference, *Journal* (1966), 2613–14.

45. The Methodist Church General Conference, *Journal* (1966), 2616.

46. The Methodist Church General Conference, *Journal* (1966), 2616.

47. The Methodist Church General Conference, *Journal* (1966), 2617.

48. The Methodist Church General Conference, *Journal* (1966), 2618.

49. The Methodist Church General Conference, *Journal* (1966), 2621.

50. The Methodist Church General Conference, *Journal* (1966), 2622.

51. The Methodist Church General Conference, *Journal* (1966), 2624.

52. The Methodist Church General Conference, *Journal* (1966), 2625.

53. The Methodist Church General Conference, *Journal* (1966), 2625.

54. South Carolina Annual Conference Southeastern Jurisdiction, *Journal and Yearbook* (1954), 158–59.

55. Martin Luther King Jr., *Letter from the Birmingham Jail* (New York: HarperCollins Publishers, 1994), 15–16.

56. Quoted in Mary L. Dudziak, "*Brown* as a Cold War Case," *Journal of American History* 91 (June 2004): 34. The literature on the intersection on the Cold War and civil rights is quite developed. See, for instance, Thomas Borstelmann, *The Cold War and The Color Line: American Race Relations in the Global Arena* (Cambridge, MA: Harvard University Press, 2001); Mary L. Dudziak, *Cold War Civil Rights: Race and the Image of American Democracy* (Princeton, NJ: Princeton University Press, 2000); Penny Von Eschen, *Race against Empire: Black Americans and Anticolonialism* (Ithaca, NY: Cornell University Press, 1997); and Brenda Gayle Plummer, *Rising Wind: Black Americans and U.S. Foreign Affairs, 1935–1960* (Chapel Hill: University of North Carolina Press, 1996).

57. The Methodist Church General Conference, *Journal* (1966), 2623.

58. South Carolina Annual Conference Southeastern Jurisdiction, *Journal and Yearbook* (1964), 99.

59. South Carolina Annual Conference Southeastern Jurisdiction, *Journal and Yearbook* (1964), 99.

60. South Carolina Annual Conference Southeastern Jurisdiction, *Journal and Yearbook* (1964), 106.

61. South Carolina Annual Conference Southeastern Jurisdiction, *Journal and Yearbook* (1965), 201.

62. South Carolina Annual Conference Southeastern Jurisdiction, *Journal and Yearbook* (1965), 201.

63. South Carolina Annual Conference Southeastern Jurisdiction, *Journal and Yearbook* (1966), 91; Murray, *Methodists and the Crucible of Race*, 194–95.

64. "A Layman's Report on the Southeastern Jurisdictional Conference," Box 22, William D. Workman, Jr. Papers, South Carolina Political Collections, The University of South Carolina.

65. "A Layman's Report on the Southeastern Jurisdictional Conference," Box 22, William D. Workman, Jr. Papers, South Carolina Political Collections, The University of South Carolina.

66. "To the Delegates of the South Carolina Annual Conference," Box 22, William D. Workman, Jr. Papers, South Carolina Political Collections, The University of South Carolina.

67. "To the Delegates of the South Carolina Annual Conference," Box 22, William D. Workman, Jr. Papers, South Carolina Political Collections, The University of South Carolina.

68. South Carolina Annual Conference Southeastern Jurisdiction, *Journal and Yearbook* (1969), 132.

69. "Remarks at South Carolina Annual Conference," May 27, 2001, Box 3, Rhett Jackson Papers, South Caroliniana Library, The University of South Carolina; Rhett Jackson to J. Russell Hawkins, April 9, 2007, letter in author's possession.

70. Dan Albergotti to Workman, July 11, 1969, Box 23, William D. Workman, Jr. Papers, South Carolina Political Collections, The University of South Carolina.

71. Workman to Don Herd Jr., June 13, 1969, Box 22 William D. Workman, Jr. Papers, South Carolina Political Collections, The University of South Carolina.

72. Dan Albergotti to the Editor of the *South Carolina Methodist Advocate*, July 20, 1970, Box 23, William D. Workman, Jr. Papers, South Carolina Political Collections, The University of South Carolina.

73. "The United Methodist Church Had Two Annual Conferences in South Carolina," undated document, Box 4, Rhett Jackson Papers, South Caroliniana Library, The University of South Carolina

74. Untitled press release, March 24, 1970, Box 22, William D. Workman, Jr. Papers, South Carolina Political Collections, The University of South Carolina.

75. South Carolina Annual Conference Southeaster Jurisdiction, *Journal and Yearbook* (1970), 117.

76. South Carolina Annual Conference Southeaster Jurisdiction, *Journal and Yearbook* (1970), 127.

77. South Carolina Annual Conference Southeaster Jurisdiction, *Journal and Yearbook* (1970), 176.

78. Hawkins, "Religion, Race, and Resistance," 14–66.

79. "The United Methodist Church Had Two Annual Conferences in South Carolina," undated document, Box 4, Rhett Jackson Papers, South Caroliniana Library, The University of South Carolina.

80. "Recommendation from the Council on Ministries to the Administrative Board," undated document, Box 23, William D. Workman, Jr. Papers, South Carolina Political Collections, The University of South Carolina.

81. "Questions about Merger," undated document, Box 23, William D. Workman, Jr. Papers, South Carolina Political Collections, The University of South Carolina.

82. "The United Methodist Church Had Two Annual Conferences in South Carolina," undated document, Box 4, Rhett Jackson Papers, South Caroliniana Library, The University of South Carolina

83. B. B. Black to Workman, November 9, 1970, Box 22, William D. Workman, Jr. Papers, South Carolina Political Collections, The University of South Carolina.

84. Lippy, "Towards an Inclusive Church," 222.

85. South Carolina Annual Conference Southeastern Jurisdiction, *Journal and Yearbook* (1971), 76.

86. South Carolina Annual Conference Southeastern Jurisdiction, *Journal and Yearbook* (1971), 76–77.

87. Dan Albergotti to the Editor of the South Carolina *Methodist Advocate*, June 16, 1970, Box 23, William D. Workman, Jr. Papers, South Carolina Political Collections, The University of South Carolina.

88. Workman to the Joint Committee on the Merger, January 7, 1971, Box 23, William D. Workman, Jr. Papers, South Carolina Political Collections, The University of South Carolina.

89. Workman to the Joint Committee on the Merger, January 7, 1971, Box 23, William D. Workman, Jr. Papers, South Carolina Political Collections, The University of South Carolina.

90. Workman to the Joint Committee on the Merger, January 7, 1971, Box 23, William D. Workman, Jr. Papers, South Carolina Political Collections, The University of South Carolina.

91. Workman to the Joint Committee on the Merger, January 7, 1971, Box 23, William D. Workman, Jr. Papers, South Carolina Political Collections, The University of South Carolina.

92. "The United Methodist Church Had Two Annual Conferences," undated document, Box 4, Rhett Jackson Papers, South Caroliniana Library, The University of South Carolina. Once the plan of merger had been defeated, a committee compiled a list of contributing reasons. A primary reason people gave for voting against the merger dealt with questions of the constitutionality of the mandated racial ratios and appointments. In addressing these concerns the following day, Bishop Hardin stated that, as far as he knew, nothing in the plan was unconstitutional. It is possible that the question of constitutionality was raised prior to the vote and the delegates chose not to believe their bishop's opinion. It is also possible that the point was never raised prior to the vote so that the question of constitutionality could remain in play for delegates looking for a reason to vote against the plan. See South Carolina Annual Conference Southeastern Jurisdiction, *Journal and Yearbook* (1971), 99–100.

93. South Carolina Annual Conference Southeastern Jurisdiction, *Journal and Yearbook* (1971), 77; "The United Methodist Church Had Two Annual Conferences," undated document, Box 4, Rhett Jackson Papers, South Caroliniana Library, The University of South Carolina.

94. "The United Methodist Church Had Two Annual Conferences," undated document, Box 4, Rhett Jackson Papers, South Caroliniana Library, The University of South Carolina.

95. South Carolina Annual Conference Southeastern Jurisdiction, *Journal and Yearbook* (1971), 99–100.

96. Lippy, "Towards an Inclusive Church," 222.

97. Lippy, "Towards an Inclusive Church," 222.

98. Lippy, "Towards an Inclusive Church," 222–23.

99. Lippy, "Towards an Inclusive Church," 223.

100. "The United Methodist Church Had Two Annual Conferences," undated document, Box 4, Rhett Jackson Papers, South Caroliniana Library, The University of South Carolina; Lippy, "Towards an Inclusive Church," 222.

101. Edward L. Tullis, "A Review of a Merged Conference, 1972–1977," undated report, Box 4, Folder "Conference Papers—Merger Documents 1968–1974," South Carolina Annual Conference United Methodist Church Records, 1960–2009, Archives, Sandor Teszler Library, Wofford College.

102. Edward L. Tullis, "A Review of a Merged Conference, 1972–1977," undated report, Box 4, Folder "Conference Papers—Merger Documents 1968–1974," South Carolina Annual Conference United Methodist Church Records, 1960–2009, Archives, Sandor Teszler Library, Wofford College.
103. Mitzi Matthews to Workman, August 1, 1972, Box 22, William D. Workman, Jr. Papers, South Carolina Political Collections, The University of South Carolina.

Chapter 5

1. Quoted in Eric Foner, *Reconstruction: America's Unfinished Revolution 1863–1877* (New York: Harper & Row, 1988), 570.
2. Quoted in Foner, *Reconstruction,* 570. For black gains in South Carolina during Reconstruction, see W. E. B. DuBois, *Black Reconstruction in America 1860–1880* (New York: Free Press, 1998), 381–430.
3. Foner, *Reconstruction,* 574.
4. "The Christian Idea and the Character of a Gentleman," Box 14, William D. Workman, Jr. Papers, South Carolina Political Collections, The University of South Carolina.
5. "Report of Committee Investigating the Establishment of Private Schools," 5, Box 28, William D. Workman Jr. Papers, South Carolina Political Collections, The University of South Carolina.
6. Roy Lowrie Jr., "Your Child and the Christian School," ed. National Association of Christian Schools, quoted in Seth Dowland, *Family Values and the Rise of the Christian Right* (Philadelphia: University of Pennsylvania Press, 2015), 44.
7. John W. White, "Managed Compliance: White Resistance and Desegregation in South Carolina, 1950–1970" (PhD diss., University of Florida, 2006), 45–46.
8. *Southern School News* (May 1957), 3.
9. Quoted in Paul Wesley McNeill, "School Desegregation in South Carolina, 1963–1970" (EdD diss., University of Kentucky, 1979), 13. For information on L. Marion Gressette and the "segregation committee" he headed in South Carolina for more than fifteen years, see White, "Managed Compliance."
10. *Southern School News* (February 1955), 3; (April 1955), 13.
11. Herbert P. Moore to Strom Thurmond, January 14, 1958, Box 6, Folder "Private Schools," Subject Correspondence Series 1958, Mss 100, Strom Thurmond Collection, Special Collections, Clemson University Libraries; "Statement by Senator Strom Thurmond on Senate Floor, March 10, 1958," Box 24, Folder "Segregation I," Subject Correspondence Series 1958, Mss 100, Strom Thurmond Collection, Special Collections, Clemson University Libraries.
12. L. Marion Gressette to Sam C. Augustine, November 13, 1958, Box 20, Folder "Segregation, Gressette Committee, 1954–1959," Ernest F. Hollings Papers, South Carolina Political Collections, The University of South Carolina.

13. "Address by Donald Russell to the Citizens Council, Olanta, S.C., March 7, 1958," Box 24, Folder "Segregation I," Subject Correspondence Series 1958, Mss 100, Strom Thurmond Collection, Special Collections, Clemson University Libraries.

14. *Southern School News* (November 1958), 5.

15. *Southern School News* (November 1958), 13.

16. *Southern School News* (November 1958), 13.

17. *Southern School News* (December 1958), 16.

18. *Brown v. Board of Education of Topeka*, 349 U.S. 294 (1955).

19. Gerald N. Rosenberg, *The Hollow Hope: Can Courts Bring About Social Change?* (Chicago: University of Chicago Press, 1991), 50. See also Benjamin Muse, *Ten Years of Prelude: The Story of Integration Since the Supreme Court's 1954 Decision* (New York: Viking Press, 1964).

20. *Southern School News* (February 1963), 8; Maxie Myron Cox Jr., "1963—The Year of Decision: Desegregation in South Carolina" (PhD diss., University of South Carolina, 1996), 144–69; Raymond Wolters, *The Burden of Brown: Thirty Years of School Desegregation* (Knoxville: University of Tennessee Press, 1984), 149.

21. "Address by Donald Russell to the Citizens Council, Olanta, S.C., March 7, 1958," Box 24, Folder "Segregation I," Subject Correspondence Series 1958, Mss 100, Strom Thurmond Collection, Special Collections, Clemson University Libraries.

22. *Southern School News* (February 1963), 8; Cox , "1963—The Year of Decision," 144–69.

23. *Southern School News* (February 1963), 8.

24. *Southern School News* (February 1963), 8; *Southern School News* (April 1963), 14.

25. *Southern School News* (March 1963), 16.

26. *Southern School News* (June 1963), 14.

27. Quoted in Cox, "1963—The Year of Decision," 167–68.

28. *Southern School News* (September 1963), 22; Wolters, *The Burden of Brown*, 145–48.

29. *Southern School News* (October 1963), 16.

30. "Summary Abbeville County School District, Freedom of Choice Plan," Box 118, Folder "Topical, 91st Education, Desegregation," Ernest F. Hollings Papers, South Carolina Political Collections, The University of South Carolina.

31. McNeill, "School Desegregation in South Carolina," 39. For more on the history of HEW guidelines and freedom-of-choice plans, see J. Harvie Wilkinson III, *From* Brown *to* Bakke: *The Supreme Court and School Integration: 1954–1978* (New York: Oxford University Press, 1979), 102–18.

32. "Table 1-A Negroes by State," Box 117, Folder "Topical, 91st Education, Desegregation," Ernest F. Hollings Papers, South Carolina Political Collections, The University of South Carolina.

33. For a thorough account of the demographics of New Kent County, Virginia, and background of the NAACP's lawsuit against the county, see Wolters, *The Burden of Brown*, 155–56.

34. *Green v. County School Board of New Kent County*, 391 U.S. 430 (1968).

35. *Green v. County School Board of New Kent County*, 391 U.S. 430 (1968).

36. C. C. Duncan to Strom Thurmond, October 23, 1969, Box 4, Folder "Civil Rights VII," Subject Correspondence Series, Mss 100, Strom Thurmond Collection, Special Collections, Clemson University Libraries.

37. *Alexander v. Holmes County Board of Education*, 396 U.S. 19 (1969).

38. McNeill, "School Desegregation in South Carolina," 39, 69; "Private Schools in South Carolina: A Case Study," ii, Box 11, M. Hayes Mizell Papers, South Caroliniana Library, The University of South Carolina. For details on the *Alexander* ruling, see Wilkinson, *From* Brown *to* Bakke, 119.

39. John Egerton, "Seg Academies, with Much Church Aid, Flourish in South, as Other Private Schools Wane," *South Today* (September 1973), 6.

40. Naomi Floyd to Strom Thurmond, July 29, 1969, Box 3, Folder "Civil Rights V," Subject Correspondence 1969, Mss 100, Strom Thurmond Collection, Special Collections, Clemson University Libraries.

41. Mrs. Eugene H. Hill to Fritz Hollings, February 2, 1969, Box 118, Folder "Top., 91st Ed. Deseg., Counties, Berkeley-Clarendon," Ernest F. Hollings Papers, South Carolina Political Collections, The University of South Carolina.

42. Mrs. Harry Balry to Fritz Hollings, June 27, 1969, Box 118, Folder "Top. 91st Ed., Deseg., Counties, Greenville-Horry," Ernest F. Hollings Papers, South Carolina Political Collections, The University of South Carolina.

43. Edna Heyward to Strom Thurmond, July 16, 1969, Box 3, Folder "Civil Rights V," Subject Correspondence 1969, Mss 100, Strom Thurmond Collection, Special Collections, Clemson University Libraries.

44. Stephen Harold Lowe, "The Magnificent Fight: Civil Rights Litigation in South Carolina Federal Courts, 1940–1970" (PhD diss., Michigan State University, 1999), 311.

45. See *Swann v. Charlotte-Mecklenburg Board of Education*, 402 U.S. 1 (1971).

46. Kitty Terjen, "Close-up on Segregation Academies," *New South* (Fall 1972), 50.

47. Nevin and Bills, *The Schools That Fear Built*, 9.

48. Jim Leeson, "Private Schools for White Face Some Hurdles," *Southern Education Report* (November 1967), 15.

49. McNeill, "School Desegregation in South Carolina," 34–43.

50. Mrs. Luther C. Mitchell to John West, June 8, 1970, Box 3, Folder "Public School Desegregation, 1970, April–November," John C. West Papers, South Carolina Political Collections, The University of South Carolina.

51. Robert Joseph Steeley, "A History of Independent Education in South Carolina" (EdD diss., University of South Carolina, 1979), 94–95.

52. Tom Turnipseed telephone interview with the author, February 21, 2008.

53. Tom Turnipseed telephone interview with the author, February 21, 2008. For more on Tom Turnipseed and the shift in his racial attitudes, see Tom Brokaw, *Boom!: Voices of the Sixties* (New York: Random House, 2007), 62–68.

54. G. Thomas Turnipseed to Strom Thurmond, May 20, 1965, Box 4, Folder "Private Schools," Subject Correspondents Series 1965, Mss 100, Strom Thurmond Collection, Special Collections, Clemson University Libraries.

55. Tom Turnipseed telephone interview with the author, February 21, 2008.

56. *Southern School News* (November 1964), 1.
57. "Report of Committee Investigating the Establishment of Private Schools," 5, Box 28, William D. Workman, Jr. Papers, South Carolina Political Collections, The University of South Carolina.
58. Tom Turnipseed telephone interview with the author, February 21, 2008.
59. Steeley, "A History of Independent Education in South Carolina," 90.
60. Interview with Donald D. Roberts, May 24, 1972, quoted in Margaret Rose Gladney, "I'll Take My Stand: The Southern Segregation Academy Movement" (PhD diss., University of New Mexico, 1974), 134.
61. Tom Turnipseed telephone interview with the author, February 21, 2008; "Private Schools Developments in South Carolina," Address by T. Elliott Wannamaker before the Annual Conference of the Citizens' Councils of America, January 7, 1966, Box 27, William D. Workman, Jr. Papers, South Carolina Political Collections, The University of South Carolina.
62. "Private Schools in South Carolina: A Case Study," 38, Box 11, M. Hayes Mizell Papers, South Caroliniana Library, The University of South Carolina.
63. "A Statement Opposing the Granting of Church Facilities for Private School Purposes," Box 4, Folder "The Church and Race Relations," Christian Life Commission Resource Files, Southern Baptist Historical Library and Archives.
64. "Private Schools in South Carolina: A Case Study," 37, Box 11, M. Hayes Mizell Papers, South Caroliniana Library, The University of South Carolina.
65. "Strom Thurmond Reports to the People," June 4, 1967, Box 27, William D. Workman, Jr. Papers, South Carolina Political Collections, The University of South Carolina.
66. Numbers from Terjen, "Close-up on Segregation Academies," 54.
67. "1974 General Information Handbook for the Southern Council Academy," University of Iowa, *The Right Wing Collection of the University of Iowa Libraries, 1918–1977*, microfilm edition, 177 rolls (Glen Rock, NJ: Microfilming Corporation of America, 1978), roll 127, frame S77.
68. Joseph Crespino, "Segregation Academies or Church Schools?: Race, Religion, and Taxes in Mississippi, 1970–1982," unpublished paper presented at the Southern Historical Association, Memphis, Tennessee, November 5, 2004 (in author's possession), *passim*. For the ramifications of private schools on IRS tax policy from the mid-1960s through the early 1980s, see Joseph Crespino, *In Search of Another Country: Mississippi and the Conservative Counterrevolution* (Princeton, NJ: Princeton University Press, 2007), 237–66.
69. Nevin and Bills, *The Schools That Fear Built*, 17.
70. Fred Atkinson to John West, July 3, 1970, Box 3, Folder "Public School Desegregation, 1970, April–November," John C. West Papers, South Carolina Political Collections, The University of South Carolina.
71. C. C. Duncan to Ernest Hollings, October 23, 1969, Box 118, Folder "Top., 91st, Ed., Deseg., Counties, Orangeburg," Ernest F. Hollings Papers, South Carolina Political Collections, The University of South Carolina.
72. John Egerton and Jack Bass, "Hayes Mizell, School Board Member," *Race Relations Reporter* (March 1973), 32.

73. Quoted in Dowland, *Family Values*, 44.
74. Quoted in Gladney, "I'll Take My Stand," 126.
75. Sociologists Donald Kinder and Lynn Sanders have labeled this phenomenon of nonracialized justifications used to support ideas that are clearly based on racist assumptions as "symbolic racism" and explain it as follows: "A new form of prejudice has come to prominence, one that is preoccupied with matters of moral character, informed by virtues associated with the traditions of individualism. At its center are the contentions that blacks do not try hard enough to overcome the difficulties they face and that they take what they have not earned. Today, we say, prejudice is expressed in the language of American individualism." See Donald R. Kinder and Lynn M. Sanders, *Divided by Color: Racial Politics and Democratic Ideals* (Chicago: University of Chicago Press, 1996), 106. Kinder and Sanders's expression of "symbolic racism" neatly syncs with the rise of colorblind individualistic arguments that religious conservatives started touting in the late 1960s to avoid racial integration.
76. William F. McIlwain, "On the Overturning of Two School Buses in Lamar, S.C.," *Esquire* (January 1971), 98–99.
77. McIlwain, "On the Overturning of Two School Buses In Lamar, S.C.," 102.
78. Mrs. M. V. Thomas to Robert McNair, March 16, 1970, Box 31, Folder "Desegregation, Public Schools, Lamar Incident, 1970," Robert E. McNair Papers, South Carolina Political Collections, The University of South Carolina.
79. Mr. and Mrs. Rufus E. Phillips to Robert McNair, March 10, 1970, Box 31, Folder "Desegregation, Public Schools, Lamar Incident, 1970," Robert E. McNair Papers, South Carolina Political Collections, The University of South Carolina.
80. "Memo Concerning the Use of Church Buildings by Private Schools," Box 10, Folder 680, Christian Action Council Papers, South Caroliniana Library, The University of South Carolina.
81. "Memo Concerning the Use of Church Buildings by Private Schools," Box 10, Folder 680, Christian Action Council Papers, South Caroliniana Library, The University of South Carolina.
82. "Editors Warn of Private School Danger," Box 2, Folder "1970—Clippings, Notes, Posters, Press Releases," Race Relations and Southern Baptists, Southern Baptist Historical Library and Archives.
83. McIlwain, "On the Overturning of Two School Buses . . . ," 103.
84. McIlwain, "On the Overturning of Two School Buses . . . ," 102.
85. "Private Schools In South Carolina: A Case Study," 23, Box 11, M. Hayes Mizell Papers, South Caroliniana Library, The University of South Carolina.
86. Bright L. Stevenson to Workman, January 29, 1970, Box 27, William D. Workman, Jr. Papers, South Carolina Political Collections, The University of South Carolina.
87. Wanda L. Forbes to Workman, December 10, 1973, Box 2, William D. Workman, Jr. Papers, South Carolina Political Collections, The University of South Carolina.
88. Jack Bass, "Massive White Flight in Summerton," *Race Relations Reporter* (May 1972), 16.
89. "Private Schools in South Carolina: A Case Study," Box 11, M. Hayes Mizell Papers, South Caroliniana Library, The University of South Carolina.

90. Walker Percy, *Love in the Ruins: The Adventures of a Bad Catholic at a Time Near the End of the World* (New York: Farrar, Straus and Giroux, 1971), 12.

Epilogue

1. David K. Chrisman, "Religious Moderates and Race: The Texas Christian Life Commission and the Call for Racial Reconciliation, 1954–1968," in *Seeking Inalienable Rights: Texans and Their Quest for Justice,* ed. Debra A. Reid (College Station: Texas A&M University Press, 2009), 115.
2. Lyndon Johnson, "Remarks to the Christian Citizenship Seminar of Southern Baptist Leaders," https://www.presidency.ucsb.edu/documents/remarks-the-christian-citizenship-seminar-southern-baptist-leaders (accessed July 14, 2019).
3. Johnson, "Remarks to the Christian Citizenship Seminar of Southern Baptist Leaders."
4. Johnson, "Remarks to the Christian Citizenship Seminar of Southern Baptist Leaders."
5. Johnson, "Remarks to the Christian Citizenship Seminar of Southern Baptist Leaders."
6. Andrew M. Manis, "'Dying from the Neck UP': Southern Baptist Resistance to the Civil Rights Movement," *Baptist History and Heritage* 34, no. 1 (Winter 1999): 33.
7. Quoted in Curtis J. Freeman, "'Never Had I Been So Blind': W. A. Criswell's 'Change' on Racial Segregation," *Journal of Southern Religion* 10 (2007): 1 http://jsr.fsu.edu/Volume10/Front10.htm (accessed July 14, 2019).
8. Freeman, "Never Had I Been So Blind," 10.
9. Quoted in Freeman, "Never Had I Been So Blind," 1–2.
10. For the importance the Southern Manifesto played in raising Thurmond's stature among southern segregationists, see John Kyle Day, *The Southern Manifesto: Massive Resistance and the Fight to Preserve Segregation* (Jackson: University Press of Mississippi, 2014).
11. Quoted in Freeman, "Never Had I Been So Blind," 4.
12. Quoted in Freeman, "Never Had I Been So Blind," 6.
13. W. A. Criswell, "The Two-Edged Sword," 1969 SBC Presidential Address, https://wacriswell.com/sermons/1969/two-edged-sword/ (accessed July 10, 2019).
14. Freeman, "Never Had I Been So Blind," 10.
15. Quoted in Freeman, "Never Had I Been So Blind," 11.
16. Freeman, "Never Had I Been So Blind," 11.
17. Quoted in Freeman "Never Had I Been So Blind," 12.
18. Nancy D. Wadsworth, *Ambivalent Miracles: Evangelicals and the Politics of Racial Healing* (Charlottesville: University of Virginia Press, 2014), 15–16.
19. Kevin D. Dougherty, Michael O. Emerson, and Mark Chaves, "Racial Diversity in U.S. Congregations, 1998–2019," *Journal for the Scientific Study of Religion* 59.4 (2000): 651–662.
20. Wadsworth, *Ambivalent Miracles*, 15–16.
21. Michael O. Emerson, "Still Divided by Faith," unpublished talk given at Mosaix National Tri-Annual Conference, Dallas, Texas, November 6, 2019.

22. Wadsworth, *Ambivalent Miracles,* 257–64.

23. Michael O. Emerson and Christian Smith, *Divided by Faith: Evangelical Religion and the Problem of Race in America* (New York: Oxford University Press, 2000), 170.

24. Emerson and Smith, *Divided by Faith,* 76.

25. Emerson and Smith, *Divided by Faith,* 91.

26. Untitled press release, March 24, 1970, Box 22, Folder "Methodist Christian Fellowship," William D. Workman, Jr. Papers, South Carolina Political Collections, The University of South Carolina.

27. Emerson and Smith, *Divided by Faith,* 91. Emerson and Smith define a racialized society as one "wherein race matters profoundly for differences in life experiences, life opportunities, and social relationships," *Divided by Faith,* 7.

28. Robert P. Jones, *White Too Long: The Legacy of White Supremacy in American Christianity* (New York: Simon and Schuster, 2020).

29. "College Choice of Minority Students Admitted to Institutions in the Council for Christian Colleges and Universities," https://files.eric.ed.gov/fulltext/EJ992993.pdf (accessed July 14, 2019).

30. "Statement on Social Justice and the Gospel," https://statementonsocialjustice.com/ (accessed July 14, 2019).

31. Nikole Hannah-Jones, "Segregation Now," https://www.propublica.org/article/segregation-now-full-text (accessed October 1, 2016).

32. Bob Smietana, "Sunday Morning Segregation: Most Worshippers Feel Their Church Has Enough Diversity," http://www.christianitytoday.com/gleanings/2015/january/sunday-morning-segregation-most-worshipers-church-diversity.html (accessed October 1, 2016).

33. John Perkins, *Let Justice Roll Down* (Ventura, CA: Regal Books, 1976), 11.

Index

For the benefit of digital users, indexed terms that span two pages (e.g., 52–53) may, on occasion, appear on only one of those pages.